CRISIS

CRISIS

BY NICKY PERFECT

AND ELIZABETH SHEPPARD

ONE PLACE. MANY STORIES

This is a work of non-fiction, based on real events. Names
and identifying characteristics and details have been changed
to protect the identity and privacy of individuals.

HQ
An imprint of HarperCollins*Publishers* Ltd
1 London Bridge Street
London SE1 9GF

www.harpercollins.co.uk

HarperCollins*Publishers*
Macken House, 39/40 Mayor Street Upper
Dublin 1, D01 C9W8, Ireland

This edition 2023

1
First published in Great Britain by HQ,
an imprint of HarperCollins*Publishers* Ltd 2023

Copyright © Nicky Perfect 2023

Nicky Perfect asserts the moral right to be
identified as the author of this work.
A catalogue record for this book is
available from the British Library.

ISBN: 978-0-00-856116-1

This book is produced from independently certified FSC™ paper
to ensure responsible forest management.

For more information visit: www.harpercollins.co.uk/green

This book is set in 10.6/15.5 pt Sabon by Type-it AS, Norway

Printed and bound in the UK using 100% Renewable Electricity at
CPI Group (UK) Ltd, Croydon, CR0 4YY

For Jayne Stratton, 1968–1998.
Gone but never once forgotten.

Contents

Chapter 1

DO YOU WANT TO SAVE A LIFE?

'He's got the knife to his throat again. He's had a lot to drink. Wife left yesterday. She took both the kids.'

I've already been briefed on the crisis by my negotiator co-ordinator Jason, over the phone. But as I arrive at the Rendezvous Point (RVP), I check in with the incident commander and get an update. A police incident commander sets up an RVP for all units attending, keeping a record of everyone who's there and what department they're from. I hear the RVP telling the control room that the negotiator is now on the scene.

The subject is male, alone in his home, armed with a large kitchen knife and threatening to slit his throat if he's approached. Home is a small modern house at the end of Murdock Close, a cul-de-sac in east London. The police are here because this guy rang a relative and she was so scared by how distraught he sounded that she called 999. It's also Christmas night – a really bad time to be drinking far too much on your own.

Police activity always creates a buzz. The Territorial Support Group – six specially trained constables and their supervisor – is clustered for a briefing. Alongside their van sit two blue-light cars and an ambulance. Radios are crackling. White and blue tape seals off the street. If the man with the knife shows any sign that he's about to harm himself, or barricades the house, or poses an immediate threat to an officer or to me, the TSG will take immediate action. I quickly call my negotiator co-ordinator Jason to let him know that I've arrived.

'One vital thing,' I ask the incident commander. 'What's this guy's name?'

'He's called Sam. Are you happy to engage?'

'Yes,' I say. 'I am.'

He's in crisis and he needs help. I'm here to listen to Sam, to calm him, to get him to trust me and to bring the stand-off to an end. This is the job of a hostage and crisis negotiator.

*

Christmas Day at my sister Dani's in west London has been lovely. My parents joined us, my brother-in-law cooked great food, I played with my niece, and I'd also taken Cora, my German Shepherd, who gets nervous if she's left alone all day. The family's been chilling – except for me. That's because I've been on call across the holiday period, and on call there's a bit of your brain that never quite turns off – an extra edge of alertness. Of course you don't drink. From time to time you touch your pocket, making sure the work mobile's with you. You keep on glancing just to check that the ringer's still turned on because if that phone screen lights up, it's an emergency and everyone will be under pressure. You don't want to put the rest of the team to extra trouble trying to get hold of you.

As the light begins to fade and what's left of the turkey is wrapped carefully in tin foil, I'm surprised that the phone has stayed silent. When I finally hear it in the late afternoon, I feel a prickle of excitement. 'The day you don't respond like that,' my instructor once said when I was training, 'the day you don't just want to drop everything and go to work – that's the time to ask yourself: should I still be a crisis negotiator?'

As I pick the phone up, I see Jason's name and I know what he will say. 'Do you want to save a life?' he always asks, cutting to the quick of what it means to do this job. 'Yes, I do,' I answer. Then he tells me what I'm faced with, and where I need to be. I briefly explain to my family what's happening ('I've got a negotiation.' 'How long will you be, Nick?' 'No idea, Dad – but you already knew that.' 'Yeah, you're right, I did'). And I ask them if they mind if I leave Cora there (which they don't, of course, bless them). My mind's already on the situation ahead. I'm thinking about what might be going on in this guy's life, and what could have driven him to this point of crisis. I'm recalling previous, similar scenarios, starting to work out what I might say.

I contact the pan-London police supervisor who sends a fast car to pick me up and take me to the scene. It's not long before I'm sitting in the back, the accelerator is floored, and the driver flicks the switches to activate the police siren and lights. Blues and twos across the city.

*

Murdock Close is dark. As I walk along the pavement, the outside world drops away. My colleagues' voices, the hiss of radios, the festive lights in windows are gone. There's only the tap of my footsteps and the sound of my breath. The guy with the knife lives in number 6, and I can see a half-inflated child's football on the little patch of grass along with quite a bit of rubbish. It's sad how un-Christmassy the place looks – no one has bothered with a tree or decorations, or even to straighten things up. Perhaps they don't celebrate 25 December. Or things have got so bad between the husband and wife that it just hasn't seemed worth celebrating.

The subject is standing in the doorway. It's hard to make him out because the street is so dark and there's a light right behind him in the hall. Until my eyes adjust, he's in silhouette. But I can clearly see the knife that he's clutching. I walk up to the uniformed officer positioned on the pavement at the end of the path.

'Can you check if Sam minds you having a word with me?' I ask. The constable takes a few steps up the path so that he can put the question to the figure in the doorway. I do this because I want Sam to feel that he has some say in what's happening and that he's being consulted – after all, he's lost control of everything else. He didn't want the police here – someone else has called them, and as far as he's concerned, they're intruding in his life without his consent. And if you're highly emotional, especially if alcohol's involved, and then you see people talking about you, it's pretty easy to end up feeling paranoid. The constable walks back to me.

'Yeah – he's okay with that.'

'What's Sam been telling you?' I ask him, and the constable explains how the guy's spent Christmas Day by himself, how he's been drinking, and he says he doesn't want to be here any more. He's repeatedly stated that he wants to die. 'If the police come any closer, he says he'll cut his throat. He's said that more than once. I think he's pretty scared.'

'Have you got a relationship with him, would you say?'

'No – it's very new.'

'Do you mind if I take over?'

'Of course not.' If I can see that another officer has really got in tune with someone in crisis, I'm totally prepared for them to go on doing the talking. Once trust has been developed, it's better not to change the dynamic. But there's not been enough time here for the two of them to have built a rapport.

'Stay here, please,' I tell the constable. 'We'll do this together. If I move towards him, stay with me.'

The role of negotiator is all about listening. It's about being in the space with someone who is desperate. It's not about you, or what you think, or how you're going to fix everything, or what a hero you are. The negotiator's role is to hear what this person is saying, how they're feeling, what exactly has gone wrong, how their problem has blown up into this moment of extremity. And then to help them find a way out of it.

*

I take a few steps up the path. This lets me look at Sam more closely, although the deep shadows round us still aren't helping. He's in his late twenties, I'd say, with dark, dishevelled hair. What I see is desperation, not aggression. He just looks totally lost and confused. I don't think this level of misery is likely to turn into suicidal violence, but I also notice how tightly the blade of the knife he's holding to his throat is pressed to his skin. *If he panics*, I think, *he just might do it*.

'Hi, Sam,' I say. 'My name is Nicky. I've been talking to this guy here' – I point to the constable – 'and he's told me that you've been feeling pretty rubbish today. And it looks like you've been drinking.' I don't use the word 'colleague' for my fellow officer because I know that Sam is frightened of the police and I don't want him to identify me with them. If he thinks I'm just another one who's here to arrest him, there's zero chance he'll trust me.

Sam drops the hand that's holding the knife to his side and takes several jerky strides forward towards me. It's a very sudden move and it does seem quite threatening, but I'm watching his face and his expression is terror. I think he's shocked that I've approached him and doesn't know what to do. I step back and raise my voice.

'Put the knife down, Sam,' I say loudly. 'Please don't walk towards me. You're frightening me.' My voice will alert my colleagues round the corner to what's happening. I know my negotiator coordinator Jason will be on the scene by now – he's a chief superintendent and highly experienced. The whole team will be watching from a distance, keeping everyone updated. Sam retreats to his doorstep and stands there, staring at me.

'You look lonely,' I say to him. 'You must be feeling sad about what's happened today, and yesterday.'

There's a very long pause. I give him time.

'Go 'way!' he mumbles. His voice is very slurred. 'I don' wan' you here.'

'I'd like to stay and help you,' I say. 'Can you put the knife down? I think that would be safer for everyone.'

He mutters something I can't catch. He's barely coherent. Then he slowly lowers the hand with the knife to his side and sits down heavily on the step. I try another careful step towards him, but he immediately raises the knife again and holds it back against his throat. This threat of self-harm is the only way that he can feel in control.

'Sam,' I say, but then he staggers to his feet and disappears into the house.

I'm losing track of how long I've been here and I don't look at my phone. I keep my focus entirely on the present. When you negotiate, time vanishes: there's just the moment that you're in and the next decision that you're making. I even lose peripheral vision sometimes as the world contracts into only what's in front of me. But it's night-time in midwinter and I can feel the temperature dropping. Fortunately, I'm wearing a very warm coat for situations just like this one, because a lot of negotiations happen out of doors. I keep snacks in my crisis situation back-pack too (I don't remember exactly where I heard the saying *Any fool can get cold, wet and hungry* – but it made me determined never to be that fool), along with my dictaphone. When I have that backpack with me, I'm ready for anything.

Now Sam's gone inside, I'm worried he might drink even more. He could take tablets, pick up another knife, make this situation even more unstable. Through the kitchen window I watch him stumbling around but then he moves away. From what I can see, the place is in a mess. I stand and wait, acutely aware of the silence. A minute or two later, he comes out. He's still got the knife, but at least now the blade isn't against his neck. He's looking down at it, turning it over and over in his hands.

'Sam,' I say to him, 'I don't know if you're drinking more alcohol but that might make this situation worse. It's not the best idea.'

'Don' tell me wha' to do,' he slurs. ''s my life. Don' tell me not to drink.'

'I'm not telling you that you can't drink. It's just that it makes it harder to work out what's going on and to help you.'

He doesn't answer but again he sits down on his front step. His movements are sluggish: it's not just the drink, I think. It's exhaustion too. He can't have slept last night.

'I can see you're having a desperate day,' I say to him, 'and I would really like to help you.' He turns his head towards me and again I step a little closer, into the shaft of light that's falling from the door.

'You wanna 'rest me,' he mumbles.

'We don't want to arrest you. There's an ambulance round the corner. They're here for you. The paramedics can help you.'

I can see him trying to weigh me up. He's highly agitated so his actions are hard to predict – everything's coming from his emotional brain right now. It can be difficult to get people back from this kind of altered consciousness so that they can use their reason. That's why the TSG is standing by: if Sam suddenly barricades himself in, or uses violence, they can storm the house – which is called dynamic entry – with their shields, protecting him from harm without endangering themselves.

'You jus' get back or I'll do it!' Sam shouts out suddenly. 'I'll cut my throat! Get back right now or I'll kill myself!'

I don't think he will. His threats seem half-hearted. But I don't rely on my instinct – I've known situations where it's been totally wrong, and those cases have taught me to trust my training and experience instead. The crucial issue here is the same as in every negotiation, every stand-off, every moment of crisis. How can I get him to trust me?

'I know you're feeling upset right now,' I say. 'And it's getting really cold, and you must be tired. If you put down the knife, we could move away from here.'

Again Sam jumps to his feet and takes several strides towards me, wildly brandishing the knife. The closer he gets, the more clearly I can see his desperation. His eyes are staring, his hair's up on end, he's distraught. He looks like a man who has lost his whole world, so frightened and broken that it's impossible to be afraid of him. I go on speaking calmly.

'If you put down the knife and come with me, I'll tell the officers that you're not going to do anything. We can walk to the ambulance together.'

He lifts his hands towards his face again, but this time he doesn't press the knife against his throat. Now he's just standing there in the middle of the path, holding his head in his hands. His shoulders start to heave with sobs.

'It's okay, Sam,' I say to him. 'Make sure you put the knife on the ground. Keep your hands where I can see them.' I hear the knife clatter as it falls. I walk towards him and the constable who's been a few steps behind me comes forward too.

'This police officer here just needs to pat you down, to make sure you don't have anything else on you,' I tell him. Sam doesn't seem a threat to anyone's safety except his own, but he could still have a concealed weapon, so he can't get into the ambulance until we've checked. Then we walk around the corner side by side towards the paramedics and the TSG officers who are waiting there. No one's had to jump on him and he won't be arrested. The outcome here is good: he's alive and now the doctors can help him.

*

As soon as any crisis is resolved, there's a debrief. I report, explaining what has happened, and that until now there hasn't been a moment when I could have broken contact with the subject to give an update. (I've been in other stand-offs with natural breaks, where people ask for cups of tea and cigarettes and everybody stops for a breather.) Our debrief is recorded and now it will go to be stored for future training, to teach future negotiators best practice. It doesn't take too long and I won't have further contact with Sam. I know from previous experience, however, the effort it will take not to carry the suffering I've witnessed away with me. But my role here has been to save his life, to de-escalate the crisis. Job done.

Before too long, I'm driven back to Dani's to get Cora. By now it's getting late on Christmas Day. The centre of the capital is never quiet but there are fewer people on the roads than usual and my journey across town is quick and easy. By the time I arrive, my parents have already headed home and my niece has gone to bed. I thank my sister and brother-in-law for a lovely day, make a big fuss of Cora who's delighted to see me, then head towards my own home in south London. As I drive, I'm still running over the negotiation in my mind, evaluating my actions, my decisions, my choice of words. I chat over it with Cora, who's always an excellent listener.

Many things went well. The constable on duty outside the subject's house did a brilliant job – I was aware of his presence the whole time and felt safe, which in turn allowed me to do my own job properly. But could I have briefed him better? I consider my own actions, looking for ways to improve them. In policing, people come together – it doesn't matter who you are, there's immediate teamwork and unspoken acceptance. I also think about the family Christmas I've just had, surrounded by people I love and who I know will always be there for me, and then about Sam who spent the day drinking all alone in his house and ended up screaming threats of harm against himself. I know I have so much to be grateful for.

At least he's alive. He's in hospital now, getting assessed and receiving help. It's time to let go. I can't go on worrying about him, or feeling the emotions that are tearing him apart. My job is to use the skills I have to save his life, then trust the professionals who come after me: they are the ones who will know how to help him. As a human being with an impulse to rescue others – something I know that I have in me – that's been a tough lesson to learn. But part of this job – a vital part – is the strength to draw a line and walk away.

I'm very tired but I'm pleased with the way the call-out went. There's no other job like crisis negotiation. It's a quarter to midnight as I open my front door and step into the hall. As my hand reaches out for the light switch, the work phone rings again.

'Do you want to save a life?' Jason's voice asks.

'Yes,' I say again. 'Yes, I do.'

Chapter 2

'*Active message, Papa 5.*'

It was 6.30 in the morning – not a time when you'd normally expect much activity on police radio. Sitting in the area car with my partner Tim at the start of our early turn, I could hear communications between all the south London patrol cars and Control.

'*Papa 5 – go ahead.*'

'*Stolen vehicle also believed involved in a burglary last night. Vehicle reg CAR123B. Vehicle heading north on Bromley High Street towards the A21.*'

Papa 5 was the pursuit car giving chase. Tim and I were in Papa 3. I immediately spoke into the radio: 'All units be aware. Papa 5 currently chasing vehicle towards Catford on the A21,' and heard the other cars respond.

'*Received, Papa 5. All units aware. Papa 5 – go ahead with your commentary.*'

'*Vehicle now turning right on A21 towards Catford.*'

I had a map of south-east London on my knee – no satnav

back then – and I quickly plotted the route of the car. 'Hey,' I told Tim, 'unless this guy turns off, he's coming our way.'

'Let's get ahead of him,' Tim said. We moved forward along the quiet morning roads, listening for updates from the pursuit car and Control.

'*Vehicle continuing on A21 doing up to sixty miles an hour in a thirty miles an hour limit, also overtaking on the wrong side of the road. Vehicle failing to stop for police or traffic lights.*'

We'd got ahead of him now and were sitting on a junction with the A21. In less than two minutes he appeared, tearing along in a battered navy Ford Escort which I knew without a doubt would turn out to be stolen. He shot straight past us with Papa 5 on his tail.

'Papa 3 requesting permission to join pursuit,' I said. I was carefully keeping my voice level, but this was my first big car chase and I felt a rush of excitement.

'*Roger, Papa 3.*'

Okay then. Here we go.

'Active message from Papa 3. Joining vehicle pursuit behind Papa 5.'

The arrival of a second police car on his tail must have panicked the suspect and he started trying to shake us off. He turned into White Foot Lane towards the Downham Estate, then swerved right into Moorside Road and right again. But he'd made a bad decision – on these smaller, narrow roads he was forced to drop his speed.

'*Vehicle slowing,*' reported Papa 5. '*Suspect looking to decamp.*'

As Papa 5 and Papa 3 turned the corner, we saw the suspect's car abandoned, slewed across the pavement with the driver's door swinging open. Tim braked and I jumped out.

'Suspect has decamped,' I said into my radio. '410 Papa Delta' – that was my call sign – 'continuing pursuit on foot.'

I quickly looked around me, working out where the suspect might have gone. He had to have headed over Downham Fields, a little nearby park, so I set off at a run with another officer who'd jumped out of Papa 5 just behind me. Even in my uniform skirt – no trousers option in those days – I covered the ground fast but when I reached the other side of the park, the suspect was nowhere to be seen.

No way has this guy made a getaway, I thought. *He's not had time. He has to be close. He's hiding.* I glanced behind me, expecting to see the other officer giving foot pursuit, but my sprinting had left him far behind. I needed backup. Tim would have driven round the edge of the park towards my location by now. He must have been seconds away.

'410 Papa Delta. I've lost sight of the suspect,' I said into my radio. As I moved forward, scanning the gardens of the houses in Moorside Road, I heard Tim's response.

'*383 receiving.*'

This guy was close – I knew it. I dropped to my knees and spotted him immediately. He'd rolled underneath a parked car.

'Stop!' I yelled a warning. 'Police! Stop! You're surrounded!'

By the time my fellow officers arrived, I had the suspect in cuffs without further resistance. The goods he'd burgled overnight were still in his car and I was pleased with my part in the arrest.

I was in my early twenties, enjoying my career, using my strengths in police work and making a difference just like I'd wanted to when I started my cadet training. It felt good. My personal life was settled and my partner, Brian, was a kind, supportive man. I felt secure, and sometimes I felt happy.

If you like doing jigsaws, you'll know that there are three sorts of pieces. There are the ones that just snap into place: there's no doubt at all where they go. There are the mystery pieces that won't fit anywhere. (They usually turn out to be part of the sky and you're left with a heap of them which no one knows what to do with.) And then there are the pieces which *very nearly* fit – but not quite. They're the trickiest. If you push down hard, you can kind of force them in . . . but the edges still won't quite line up. So you think – well, okay. Perhaps they weren't made right.

I felt like that piece of the jigsaw. Secretly, I always had. I very nearly fitted into the world around me – but in my heart of hearts, I knew I didn't. Something was wrong, but what was it? This feeling nagged away at me, but there didn't seem to be an answer. The only thing to do was to push it to the back of my mind.

*

My police career had begun on Friday 5 December 1986 when Mum and Dad drove me from Ealing in west London, where Dani and I had grown up, to the Hendon Police College to start cadet training. The idea of joining the police came from Dad, who'd read an article about the cadets and thought it might suit me better than the A level courses I was half-heartedly taking at school. When I visited the careers office at Scotland Yard and saw videos of cadets canoeing and abseiling, I couldn't believe anyone would pay me to do something as much fun as this, but once I found out they would, I was sold.

I was eighteen. The course was residential and once it started there was no home leave for a month. It was a real shock: we slept in dormitories, we had to get up very early, and there was masses of PE and military-style discipline. Not quite as much fun as I'd expected. Two weeks in, I felt I'd had enough and I telephoned my parents, feeling sure it would be Mum who took the call because she always, always answered the phone. I was certain she'd sympathise and tell me it was fine to come home if being a cadet wasn't for me. But instead, I got Dad. I took a deep breath, ready to launch into my sob story, but Dad just said, 'I'm sure you're doing great, love – you'll be fine,' and hung up! I still wonder what would have happened if it *had* been Mum who answered and I'd persuaded her that I should leave Hendon.

Dad used a bit of tough love on me that day, and he was right. Once I'd got used to it, I had a wonderful time as a cadet, one of twelve women and twenty-four men in our intake – the highest number of female trainees there'd ever been in one group. I'll never forget my relief when I first entered our dorm and immediately got talking to my friend Jayne – she was so chatty and we headed off to the cafeteria together, both of us secretly relieved that we didn't have to go down there by ourselves. And once our social group had formed, everything was so much easier; we had a year of growing up and I made friends I'm still close with to this day. By the end of it, I was super-fit and strong, ready to progress to the next stage: training school.

In January 1988 I moved on to the next level of police training as part of Hendon's yellow intake. This was very, very different from cadet life, with lots of time in classrooms learning all about the laws we would have to enforce, and tests and exams to revise for. Not quite my thing, but I managed to motivate myself just enough to pass. We were tested in role-play situations, acting out what we would do as police officers on the streets, and we practised giving evidence in a mock court, and learned how to make interview notes that could stand up to a barrister's questioning. Some of the trainees were older and they'd had other jobs and even careers before joining the police, so now we were treated in a much more adult way. Perhaps that's why I felt much lonelier in training school than I'd been as a cadet. But I never thought once about leaving. I'm quite a dutiful person by nature, and policing was the path that I had chosen. It was as though the die had been cast. Just because it was tough sometimes, that was no reason to turn back.

Then, quite early on in my police training, I met Brian. He drove the van on an outward-bound course in the Lake District and I vividly remember him laughing and joking on that first trip. There was nothing romantic between us at first, but we chatted and over the next few months we started seeing each other. He met my mum and dad, our families got on, and the two of us became an item.

After twenty weeks at Hendon, it's decision time: you have to make up your mind what area you want to apply for. Brian was based in Kent and the two of us were serious by now, so I chose the southern region and was posted to Catford, south-east London, for my first station. A female officer who supervised the trainees gave me a talk about my future. 'Most female officers end up as the station bike or the station dyke,' she said. 'So which will you be?'

Her words – which sound incredible now – were a warning. Not about the police service as a whole, but definitely about the behaviour of a few of Catford's old-school officers. Some of their values and beliefs didn't fit with mine (to say the least). As female officers, we faced more obstacles than the men and even our uniforms got in the way: women still all had to wear A-line skirts. Our instructors could be negative, which was discouraging, and the way we were expected to learn seemed harsh – or was I just very soft? Even after the army-style training that I'd had, I was still only nineteen and I felt anxious under the spotlight. One sergeant in particular seemed to take against me and would shout at me across the canteen: 'Oi, you! I'm talking to you!' I remember worrying and wondering what it was about me that he disliked.

But I still loved policing. In Catford, I was working a tiring four-week shift system with regular night duties – tough, but I was young and full of energy and could handle long hours. I enjoyed getting out and about on my patch, feeling that I was helping people, and I focused on the positive parts of the job, refusing to be dragged down by the cynical, negative attitudes of a few others.

Not everyone saw us female officers as equal to our male peers. When I was first posted onto an area patrol car, I was excited – as well as extremely nervous – then crushed when I got a long lecture from the area car driver on my very first day. 'You're a girl. Nothing personal – but I didn't want a girl on the car. You can't help if there's a fight or if I need support. You'll have to stay in the car and not get involved in any violence.'

At a colleague's barbecue, I found myself chatting with the

wife of one of the guys from the station. She told me very honestly that she didn't want me to be posted with her husband because she didn't think I could back him up physically if he was in trouble. I didn't challenge what she was saying because she was only telling me how she felt, but I remember feeling sure that she was wrong. As I listened, I was thinking: *Yes – but I bring something to this job. You don't need to worry. I'm not going to let anything happen to him.*

Looking back, I can see that I was learning to use my communication skills. I could read people, observe and anticipate what they might do next. I prided myself on the way I could often de-escalate tense situations. I was also very lucky to be part of a wave of change moving through policing. The number of women in the force was rising, and the old assumption that a female trainee would serve for five years then leave to marry and have children was being challenged. My fellow female trainees and I wanted careers, and we didn't see why there should be limits on how far we could progress.

There were other changes too – the digital world was just around the corner. Our inspector had a mobile phone now – just the one – which was huge and was carried around in a briefcase. If he needed to use it for a call, the case would be carefully opened, and to be honest having it available at all was a huge novelty. But we didn't record crime on computers yet – we still used paper files, writing details of arrests in red pen.

The other big change in my life when I moved to south London was personal. By now I was living with Brian, who'd been married before and had children; two of his three boys were still around at home with him, and I found myself looking after teenagers only a few years younger than I was. Trainee police officer, step-mum, living miles from family and friends, doing long hours in a demanding shift system . . . it was a lot for me to handle. I noticed my drinking and smoking creeping up, just to relieve the tension I was feeling. I wanted to fit into this life and I was trying my best. But that image of myself as a slightly wonky piece of a jigsaw was hard to get out of my mind.

It wasn't just policing that was changing around me: the criminal world was changing too. These days street crime and robberies are often drugs-related, but not so many years before, the London estates we were patrolling had been run by the famous East End gangsters, Ronnie and Reggie Kray, and their bitter rivals, the Richardsons. There was much less gun crime then, and we still met old-school types from those days who told us how they'd never hit a female copper and that they understood the job the police had to do. I remember sitting in the back of the van with one proper 'sarf London geezer' I'd arrested, listening while he complained how young criminals these days don't show no respect. When we got to the station, I made him a cup of tea and we continued our chat: I'd found that I could learn a lot by listening to him.

As soon as my probation was completed, I joined C Relief over in Sydenham and felt at home right from the start. There were quite a few older women on the team there and they took me under their wings. Shift work was still pretty shattering but everyone looked out for each other as we worked and played together and the team began to feel like family – at any given moment I was either on duty, out socialising with workmates, or fast asleep. I also still loved sport and had a passion for hockey, playing on a south London team and going touring.

Brian was in the City of London force but he'd often join in with whatever the Sydenham guys had planned. The two of us had fun, we had lots of things in common, and we decided to get married. This wasn't some big romantic scene – more a chat over a glass of wine when we agreed that it had been four years now and, well, marriage was the next step in life, wasn't it? He was kind, he was funny and my mum had also married when she was twenty-two, so this seemed like a natural progression. Underneath, though, was a slightly different feeling. I was like that jigsaw piece again, still not quite lining up. But if I just kept pressing down, pretty soon I was sure that I would fit.

*

Anne was a member of my hockey team. I'd got to know her a little, but we'd never really talked. That all changed in the autumn of 1994.

Hockey tours were great fun – boozy and relaxing with parties in the evening and lots of opportunities to let our hair down. Over the course of a few days away, the two of us started chatting – just banter and kidding around, nothing serious or heavy. She made me laugh a lot and we definitely had a connection: I could feel it. Now that I look back, it must have been obvious to everyone around us on that tour what was happening – just not to me.

I'd done police diversity training, noticing, for example, that the Met was pretty white although London really isn't, and thinking that this should change. The training talked about the gay community too, but the focus was so much on men in those days that lesbians were kind of invisible. Not Anne. She was absolutely out, funny and flamboyant and totally herself. On the last night of the tour, the two of us were sitting in the bar after everyone else had gone upstairs, chatting and laughing just like we'd been for days. I remember the thought coming into my head that I was so happy here – I just didn't want to go home. And then she reached out and took my hand.

It doesn't sound like much, but to me it felt like everything. It threw me into absolute confusion. And tingling excitement. And overwhelming guilt. I was married, so of course this was wrong. But the feeling of right-ness was intense. I'd always had what I called crushes on women – my history teacher at school had been one of them – but I'd told myself that this was admiration, that I put girls on pedestals and liked them in that way. Then one year I'd been policing the Gay Pride Parade in London and someone called me out as I walked with the procession. 'Check her out – she's so gay!' this woman said, and I could hear her friends laughing, not in a mean way but it made me feel so uncomfortable. I knew that I liked Pride, I liked being there, but it hadn't seemed like something I was part of. Now everything had changed. This was who I was – this was who I'd always been – and I knew it. I'd been the jigsaw piece that never fitted – and like a brilliant flash of lightning, I could understand why.

Looking back, it was really, *really* sudden. On Friday night I was happily married, living my life with my husband. By Sunday evening I was questioning everything I'd ever believed to be true about myself, my marriage, and my future. The most painful part was how innocent Brian was in all this – it had nothing to do with him at all. This was simply who I was. But who exactly was that? It was scary to realise that I couldn't answer this question.

I'm intuitive and when I take decisions, I move quickly and I follow them through. I'd no idea what was going to happen next, or how my family would react, or what my friends or my workmates would say. But this incredible discovery wasn't something I could put back in a box. I was absolutely clear that I would have to face up to a new reality, and that I'd had enough of that strange, tiring feeling that I didn't quite fit in. In the end I didn't have a choice anyway because Brian knew something was wrong as soon as I walked through the front door. I was distant, distracted, unhappy, just emotionally so far away that he even *looked* different to me – as though I was suddenly seeing him from a distance. I was also secretly texting Anne.

'You okay, Nick?' Brian asked me. And asked me again.

I remember saying, 'I don't know. I just don't know.' Then I told him that I'd made a new friend at the weekend and he seemed okay with that. But we couldn't get back to where we were, and quite honestly I didn't want to try. A few weeks later, Brian and I split up and I moved out of our lovely house into a not-so-brilliant flat-share with all my stuff in carrier bags.

For a few crazy weeks after that, I thought that Anne and I were madly in love, but it turned out we weren't. She was just a catalyst and once we were dating, things quickly fizzled between us. I did say to her, as we were breaking up, 'I left my husband for you,' and she immediately shot back, 'I never asked you to!' It was a pretty bleak moment. Then a week or so later, I saw her at a party with somebody else. I just had to face it: she'd changed everything for me but to her, I'd meant nothing.

*

I missed Brian. There were even times I wanted to move back. I didn't miss my straight life, always feeling like the wrong piece of a jigsaw, but sometimes I did long for the steady feeling I'd had with him and the simplicity and certainty of being in a marriage. Most of all I missed the way I'd been open with everyone about everything without giving it a second thought. Life was much more complicated now.

No one around me knew why I'd left my husband. I didn't tell my workmates or my parents, who both regarded Brian as part of the family and were deeply upset about our split. They thought we'd had some really awful fight and would sort it out in time. I didn't even want to tell Dani, although we'd always been close. But a month or so later, she came to a hockey do with me and we were chatting outside when she suddenly gave me a stern look and said, 'Right then – why don't you tell me the *real* reason why you've split up with Brian?' I managed to come up with an answer but it obviously wasn't convincing. 'Nick,' she said, 'I know that isn't right.' So I told her, then insisted that this absolutely must not go further. She saw how desperate I was, and said okay. For me, being gay just had to be the best-kept secret in the world.

Or at least, I thought it did. A few weeks later my friend Caron gave me a lift to a hockey match and as we were driving along, she said to me quietly, 'Did you know that Diane and I are together?'

'Together? You and Diane? You mean –?'

'Yeah. I mean that we're a couple. And I thought – we both thought – it might help you to know that.'

She was so gentle and kind that I burst into floods of tears. Right there in the back seat, I stuttered out that I'd been having a relationship with another woman and that was why I'd left Brian. While I was sobbing, it dawned on me that Caron had already worked this out. And obviously Diane had too. *Okay. So perhaps it's not the world's best-kept secret after all.*

But whatever those around me might have guessed or might have known, I definitely didn't want to talk about it. This was the Nineties, after all, and I was gripped with shame and fear and real dread that anyone would find out the truth. One time a colleague mentioned rumours: 'Nick,' he said, 'I heard you might be gay, and if I find out you are I'll be absolutely devastated.' I was haunted by his words. I think he probably meant well and was just trying to warn me to be careful, but it reinforced my belief that I must never, never tell. I stopped attending social events – after all, the last thing I wanted was for my colleagues to really get to know me – and my secrecy pushed a wedge into the close-knit teamwork I'd always relied on.

My life had split in two. My career was going really well: I was already seeing women becoming advanced drivers and this seemed a great direction to go in, so I did a six-week course back at Hendon. Learning cool new skills like pursuit driving and fast cornering was thrilling, I loved it and I passed as a Class 1 – the highest driving qualification it was possible to have at the time. In my new role I responded to car chases and bank robberies and was able to make my own decisions more often. I found I could think quickly and clearly under pressure and my confidence rose. Whatever might be simmering away in my personal life, in my professional world I knew that I belonged.

But nobody I worked with knew anything about the emotional turmoil I was in. Home life did get easier as I moved into Caron and Diane's spare room and they helped me pick up the pieces after my break-up with Anne. I was lucky with Brian too – we were still able to talk to each other and we divorced two years later without bitterness or blame. By now I'd also discovered that gay life could be great: I'd started going out to clubs and having fun. But it was still a very separate, secret world – and hiding the truth makes you lonely. I could feel the distance steadily growing between me and many of the other people around me.

I've thought about this feeling many times in my career when I've been faced with individuals in crisis. *Don't be fooled by appearances; things might not be as they seem.* There can be drama going on in someone's life that even those who see them every day are unaware of. Even the ones who are closest – and sometimes especially those people – do not always know.

*

The first time I tried to get into the Territorial Support Group – the unit that carries out public order policing – I didn't pass the interview. But on the panel was Inspector Robbins, who liked what I'd said and gave me some very helpful feedback about how to prepare for when I tried again. In 1996 I made it and enjoyed my first year of duties, but then came a huge setback: I suffered a prolapsed disc while I was out running, which made one of my legs completely give way under me. It was very scary, I struggled home and eventually I was referred to a specialist. While I was waiting, off work sick, I didn't get a whole lot of sympathy: in those days the police service was sceptical about two kinds of sick leave in particular – the stress-related kind and the back-trouble-related kind. Perhaps these injuries just weren't visible enough to be taken seriously.

When the specialist did finally see me, the news was incredibly upsetting. He told me that I wasn't going to be able to run again, and that my career in the police was over because I'd never get back the fitness and strength I needed. So I'd have to find another career, he said, but he didn't give me any advice about exactly what that might be, and showed no empathy whatsoever about how devastated I would feel.

The next few months were awful. My back pain was chronic and nothing seemed to ease it except lying on the floor. All alone at home, I smoked too much, drank too much, and steadily sank into a deep hole of self-pity, not helped by the behaviour of Pippa, my girlfriend at the time. Things got even more miserable when Mum asked me why I wasn't ringing her back although she was leaving messages for me – and I realised that I wasn't getting these messages because Pippa wasn't passing them on. (Mum, of course, had no idea she was my girlfriend.) Pippa was pretty insecure, and I think she was trying to make me more dependent on her by cutting me off from other people who supported me. She was also hiding who she was, and demanded absolute secrecy about our relationship to the point where she wouldn't let me park my car outside her house. It meant that both of us were terribly alone.

I couldn't do the work that was the heart of my identity, and

I might never be able to do it again. My personal life could hardly be described as a success. I was in chronic pain, could barely move, and some days I didn't even open the living room curtains. There were times when I honestly felt: what's the point?

*

I'd kept in touch with quite a few of the girls from cadet school down the years. A group of us stayed close until around the time that I left Brian, but when all the secrecy began, I'd pushed the gang away. But I did find out that Jayne – my very first cadet friend, the lovely, friendly girl I'd got talking to when I arrived in the dormitory – had been diagnosed with a brain tumour, which had been successfully treated. Still, I'd missed out on knowing about this while it was going on, and I knew it was my obsession with hiding everything and keeping people at a distance that had cost me the chance to be there for my friend when she needed me. I felt so badly about this, and I trusted her without question – so I got in touch and told her. Jayne – of course – was cool ('You could have said all this before, Nick – I really wish you had!') and our friendship got back on track. And then her cancer symptoms returned, except that this time they were worse.

She'd started bumping into things. She had an awful pain in her back. It was clear pretty quickly that the outlook for her was bleak – but she was young, the same age as me, and she struggled to find any kind of acceptance. Instead she was overwhelmed with anger, desperate to prolong her life in any way she could. But this was a battle that nobody could win.

I went to visit her in the hospice that was caring for her, and as I left, I knew I wouldn't see her again.

Jayne died aged thirty, on 2 October 1998, and a few days after that, I had a dream. In the dream, I heard her speaking – not sounding peaceful and saintly and accepting, but full of the rage that I knew she had been feeling as her life slipped away. Sounding, in other words, just like the fierce and vital woman Jayne had really been. 'For God's sake, Nick,' the voice in the dream said to me indignantly, 'you're still alive!'

At her funeral, the group of us all came back together. I still hadn't told them I was gay, but I realised very clearly that day that it simply didn't matter. We were all just the same as we'd been when we'd met twelve years before, so young back then, so optimistic, so excited. My friends loved me, and they were such good people. They weren't going to judge me. I took great strength from that thought. And I knew now that life was so precious – and so fragile.

For God's sake, Nick, you're still alive! I realised that I had what Jayne had wanted most and couldn't have, the only thing that matters and the one thing that money cannot buy. I had time. So right then and there, I decided that somehow, no matter what problems I was faced with – prolapsed disc or not, police career or not, difficult personal life or not – I'd had enough of lying on the floor in the gloom thinking about what a terrible time I was having and feeling sorry for myself. I'd had enough of hiding too, and of feeling I must stay away from everyone. From now on I would honour my friend by fighting for my future and making my life the very best that it could be. From now on, I was done with secrets.

But concealment is something that becomes a part of you. Even now I wanted to be more open, it still felt like a struggle. The only way was one step at a time. Was the police force still my future? I knew I had to find out for sure, which meant going to see the Chief Medical Officer – the one with the power to tell me I could stay or that I'd have to leave. I'd been putting off and putting off my visit, in case I heard bad news. I even put a backup plan in place, studying for an HNC in Business Management at Bromley College in case I had to leave the police – but it turned out that I needn't have worried. The CMO told me that I'd recovered from my injury sufficiently to allow me to be operational in the force full-time, but the Territorial Support Group was out because I wouldn't be able to handle shields and other heavy equipment. What I needed was to find a different role.

Once I knew I hadn't lost everything, I felt more confident about getting help and I stayed for a while at the Flint House Police Rehabilitation Centre in Goring, Berkshire. I had intensive physio there and was finally able to walk without pain – and emotional support was available too, though I still found it hard to receive it. I remember a session with a counsellor and how much I wanted to talk about what was going on – about Jayne's death, about a painful relationship break-up I'd been through. But I couldn't get the words to come out. I'd been holding my secrets for so long – it was a really tough stretch to let them go.

Flint House got me ready to go back to work, which meant applying for promotion to sergeant. Instead of being a front-line officer sent out to incidents, I'd be supporting and directing those who did. My first post was in Walworth in 1999 – a tough, inner London area where life was certainly intense. Every day we handled stabbings, road traffic accidents, and violent crime of many kinds, and I found myself in charge of murder scenes, car chases, and calls by officers for urgent assistance. I learned a huge amount and had a team of really brilliant, dedicated people.

But the best thing of all about Walworth was its openness and freedom. There were openly gay people there, and everyone was accepted. Workmates asked each other about their dates – all sorts of dates – and even laughed and joked about it. You could just be who you were, and I began to feel a bit more relaxed. If I could be like this at work, then maybe I could do it in other places too, with the most important loved ones in my life.

*

Now. Just do it now. It'll be easier to talk to Mum on her own.

I looked at my own face in the bathroom mirror, noticing the clenching of my jaw and the furrow in my forehead. I was in my parents' house, and I could faintly hear a radio chattering away downstairs. Dad had gone out to get some extra groceries while Mum was pottering about in the kitchen fixing dinner.

But the thought was just so scary. *What if?* my mind kept whispering. *What if?* Of course I didn't think that she'd be livid if she found out I was gay. I knew she wasn't going to scream insults at me, or order me out of the house. *But . . . what if she tries to smile and she says it's okay, but just for a second I can see in her face that she's sad and disappointed? That I'm less in her eyes than before? That I've let my family down? What if she's ashamed of me, embarrassed about telling her friends that her daughter is a lesbian?*

But how long is it now since Mum and I really had a proper chat? Since we felt close, since I confided in her? It's been years. I've let this awful distance creep in between us. I've lost so much, just because I'm scared to tell the truth. We all have. Enough already.

I gave myself a shake. *This is ridiculous. She's your mum. Just go down there and tell her. Before Dad gets back.* I squared my shoulders, cleared my throat and headed down the stairs.

'Mum?'

'Yes, love?' She was chopping the leeks.

'There's something I've been meaning to tell you.'

'So what's that then, love?'

My stomach was churning. Suddenly I felt my eyes filling up with tears.

'Nick?' She looked up from her chopping and all I could see in her face was love and worry. 'What is it? You're not ill, are you, love?' That was too much and I burst out crying. 'Oh, Nicky! What's wrong?'

'Don't worry, I'm not ill!' I tried to rub the tears from my cheeks. 'Um – so – it's – there's something – I've been worried that you might not be too happy if I told you. And, um, Dad. Dad might not be happy either.'

'Well,' Mum said in her practical way, 'why don't you try me first?'

I took a very deep breath. *This is it. Say it, Nick. Just say it.*

'Remember when I left Brian, Mum?'

'Of course.'

'So – um – there was a reason why but I didn't tell you. I left him because I'm gay.'

'Ah,' replied mum, without missing a beat. She put the knife down on the chopping board, walked over to me and put her arm round my shoulder. 'Yes, we thought it might be that.'

Of all the ways I thought she might react, this was the very last response that I'd expected.

'What? *You thought it might be that?!*'

'Yes,' she went on. 'Me and Dad were having a chat about you and we both said, yes, we think she's gay. That's fine, love.'

'It's fine?'

'Of course it is.' She gave me a beaming smile. 'Don't be daft. We just want you to be happy.'

'So – why didn't you ask me – if you thought –?'

'Well – Dad and me – we said if we're wrong, you might feel we'd made a judgement on you. And we'd never do that. So it was better to leave it to you.'

Would I have told her if she'd asked me any sooner? Looking back, I wish she had, but I'll never really know. My parents were both brilliant. Mum finished chopping the leeks and I sat at the kitchen table wiping my eyes and feeling so much better, so much happier and safer and stronger – ready to take on the whole world. Whatever the future might hold, I now knew just how lucky I was.

Chapter 3

'*306. Suspect observed not wearing a seat belt,*' reported the radio. 306 was the number of PC Samantha Evans out on patrol, a really good copper who'd take on any case and more often than not would get the bad guys. A few minutes later, the radio crackled into life again with an update: '*306. Suspect failing to stop.*'

This spring morning in 2003 had been quiet up to now. I was the skipper in charge and I'd decided that the two probationers based at our station in Walworth, south London, should go out on patrol with Samantha to gain more experience. Fifteen minutes earlier I'd watched as the three of them drove out through the back gate. This sounded like a pretty routine traffic stop – it would be useful training. A minute or two later, another report came in from Samantha.

'*306 chasing suspect following failure to stop.*'

I was working in the relative calm of the sergeant's office when suddenly the radio burst into life. I heard Samantha's voice again – but now she was yelling in a way she'd never do unless something was drastically wrong. Her voice was choppy and breathless as though she was running, but I couldn't make out what she was saying.

'306, where are you? Where are you?'

No reply. Then another shout from Samantha. This time we all picked up one word. The word was '*gun*'. The calls to back her up went out straightaway.

'All units, Mike Sierra. 306 requires assistance. Does anybody know where she is? Last location was Cooks Road.'

I ran out into the station car park and jumped into the car. I knew that other units were also on their way because I could hear them over the radio, all trying to locate 306.

'*306 where are you? Tell us where you are. Does anybody know where she is?*'

And then: '*Call from a member of the public reporting an armed man running in Kennington Road.*' My foot went to the floor. When I got there minutes later I saw Samantha, the suspect, and a second man in jeans and a leather jacket, all of them on their feet, which was an incredible relief. Two officers who'd made it just before me were sealing off the small green as a crime scene, and as I drew up alongside, the van to remove the suspect also arrived. Samantha's and the suspect's eyes and noses were streaming from CS gas. I had no idea what had just happened.

As I found out, I felt horror. A simple traffic stop had changed in seconds from routine to shocking violence and attempted murder (which was the charge the suspect eventually faced). Samantha Evans had pulled a man over for not wearing a seat-belt, and he'd jumped out of his car, drawn a gun and started running. She gave chase and caught up with him down a side road. As they struggled, he'd jammed the barrel against her head and pulled the trigger at point blank range. But the bullet was home-made and he'd loaded it in the chamber backwards – this was the only reason the gun didn't fire. Seconds later Samantha, showing unbelievable composure, sprayed him with CS gas from her canister. The gas got into her face as well as his, and the very brave passer-by in his jeans and jacket then assisted her to take him into custody.

Nothing could have shown me more clearly how much the world had changed. The old rules had gone out of the window – and for more and more criminals, so had any kind of compunction. When I'd joined the force, there were no stab-proof vests for police officers (Met vests, as they're known), and my handbag would have made a better weapon than my first issue truncheon – it was heavier, for sure. I didn't have a great sense of danger; in those days, offenders would mostly run if they heard sirens, and although quite early on I was half-heartedly threatened with a knife by a man who was trying to get away, it felt like an exceptional event. The murder of an officer on a routine call-out in Croydon changed that right across the capital. This was when the FBI began to pass on its second-hand Met vests to UK police forces, and I remember my mum anxiously saying that she would buy one for me. Next, everyone in each area car had to wear them. And then they became standard issue for all cops: a deep shift of culture in the first decade of the new century.

As our team was debriefed following the attempted murder of Samantha, the impact on all of us was clear. I felt it too – a sense that somehow I'd failed her, let her down, put her in harm's way. Could we have done more to help her? Found her faster?

Got there before her life was in danger? Had I put her under pressure to do the training that day with the probationers? It had been my decision, after all, to send her out. At the same time, I knew my thoughts weren't rational – I couldn't have known what would happen.

The experience brought the whole team closer together. I tended to dismiss my own reactions, though – after all, I'd been sitting in the station when it happened, not directly involved – and I focused on the guys on the street and of course on Samantha herself. She was amazingly resilient. A colleague did suggest that I get some support but I didn't take his idea all that seriously. At the time it was for me to decide if I needed it or not.

*

More gun crime. More violence. More drugs on the street. The old-school criminal code of honour I'd encountered just a short time before, down in Catford, had vanished. Central London, and Walworth in particular, was looking rougher and poorer, and the security guards on duty at the nearby Elephant & Castle Shopping Centre were the first in the country to be issued with stab vests as a normal part of their uniform.

Nothing bonds a team quite like pressure and danger. Front-line cops are just incredible. Since coming out, I was also free to be real with those around me, and the wedge that I'd felt creeping into all of my relationships was gone. I was so much happier and loved the work that I was doing: every day I could feel and see the difference I was making for the better in the local community. There was strong, supportive police leadership in Walworth too, with effective coaching and mentoring and the chance to ask for help if you needed it. The role of mentors is a great strength in policing and I'm grateful for the guidance I've received down the years.

A coach I spoke to there once asked me, 'What do you want to do with your life, Nick?' And although it seemed a huge question to answer, it was also a really powerful one.

Without thinking about it too much, I answered, 'I want to change the world.'

'Okay,' he said to me. 'So start in the street where you live.' His words stayed with me from that moment on. 'And always leave the ladder down,' he went on, 'so that others can follow you.'

I was also personally happier than ever before. I'd met a woman who was showing me how love can really be when it's founded on honesty and trust, not hemmed in by secrecy and fear. But life in Walworth could still be disturbing and frightening. When a batch of contaminated ecstasy was sold in local nightclubs, one person died from the drug, two ended up in hospital, and another was killed jumping from a building, hallucinating that he could fly. I'd not been there long when an 11-year-old schoolboy was stabbed to death by two other children only a year or so older than he was. I wasn't directly involved in investigating that case, but I'll never forget the atmosphere at the station when the two young suspects were brought in. They were brothers from a problem family, well known to the police and often in trouble, who'd always fight aggressively if any attempt was made to arrest them, and their mother made the police investigation extremely difficult, slowing down the gathering of evidence. Six years later, both of them were convicted of manslaughter.

One day, driving the van, we received an urgent call. A fight had broken out behind some shops in Liverpool Road with several combatants using knives. As my partner Ben and I reached the scene, most of them ran for it but one guy stayed put, swinging an enormous meat cleaver and yelling 'Come on then!', absolutely ready to take on the police. Ben shouted, 'Put the weapon down!' and I ran over to give support as he rugby-tackled the guy and managed to get the meat cleaver out of his hands. If he'd not been disarmed as quickly as he was, I don't know what would have happened. As I sat there on top of him, holding his head down on the ground with adrenaline racing through my body, I felt a rush of anger that he'd put us all in such danger.

Ben and I never really discussed this – he just thanked me for backing him up. But moments like that make bonds between police colleagues which aren't commonly found outside the service, except in the armed forces or the other emergency services, where the normal working day means trauma after trauma, crisis after crisis. The shared knowledge and connection this creates is very often unspoken. That day, I believe Ben saved my life.

Not every incident brought drama like that, however. I also remember a young man who was using stolen mopeds for a series of robberies. We spotted him one morning and gave chase: a lengthy pursuit around the South Circular into New Cross, with dozens of opportunities to turn off – none of which the suspect took. He had so many chances to vanish down a side road or speed away along an alleyway, where the moped would fit and a police car wouldn't, that I grew more and more amazed he didn't take them. It was very nearly funny. *What's wrong with this guy? Perhaps he really wants us to catch him.* Which of course we did.

*

It was rare for me to feel unsupported during my time in Walworth, but one occasion does cast a shadow in my memory. As a sergeant, I had to attend the scenes of sudden deaths to make sure there were no suspicious circumstances, which of course could be distressing. This one was particularly awful – a student house share in which one of the occupants, who was studying medicine at the nearby teaching hospital, somehow managed to bring home a lethal substance from a lab. He stuck a sheet of A4 paper on his door stating that he should not be resuscitated when found, and tragically committed suicide. When his flatmates got up the next morning, they saw what he'd written and rang 999 in horror.

My colleague Stewart and I opened the door to the young man's bedroom and found him dead. We had to notify his parents, stay with his body until it could be removed, then go through his possessions to check for any signs of foul play, and those few hours became one of the saddest shifts of my whole life. His housemates were distraught, repeatedly asking us and each other how they might have helped him, and clearly blaming themselves that they hadn't. I could feel the circles of pain and loss spreading wider and wider and went home absolutely drained.

Next came a phone call from Human Resources. 'Just to let you know,' said an unknown voice briskly down the line, 'that you might be at risk because you attended the suicide at Vicarage Grove. The poison has now been identified. So if you find yourself experiencing any of the following symptoms . . .'

and she listed what these might be. There was no support or sympathy for me. No understanding that I might be concerned.

I didn't get the symptoms of poisoning and nor did Stewart. But for the first time in my career, I felt really left alone and let down. My inspector, Karen, asked me a few days later if I was okay and I truthfully said no – and Stewart, who was still on probation, was struggling even more. If you're a member of a specialist department, you're more visible, and I think you're more likely to get help than an ordinary front-line copper. Police training maximises resilience and gives you a can-do attitude, and while that is important, no matter how professional you are, you can't always 'do'. No one can. Sometimes, everyone needs help.

*

After three years in Walworth, I applied for promotion to the rank of inspector. Once again I'd be facing an interview board. First time round I didn't study hard enough – revision had never been quite my thing and it still wasn't – but for my second attempt I was determined and did a lot of preparation. I remember my superintendent's words of encouragement: 'You need to stand out,' she told me firmly. 'Don't give the same drab old answers that everybody else does. Make yourself different!'

Dressed in my new suit, I was pretty keyed up about the interview and went for a nervous pee a few minutes before I was due to be called in. When my name was called, I stepped into the room with what I hoped was a confident smile, then realised as I took my seat in front of the panel of three that I hadn't done my zip up.

Damn it. What am I going to do? Okay – just be professional. Ignore it. Nobody's noticed.

The chair of the panel said a few words of welcome, then explained the areas they'd be covering in the interview.

But what if they have noticed? One of them must have. They're senior police officers – they won't miss something like this! Anyway, I've realised and now it's all I can think about. As they launched into their first testing question, I knew that if I wanted to concentrate at all, it was vital that I got that zip done up.

'Ah – excuse me,' I said, 'I'm going to have to stop you. I've bought this new suit, and ah – I just need to pop outside and adjust my zip, if that's okay.' As I shot out of the room I could hear the panel laughing. *Oh well – at least I'm memorable now.* And yes, I did get my promotion.

*

I'd made a good recovery from my prolapsed disc, but I knew that the stronger I became, the less likely it was that my back problems would return. So I stepped up my fitness routine, adding in weights for the first time, and started to notice a real increase in my strength. My next step up in the police, I decided, would be firearms training.

The Metropolitan Police Specialist Training Centre near Gravesend overlooks the Thames estuary, which sounds like an attractive location . . . except it really isn't. A sulphurous estuary smell hangs in the air all year round and gets worse in hot weather, so when I did my courses all through 2004, I had to get used to the pong. The place is huge, with mocked-up buildings for training situations and replaying incidents that have happened in the past, shooting ranges, and outdoor areas to simulate scenarios like house searches, car chases, and hostage rescue. All the courses were residential, taught from Monday to Friday while we stayed in small rooms with small windows, shared shower blocks, and slept in single beds with plastic mattress covers that crackled every time we rolled over. The food wasn't great either, except for the salad, but at least the place had a decent gym. And with trainees constantly coming and going on short and longer courses, there was a real buzz in the air.

I entered this period of training as an inspector, so for me there were three phases to it: basic firearms instruction, then the Armed Response Vehicles course – which was considerably harder – and finally the supervisor's course which prepared us to serve as tactical firearms advisers. This last one was especially testing and intense. On top of shooting and weapons maintenance – how to fire a Glock and an MP5, along with other guns that would be available to us if an incident required it – we learned tactical skills, emergency strategies, and risk assessment. Our trainers were looking for individuals who stayed calm under pressure and could show assertiveness, even dominance – but definitely not aggression – when a situation required. And as so often in policing, scenarios that might seem very scary became matter-of-fact: just new knowledge that was there for us to master.

I loved the challenge of my firearms role, but wasn't enthralled by the guns themselves. For me the satisfaction of the job lay in pushing myself and finding out where the limits of my capabilities really lay. So I was very pleased indeed when I passed all the stages of training and joined the Met Police firearms unit known now as SCO19, one of only seven women in a team 650 strong. In the almost twenty years since I'd started out as a wide-eyed cadet, I'd worked my way up the career ladder and now I oversaw forty-three men based at two stations, one in the north of London and one in the south, and was in charge of the response to any armed incident across the city – twenty-four hours a day, seven days a week.

*

On Thursday 7 July 2005 – the day that would become known as 7/7 – four suicide bombers detonated devices in central London. Fifty-two innocent people died. I'd been in firearms for only a few months.

The four explosions occurred within sixty minutes during the morning rush hour. I was on the late turn as Trojan One that day – this is the title of the inspector in charge of the armed team on duty. He or she is mobile, out in a car with a driver ready to be taken to any incident where we're needed. I didn't wait until the start of my shift that day, though – I went straight to work when I heard what was happening, to help those on duty who were having to respond. I wasn't called or asked to do this, but hundreds of my fellow officers did the same. We went because we were angry that someone had attacked our city, and determined to do whatever we could to stop it happening again. It's an outcome of our training, but it's also a trait – that police officers will walk into danger.

Our biggest fear, of course, was more attacks, and I stayed

on the move around London for the rest of the day. The centre was completely shut down and its streets were deserted – a city standing still in shock. At one point I passed the ugly wreckage of the bus with its roof blown off, right next to the British Medical Association's headquarters in the stylish central area of Bloomsbury. Heightened armed patrols were placed at key locations, and there was also reassurance patrolling: visible policemen and women on the streets where Londoners could see them, a reminder that protectors were at hand.

On a day like that, there were rumours: names of interest were mentioned, and faces or the details of vehicles were circulated. The woman I was seeing at the time was in surveillance and she was gone for days afterwards, constantly on duty either on stand-by or following possible suspects. But terrorism units and the security services handle their information on a need-to-know basis, and on 7/7 there was nothing specific: no one for the police to look out for. Somehow these four murderers had been missed, giving them the chance to do what they'd intended. It was hard not to find this disturbing, and a short while later, I told my sister Dani, who works in the middle of the city: 'If I ever ring you and tell you to leave London, don't ask me why. Just do it.'

Then, on 21 July – exactly two weeks later – there were four more attempted bomb attacks in London: the work of copycats. Three tubes and one bus: it was obviously someone's big idea to bring the horror back to life. Dani is quite certain, from photos that were shown on TV later, that she sat next to one of the four would-be bombers at Embankment underground station when he was on his way that morning. 'All the hairs on my neck stood up when he sat down next to me, Nick,' she told me.

But the copycats screwed it up: their detonators exploded but their home-made bombs didn't. Their photos were immediately circulated and now the police were looking for them

Four suspects at large, but nobody knew where – just that they were dangerous. Heightened patrols focused on key areas. Police shift times were extended from eight hours to ten or even twelve. And as well as all of this, there was normal policing to be carried out for London. The pressure was immense.

Next morning, a terrible tragedy took place. Jean Charles de Menezes was a Brazilian electrician who lived in the same block of flats in south London as one of the suspected bombers. When he left the building on his way to work next day, he was wrongly identified as a member of the group and followed towards Stockwell tube station. The Met's Gold commander ordered that he should be prevented from entering the Underground and detained as soon as possible. Armed officers were dispatched. It turned out later that Jean Charles was heading for work – he had a job up in Kilburn, north of the river. He boarded a tube train at Stockwell and was shot dead by police. I heard the news by text: *we've got one of them*, it said, and at first I felt relieved. *This will help to stop another attack*, I thought. And then, as time went by, we realised that we hadn't got one of them at all. Jean Charles de Menezes should not have been shot.

His shooting was met with waves of public concern. There was support for the police. There was also harsh criticism. As I watched and listened to all this, as an officer who carried a gun – who could have been called to Stockwell that day – I remembered a day down at Gravesend during my firearms training, and an exercise we did. Along with Graham, a colleague on my course, and observed by our tutors and classmates, we played out a scenario in one of the training centre's many locations.

The space we were in looked like the garage of an ordinary house, except that on one wall was a large video screen. The 'characters' involved in the scenario appeared on this screen and we were told to respond, work together, and deal with whatever we saw in front of us. The point of the exercise was simple – it was asking us one question, over and over again. As the scenario unfolds and the situation changes: *do I reach for my gun?*

Before we started, we'd been told that there was screaming in this house and that the neighbours had phoned the police. The garage door was open, and as we went inside we saw a woman (on the screen). She told us that everything was fine and that we didn't need to be here – except that she was clearly distressed. All of a sudden, a man jumped up behind her, grabbed her and held a knife to her throat.

Graham and I shouted out together: 'Armed police! Put the knife down! Put the knife down!' In a sudden, shocking movement, the man slashed the woman's throat then flung the knife away. He was shot in the chest and collapsed. It took seconds.

'It was you who shot him, right?' I asked Graham as we left for our assessment on the exercise. I knew I hadn't.

'No,' he answered. 'Not me. I thought you did.' This totally confused me.

'You must have,' I said.

'Honestly, I didn't. Did he shoot himself?'

'No way. Was there another gunman in the room?'

But it turned out that the person who'd shot the guy was me. As the man in the video had cut the woman's throat, I'd fired three bullets in milliseconds – an instantaneous reaction. All of them had hit him in the chest and I didn't even know. Graham had fired at him too.

That day was an absolute eye-opener to me. I'm a non-violent person, and my action was a primal instinct. It was for survival. Looking back on it now, I see this moment as the start of my fascination with the way our brains work and how we do things that we're not even conscious of. But above all, I learned how vulnerable I was as a firearms officer. The media spotlight – and a murder charge – could be the outcome of anything I did. To do my job, I was going to have to put all this to the back of my mind. *Don't worry: you know you'd always do the right thing*, is what I had to say to myself. And also: *this won't happen to me.*

When you're interviewed for firearms training, you're asked the question: *how would you feel if you shot someone?* I can tell you the answer: *until it happens, you don't know.* After any shooting, there's an investigation with the officers involved taken off duty until it's been completed. They know that they might be charged with murder, and they live with that pressure and with the consequences of their actions that can continue for months and even years.

22 July 2005 was a ripple effect – a perfect storm which started with the wrongful identification of Jean Charles de Menezes. The rest was a cascade of outcomes leading to the death of an innocent man. It's easy to reflect on all of this when you're calm and safe. And it's obvious – of course it is – what ought to have been done and known and seen when the tension has subsided. But I was there, and there's only one

word I can think of to describe how it was on the streets. It felt like war, and war was the reason for what happened.

*

Joshua was seventeen when he was shot. He'd made some poor decisions in his short life and fallen in with some scary people, and when a disagreement flared up – I never found out exactly what it was about – one of them used a gun. By the time I reached the scene, the ambulance was minutes away and the first responding officers were giving him chest compressions and rescue breathing. Then the paramedics took over with drips and used the defib machine to give a sharp electric shock to his heart. This young boy was in cardiac arrest. We alerted St Thomas' Hospital that there was an emergency on the way then travelled with the ambulance, clearing a path ahead of it through the city traffic. We had another reason for attending too: what if someone came back to make sure the job was finished? That's why when anyone gets shot, the firearms team guards the hospital where they're taken and protects the medical staff looking after a patient who has such dangerous enemies.

By the time I got to Tommy's, things were under control. Joshua had been assessed in A&E and – still just alive – he was undergoing surgery. The corridors around him had been sealed and the doors were guarded by armed officers. Then his mother arrived. I didn't have to ask who she was: the terror in her face was enough. Chaperoned by a local officer, she sat down near me, staring ahead but seeing little.

A few minutes later the door leading down to surgery opened

and the surgeon appeared. One look at his face and I knew. He went over to her and told her that her son was dead. I'd never heard a cry of agony like hers before and I never ever want to again. As a human being, my impulse was to try to comfort her – but I was wearing a police uniform, carrying a gun . . . I wasn't the right person. My team and I just faded away. We knew there was no more we could do.

*

'*Any Trojan Unit available to investigate a possible shooting in Knightsbridge.*'

I heard the message come in over the radio, and a couple of units picking it up. It was the evening of 13 September 2005, a warm day with showers of light rain. I was Trojan One, in a car with a driver, moving around London with responsibility for managing all reported firearms incidents across the city and the deployments of armed officers.

'*Looks like there's been a double shooting,*' the radio reported. '*Ground floor of a large department store. Make-up section. Male suspect has shot female and then shot himself. Murder suicide.*'

The store was in the West End Central area of London – Charlie Delta's ground. I switched my radio to Charlie Delta's frequency and heard the local Delta call signs rapidly responding.

'*Delta One. I'm on my way.*'

'*Charlie Delta from Trojan One – anybody on the scene yet?*'

'MP from Trojan One,' I said. 'We're not far away. We'll respond to that as well.'

My driver turned the car and picked up speed. Our siren went on. It only took a couple of minutes to get there, and as we travelled, I was gathering as much information from the reports as I could. It was a vital part of risk assessment to work out what the situation would be as we reached the scene. What were we going into? Could there even be another gunman?

'*Charlie Delta, we've got an ambulance running but we need two. Do you have an ETA for the first one?*'

'*Let the ambulance know this is a double shooting. Female unconscious, not breathing. Male unconscious.*'

'*Lots of calls. Witnesses reporting that this guy just walked in and fired.*'

'*Charlie Delta. Believe there are no outstanding suspects.*'

It was the number of reports coming in that told me it was going to be bad. Some reports of firearms are isolated: a witness spots a gun, or thinks they did, but then whoever makes the sighting doesn't contact us again or the suspect disappears. But this was something very big and dreadful – I knew because we were being inundated with calls. That's where training kicks in. We must go to the scene of the disaster and stay there, functioning at a high operational level and overriding our deepest human instincts for fight or flight or freeze.

It was still only minutes since the shootings and apart from two police cars at the kerb, the affluent street looked quite normal. The traffic was still flowing and as I pulled up and got out of the car, members of the public called out 'Over there!' to direct me. Inside the store, it was eerily quiet. The beauty hall had been open late and the police were evacuating the last few evening shoppers – a difficult job since some of them just stood there, motionless with shock. The security guard at the door pointed me across the gleaming beauty hall on the ground floor, a luxurious space full of mirrors and lights, to where two firearms officers from my team, who'd arrived seconds before us, were crouched by the man and the woman on the ground alongside one of the counters. Firearms officers are trained in ballistic first aid – treating gunshot wounds – and until the ambulance arrived they were doing their best to give emergency medical attention while going through considerable trauma themselves. Front-line officers are just awesome.

I immediately began organising, sealing the crime scene, taking the names of anyone who'd seen what had happened and making sure that when the paramedics arrived they would be able to work safely. My local colleagues started speaking to the witnesses, all of whom repeated the same thing though quite a few could barely get their words out because they were so stunned. The man, they said, had walked up to the woman as she was standing alongside one of the counters. He'd shot her in the head before turning the gun on himself. It was therefore unlikely that any other armed individual was still present. The two ambulances arrived and the police officers who'd given first aid travelled to hospital with the casualties, keeping both in their sight at all times so that their line of evidence could remain continuous. I followed to make sure that my team was okay. Doctors couldn't save the woman's life. Her murderer had briefly been her boyfriend, but when she'd ended their relationship he was unable to cope with this, stalked her and was charged with harassment. But he was out on bail when he decided to kill her and he died shortly after she did.

This shooting was the worst incident I dealt with in my years on the firearms team, and afterwards I struggled to share my feelings about it with anyone. In the days and weeks that followed, I noticed that my memories of the scene, although I'd taken everything in very clearly while I was present, now seemed like fragments as I tried to recall them. It's probably the trauma, I thought.

*

2006

It was years now since I'd felt like the wrong piece of the jigsaw, but I started to notice the feeling creeping back. It took me quite a while to acknowledge it. After all, I'd enjoyed my firearms training. I wanted to challenge myself in my career, and this role certainly did that. So what exactly was wrong?

It wasn't the job, I realised. It was the environment that didn't really suit me. The best way to describe the unit was 'old school' – and what that really meant was 'pretty harsh', to be honest. Firearms is an intense arena where lives are at stake and after every incident, feedback is given. It's vital to have strong debriefings to look at what's happened and take lessons from it that might help in the future; not everything goes right and people must reflect and learn. But that's not the same as blame – or at least, it shouldn't be. Too often I found that these debriefings had the feeling of finger-pointing: *you did that wrong. You didn't pass that info on. It was you.* There was no chance, it seemed, of a supportive approach: *okay, but it might have been better if you'd . . .* And if you got defensive in response to criticism, this was seen as your weakness. For me, that's not a good learning environment and I could feel my confidence starting to dip.

We were called out to a nightclub one evening after somebody spotted a gun. The place had been sealed off, the clubbers were being searched and released and we were asked to clear the building. I made a judgement call: the threat, I decided, had been minimised and in any case there had only been one report about the gun. We would holster our weapons and simply do a walkthrough. This went off without a hitch.

But in the debrief, when I said that the call-out had gone well, I faced a serious challenge from one of my PCs. 'No, it didn't,' he said flatly, 'and if you think that, you're not taking it seriously.' He took the view that if we didn't go in with weapons drawn in a situation like that one, there was really no point in our being there. I strongly disagreed, but his confrontational attitude still caught me off guard. The firearms unit was full of strong personalities like his – I think it's inevitable – and quite a few of them would openly argue with a senior officer, and even question their ability. These guys worked very hard and they were trained to the hilt, but some of them were convinced that they were always right and I was still quite new to the unit, which made it difficult for me to push back. It was hard to know how I should receive direct criticism when I wasn't deeply grounded in my role, and I constantly felt that as a leader, I *should* have all the answers. It started to get wearing.

I had another kind of people problem too: a personality clash. Two of my sergeants didn't get on at all and one in particular showed no compunction about voicing his contempt for the other to his PCs. This wasn't only unprofessional but also highly disruptive to the functioning of the team: you try to present a united front as supervisors but the bickering and badmouthing were causing unrest and the situation grew more and more unstable. I started to experience what's known as the 80/20 rule – spending 80 per cent of my time managing 20 per cent of my staff. Armed units also often wait around, working shifts where there's no immediate crisis but their readiness must be maintained, and keeping this bunch of strong, sometimes deeply divergent characters engaged during these down times was very challenging.

It was hard to pin down my unease at the time. What exactly was I doing wrong? But looking back, I see the problem much more clearly. I just didn't fit – no one's fault, but simply who I was. Firearms is a reactive role in which you respond to severe situations which are already underway. Contact with people is limited and most of the time I was only interacting with the members of my team. But my major strength is as a communicator, and I flourish best where I can initiate. The role takes controlled aggression, and I don't think I have that aggression. I lacked female mentors and may have been too young in the rank. Above all, I didn't feel that I was making much of a difference, and to do that is my biggest motivation.

I was feeling like that jigsaw piece again, just not quite lining up. Firearms wasn't my best fit. And I knew by now that it doesn't matter how hard you push – this feeling doesn't go away. My mood was getting lower for other reasons too: I'd split up with a partner after five years together, and my dad had just been scheduled for a triple coronary bypass operation. There didn't seem to be anyone I could talk to, so when I went on a training course for the next level up – in tactical support – even though I failed it, I enjoyed chatting to the guy in charge. We discussed why my confidence was taking such a knock and he helped me crystallise my thoughts: *I'm not happy here. I don't want to stay.* But if firearms wasn't right for me – what should I do next?

*

The Directorate of Professional Standards seemed kind of intriguing. Bit of a dry-sounding department title, maybe, but good for my CV, and best of all, it would use my strongest skill: communication. I was getting to know myself better and better, and this would be a people role: working in the department which investigates complaints about the conduct of police officers. I thought it might be a good next step to take.

My decision wasn't definite yet, but I discussed the idea with my mentor, Liz, a superintendent in the firearms unit, two ranks above me and part of my senior management team, which was how our mentoring relationship began. She was a very strong character, kind but very caring, and also a breath of fresh air: the very first words she ever said to me were, 'Don't call me ma'am: call me Liz,' and we just went on from there. (Mind you, it took ages for me to actually follow her instruction: from cadet training onwards, the importance of respecting senior officers had been deeply instilled in me.)

Liz could make others feel listened to, as though they were the most important person in the room when they were speaking. This really is a heck of a skill. I knew she was always observing everything that was going on very closely, and – of course – that included me.

'Come in for a minute,' she said to me one day as I was walking past the door of her office. 'We can have a quick chat. Tell me what's been happening.'

'So I'm certain that I'm not the right fit for firearms,' I told her. 'That's pretty much a definite decision now. I do enjoy the challenge, but . . . ' She was nodding, listening very carefully the way she always did. 'I'm not sure what I should do next, to be honest,' I went on. 'It's a bit of a crossroads. Just – considering how to move my career forward, really. I thought that the Directorate of Personal Standards might be one way to do it.'

'Right.' Liz looked at me thoughtfully. 'I'm sure that would suit you well, Nick.' And then she said the words that were going to change my life.

'But have you ever thought of becoming a negotiator?'

Chapter 4

SUPERHEROES
June 2008

Captain America and Thor were sitting on the roof. Two negotiators were out there with them, and everyone was drinking mugs of tea. Down in the street below, a crowd of media had gathered to cover this superhero invasion. Mics and zoom lenses were everywhere. They'd all turned up because this house belonged to a very senior politician and member of the British Cabinet.

It was the most surreal sight I'd ever seen. I was there to learn my new job.

*

The Directorate of Professional Standards did turn out to be a very good decision: I felt more comfortable there, and happier. Once again I had the satisfying feeling of making a difference to the people around me on a day-to-day basis. In firearms my team had been spread right across London, making it difficult to ever feel connected, but here I was part of a tight-knit group, listening and explaining, allaying people's fears and building good relationships. Professional Standards deals with complaints against the police and issues of conduct, and it's often about clarifying, giving information, helping people understand. For me, this role was a much better fit.

But I also knew it wasn't the limit of my abilities, and I wanted to progress until I reached that limit. Liz was continuing to give me her support, and the suggestion she'd made about negotiation training had got me thinking. People skills. Communication. But along with all of that, a job that sounded truly challenging, one that would push me to become the best I could be. *If that's what negotiation is*, I thought, *I'm up for it*.

Most negotiators are also volunteers: they work in other areas of the force but are available once they've completed their training to respond to crises. I already knew a bit about their work, having met quite a few of them as a firearms officer on calls where they were also deployed. But up to now, you'd had to hold the rank of chief inspector (one above mine) to be eligible to train, and it was Liz who'd first told me this had changed.

When a crisis situation blows up, a negotiator's phone rings and the job is theirs if they want it. That's how Liz worked, negotiating alongside her position in the firearms unit. It's one of the things I would come to love most about the role and about my fellow negotiators – that they do the job because they choose to help people and they love what they do.

*

Okay – I'm going to go for this.

Selection for negotiation training takes place in two stages,

an interview panel and a role play. My meeting with the panel
went okay, but the role play was tough. I travelled up to Hendon
and found myself standing in a corridor, closely watched by two
directors of the national negotiation course, while behind a door
was somebody in crisis, played by another of the trainers. The
situation had been briefly explained to me: a friend of this person
had called the police, worried that they seem to be depressed,
and now suddenly they're texting to say that they've swallowed
some pills. That was all the information I had. The purpose of the
role play was to test my resilience, my ability to make personal
connections, and the way I interacted. It's challenging to speak
to someone like this when you know almost nothing about them.

Controlling my nerves, I tried to start a dialogue but the
invisible person behind the door didn't want to know. I knew
I must keep going. For a long time they said nothing, then finally
I heard a woman's voice. 'Why are you here? I didn't call you,'
she demanded irritably.

'I've been told you've taken some tablets,' I replied carefully.
That just seemed to make her even more angry.

'Fuck off. Leave me alone. I've no idea why you're here.
There's nothing wrong.'

The purpose of a conversation like this is to let the person in
crisis express emotion, to deal with these emotions calmly and
patiently, and to start to make a connection. But fifteen minutes
later, I'd made little headway and didn't think I'd done very
well. I reminded myself that the assessors weren't looking for
actual skills – after all, I hadn't been taught any yet – but for my
aptitude. Did they think I'd make a good negotiation student?
Did I seem like I could learn? I didn't know.

By now I really wanted to be chosen, so I left feeling flat and disappointed, with at least a fortnight to wait for the outcome. When the call eventually came through and the answer was yes, I was overjoyed. I'd had a lot of support from my detective chief inspector at the DPS, Murray, and I shot upstairs to his office to tell him the good news too. Murray took negotiation seriously and understood what negotiators do, and the life-or-death situations they face, but his attitude isn't universal in policing even today. There are still those who think our skills are 'soft' and we're just not rough and tough enough to gain their respect. (In the exasperated words of a close colleague: 'It's like they think we work in a charity shop or something.') I knew I was extra-lucky to have Murray backing me up.

But it was going to take a while before a place was available on the course, and I wanted some hands-on experience. 'Why don't you shadow me, Nicky?' Liz suggested. 'It'll help you get a feel for the job. Next time I'm on call and something comes up, I'll give you a shout and you can watch.'

*

On Sunday 8 June 2008, I got my chance. The phone rang early in the morning.

'Nicky?' said Liz's voice in my ear. 'I've got a negotiation in south London. Politician's house. Protestors have got onto the roof. Would you like to come along?'

I felt a surge of excitement, and then – daft as it sounds – a sudden concern about my wardrobe.

'Of course. Yes. Err . . . it's hot today, though. What shall I wear?'

'Just dress casually,' Liz said. She gave me the location. 'And don't forget to bring some sun cream.'

Dress casually. Oh God. What does that mean? I think sometimes when we're nervous, we avoid the thing we're worried about (*Can I really do this? Will I mess it up? Will I fail?*) by focusing on some other thing we can control more easily: *what should I wear?* I stood staring into my clothes cupboard with the horrible expression 'smart casual' running round and round my brain. In the end I went for linen trousers, I think, and some sort of top, and then when I got there it was boiling and the rest of the negotiating team was wearing shorts.

The leafy street was cordoned off. I showed my warrant card and told the officers on duty that I was with Liz: I'd spotted her as soon as I came around the corner, outside on the pavement with the incident commander. Her role as a negotiator was to give him advice on tactics to bring the incident to a peaceful conclusion. I could also see the press gathering behind the tape at the end of the road – more and more of them every minute, reminding me that this was a national incident and a very big deal.

'This is Alison Elliott's house,' Liz told me. 'She's the Leader of the House of Commons and a member of the Cabinet. And her husband's there as well – Harry Bradford. He's in politics too.'

'Just the two of them at home?'

'Yes. There are two intruders on the roof. They're dressed as Captain America and Thor and they're from a group called Fathers 4 Justice – the same guys who climbed Big Ben, if you remember. It's part of their campaign for divorced dads to get access to their kids. They're both locals so Elliott's their MP. They're trespassing up there, so obviously they could be arrested, and I'm here to advise the incident commander on his options. Would you like to see what the negotiators are doing?'

'Absolutely,' I said. As we walked up the path towards the house, I saw a big red and white banner hanging from one end of the house. *A father is for life, not just conception,* it read. There was a bright yellow S underneath, like the one Superman wears on his chest. Liz took me into the kitchen for introductions and I recognised Alison Elliott straight away.

'Alison, Harry,' Liz said, 'this is Nicky from the negotiating team.' We all nodded and smiled. Alison Elliott was sitting at the kitchen table while Harry Bradford was busy making several mugs of tea, and both of them seemed pleasant and friendly despite the extremely strange situation. Then Harry led me up through the house, carrying the tea mugs on a tray, and out through French doors in an upper bedroom onto the roof which had a flat central section and sloping tiles each side. Captain America and Thor were directly in front of me, sitting quite close to the edge and chatting calmly with the two negotiators – Jack and Mark – off to one side. Jack and Mark didn't seem surprised to see me, so there must have been a heads-up from Liz.

'Best if you just sit out of the way and observe, Nicky,' Mark said to me, and I took a seat on one of the low brick ridges that ran across the roof. Harry Bradford handed round the mugs of tea then said politely, 'Let me know if you need anything else,' and headed back downstairs.

I got a quick update from Jack: 'We're engaging them in

conversation, nothing happening yet.' But we were within earshot of Captain America and Thor so there was no chance for me to ask any questions. I'd brought a pad and paper with me on Liz's instructions so I fished them out of my bag, hoping I could do something useful.

We were very much aware of the throng of reporters and cameramen at the end of the road. Each time Captain America and Thor made a move, it set all the cameras clacking and led to shouts of 'Look this way, guys!' and both of them were watching the media carefully, waving whenever they were asked to and striking poses. Getting on TV and in the papers was their aim here, and it looked like they were doing a good job.

'The problem,' Jack said to them, 'is you're invading someone's privacy. This isn't Alison Elliott's office, or some building in Whitehall. This is where she lives.'

'We know. That's why we chose it.'

'But that means both of you are trespassing.'

'We get that. We came here to trespass.'

'Surely you don't have to do this to talk to Ms Elliott. She's an MP – she holds meetings. You could go along to see her.'

'No point doing that,' Captain America answered flatly. 'Already tried it.'

'And I haven't seen my kids,' said Thor abruptly, 'in nearly five months. My son, he's ten. He really misses me. My little girl, she's seven.' He was only a few feet away and I could see he was getting upset as he was speaking.

'Surely there must be some way forward,' Jack said to him. 'How about the family courts? Could you go back and –?'

'Don't talk to me about the family courts,' Thor snapped.

'They're a joke. They don't care about fathers' rights. Or kids' rights, for that matter.'

'You don't have a clue, mate, do you?' Captain America said. He made his points quite reasonably and calmly. 'Elliott hasn't done anything to help. No one's taking any notice. This way' – he pointed to the crowds of reporters – 'people pay attention. So we're not coming down. We've got food and water.' He poked a bulging rucksack with his black-booted toe. 'And we're staying put. But' – he gave a grin – 'you could get us another cup of tea, maybe? That would be nice.'

'Sure,' Mark said calmly. 'I think we'd all like that. Nicky – would you mind going down? Five more cuppas. And you could let Liz know what's going on.'

Harry Bradford made more drinks: I wondered just how many times today he'd boiled that kettle. Policing very often runs on tea. But Liz was talking to Alison Elliott again and I noticed that although Alison was still polite, she seemed more tense and angry now than she'd been when I first got there.

'They've overstepped the mark,' she was telling Liz firmly. 'It's unacceptable. This is my home.' *She's in politics*, I thought, *so she must be used to being targeted and abused. But this is different. It's happening in her private space. She feels violated.* The longer the stand-off continued, I realised, the higher the tension in the house would ramp up.

It was getting on for lunchtime by now. I was starting to get hungry, and back up on the roof the midday sun began to burn my arms. Time to use that sun cream. Captain America and Thor put up a big rainbow umbrella – they really had come prepared. I heard the reporters yelling more questions at them, and they posed for another lot of photos on the edge of the roof. Mark and Jack went on chatting.

'I get that you feel Ms Elliott's let you down as your MP,' Jack said to them, 'and that the system's let you down as well. But have you considered it from her point of view? You've invaded her home. It's Sunday – her private time with her family. How do you think she feels about that?'

'Look – to be honest,' said Captain America, 'we're not bothered how she feels about it. Because nobody is bothered how we feel. Her time with her family? At least she gets some.'

'You married, mate?' asked Thor. 'Got children? 'Cos just remember – the mum has all the power in a split. She can say anything about you and the courts just accept it. She can turn your kids against you and there's nothing you can do. There needs to be a change in the law. So sure – we get that Elliott's upset. But we're upset too.'

As I watched and listened, I was trying to get a handle on the situation. *We can't just grab these two and arrest them; it would be dangerous. They know we won't try anything this high up and they're standing by the edge of the roof just to make sure. They've thought this through, they've brought everything they need, and the press is doing just what they wanted. These guys are calm – but underneath there's a lot of tough emotions. They're ready to stay put a long time.*

I was fascinated by how Mark and Jack were handling all of this. Mostly in policing you have 'authority conversations', directing people, telling them what they have to do. This was very different. The negotiators were exploring, finding out how everyone was feeling and thinking, what exactly it was that they wanted or might be willing to do. What it was that they were most afraid of. Because behind all this anger and disruption there was loss, and the fear of even more. And Jack and Mark weren't searching for the truth, because there wasn't just one truth. This was a very messy situation, so the only way forward was to listen.

It was impossible not to feel sympathy for Captain America and Thor. Of course I couldn't judge: I didn't have all the facts. There might be something else going on, some other reason that explained the mothers' actions. But they seemed like decent guys, not aggressive, not demanding, just wanting a say about the most important thing in their lives. Based on what I'd heard, I had compassion for them.

Next time I went down to the kitchen, there'd been a shift. Alison Elliott was gathering her things together. 'Harry and Alison have agreed to leave the premises,' Liz told me. 'Please can you update the team upstairs, and Captain America and Thor, of course?'

Without the famous politician in the house, the media quickly began to fade away. When the protestors realised what was happening, for the first time since I'd met them they looked taken aback. They retreated as far away from the negotiators as they could go for a discussion.

'Okay, mate,' I heard Captain America mutter, 'we got the pictures. Front pages tomorrow. We're good.'

They were ready to come down, and they carried on waving to the group of reporters who still hung around as the police cherry picker moved in: it's an aerial platform that can be raised to roof height. Once they'd safely reached the ground, the two superheroes were arrested for trespass.

Out in the quiet street, once the media had departed, Liz talked me through her thought process during the day and let me listen to the debrief with Mark and Jack.

'Mentioning the trespassing thing just didn't work,' Mark said. 'As far as they were concerned, it wasn't a threat. They'd come to break the law and be arrested anyway, so . . . '

'What worked was getting Elliott to leave.'

'Definitely. That shifted it straightaway.'

'And by then they'd got what they came for. The press is their success and tomorrow they're all over the front pages, so job done.'

'It all stayed calm and relaxed, so that was good.'

'What did you think, Nicky?' Liz asked. 'How did you find it?'

It was difficult to answer her question right then and there. This job appealed to me deeply – it was all about connection. But I didn't really feel I'd grasped the process. The main thing I'd taken from the day was how much I had to learn.

'I think I need a bit of time to take it all in,' I told her. I thought she'd appreciate my honesty, rather than just trying to say what she might want to hear. Liz nodded.

'Sure, Nick. Have a think about it.'

I drove home slowly, letting my thoughts spool through my head. It was going to take some time to fully understand what had happened. *I was expecting a suicide, and instead I got superheroes. That was just weird.*

In the past, I'd watched Liz facing challenging situations as a superintendent in firearms, and greatly admired how she dealt with them: she was personable yet able to assert herself, and she always got the job done. And I'd seen the same traits in Jack and Mark today: they weren't submissive, they weren't shouty, they just kept the channels open. I realised that what I'd really seen was a very different way of policing.

*

My hostage and crisis negotiation training took place in a freezing cold December up in Hendon. It was the hardest course I've ever done, and I'd honestly say that it transformed me.

Hendon had changed too: there were no recruits living in residential accommodation on site any more, the lovely swimming pool I remembered had been closed, and the place felt like a bit of a ghost town. The negotiation trainees stayed in old police houses behind the training centre that were being used as temporary accommodation until they could be sold for development. That meant no one was splurging any money on their upkeep, so they all looked pretty shabby and tired: the wallpaper was peeling, the kitchen was basic, and the heating didn't work. I literally had to sleep in my hat and scarf and gloves, bundled up in a sleeping bag in my icy bedroom. A guy from Saudi Arabia on the course with us was convinced that making us live in that house was part of a fiendish psychological strategy to break us down and reveal our true characters, like training for the SAS.

Luckily we didn't have to spend much time there: we were training from 8 a.m. until midnight. There were twenty-four trainees, from Saudi, from Sweden, from the Met and other British forces, and from the FBI. We would work in teams of six which constantly changed around and switched roles in a series of exercises. Debriefs followed immediately afterwards, in which everything we'd just said and done would be taken apart. *What was your thought process there? Why did you say that?* If you asked the tutors a question, they would ask a question back: *so what made you ask that?* It was all part of making us super-aware of our unconscious behaviours and those of others, and for me this was a revelation: I realised very quickly that I wanted to understand human behaviour much better, and that this training would be only the start. But it was also a shock because I'd thought of myself as a strong communicator, here to develop skills that I already had. Now the course was stripping back these beliefs, removing what I thought I knew and rebuilding it in a very different way.

It was showing me that most of the time, *I didn't really listen.* I thought I did, but what was going through my head was what *I* was going to say or do next. I think this starts at school where we're always praised for speaking, for standing in front of classmates and performing – talk talk talk – but we're not so often praised for listening. Joining the police had built on this conditioning, because as officers our natural default is to get people to do what we want them to. This had made me quick to advise, always solving problems, directing and imposing what I thought of as the right way to see a situation.

Negotiations often don't take place in daytime hours, but late at night, when everyone is tired and disorientated. They're always very stressful, and in order to qualify, we'd have to prove that we could deal with emotional and mental pressure. So the training often kept us in suspense, never knowing who we'd work with, what time we'd start, or what would happen next. It built new skills in layers until by the end, we should be able to use them all. Reflective language. Really hearing what people are saying and mirroring it back: *it sounds like you're going through a really bad time here.* Or: *it sounds like this guy really hurt you.* Or: *I can hear how hard it is for you to see a way forward.* It takes courage to be honest and direct: *are you thinking of killing yourself today?* People are often afraid to ask this in case it triggers an awful response. But many times, the real conversation can't happen until you do.

Then there's how to choose your words when every single one of them matters. Lots of us tend to say 'okay' as a filler when we don't really mean it – it just takes up space when we're talking. But if you use 'okay' to a person who's about to take their own life, they could hear it as agreement: *okay then, go ahead.* Or if you respond 'okay' to a person who's telling you they want a million quid and a helicopter, it would be a terrible strategic mistake with no way back, leading to chaos.

So – are you ready to be conscious of everything you say? Communication skills are life-saving – not soft at all, and using them tests you to the limit. The course left us nowhere to hide. It was exhausting, but also it was fun in the way it can be fun to meet a serious challenge and to find you have inside you what it takes to overcome it. I absolutely loved the training and knew without a doubt that I wanted to do this job for the rest of my life. I've taught a lot of students these very same skills since then, and I hope they'd say the same.

*

It's the final assessment on the hostage and crisis negotiation training and I'm standing in the grounds at Hendon between a row of empty police houses. I want to qualify as a negotiator more than I've ever wanted anything before. So this is do or die. I have to get this role play right and pass the course. It's also pigging cold out here, just like it's been every day. I'm not great in this weather. I'm wrapped up in a hat, a big scarf, and lots of layers of clothing, but I can still feel the wind biting through.

I know just how tough today is going to be. The role players will be harsh and they'll react to every word we say. If we make a mistake, they're going to grab onto it. It's 9 a.m. right now and this will be an all-day exercise with tension building and building as our scenario unfolds. It's going to be dramatic because it always is: a terrorist incident, perhaps, or a plane hijack at Heathrow – a scene that's highly confrontational. In negotiator training, sometimes students excel at dealing with those in crisis, and do strong suicide interventions with loads of empathy. They're great at listening skills, mirroring, talking people away from the edge. But those same trainees can struggle with aggression: dealing with people who are angry, or highly self-absorbed and narcissistic, or so intensely ideologically motivated that they're hostile to anything that's said to them. Very empathetic characters don't always know where to go with those. But as negotiators, we'll have to deal with all of them.

Two of our instructors, Karl and Grant, give us a briefing. They tell us that gunfire's been reported, and now there's a car abandoned in the road and a man standing near it with a gun. We have a firearms team in attendance to give us protection as we try to end the stand-off. I'm working in a team of four and we know the roles we each have to perform. A negotiation like this one needs a cell of four people: a lead, a coach and adviser to the lead, a liaison who keeps the incident coordinator closely informed, and a recorder who makes sure that everything is logged with precision because if someone's demanding that million quid and their helicopter to escape in, it's vital to know what time they asked for it, who responded, and exactly what was said. To start with, Grant and Karl assign me the role of Number Two, the backup, supporter and coach to the lead negotiator. After half an hour, Number One will move on and I'll step into that role. We'll continue in rotation until all of us have been assessed for every competency.

Thirty minutes in, Number One has successfully engaged with the guy who has the gun, and it's time for me to take over. He's thirty feet away from me, wearing a balaclava. He's shouting but the wind is whipping his words away and I can't hear what he's saying. I can see from his body language that he's very angry and agitated. His shoulders are hunched, his hands are curled into fists and he's spitting as he shouts.

'Get me a fucking mobile!' he yells. I frantically look round at my colleagues and mouth 'mobile', extending my thumb and little finger between my mouth and ear in the universally understood gesture that means 'phone'. But there's a big problem here: we've also been taught that mobiles distract during negotiations and in order to give our full focus to the person we are with, we shouldn't carry them with us. I briefly hope that someone might have one stashed in their pocket – but I'm pretty sure they won't. They all look back at me blankly.

'I'm afraid nobody has a mobile!' I shout back. I already

know how feeble that must sound. Gonna have to do much better than this.

Balaclava man laughs. 'You fucking liar! Of course you've got mobiles!'

My palms begin to sweat despite the cold.

'I'm telling the truth! We don't have them with us!'

'What a load of lying shit!' he yells. 'Somebody's going to pay for this!' The scenario feels so intensely real that my heart begins to speed up. I'm having the same physical reactions as I'd have in an actual situation. Now balaclava man starts striding up and down. 'Get me a mobile phone!' he screams at me.

For my entire half-hour as lead negotiator, the guy stays full-on noncompliant and aggressive. My goal is just to calm him in any way I can, first by trying to persuade him to believe me about the phone, then by getting him one. Once we've done that, the trainee who takes over from me tries to move the scenario indoors. If we can all get out of the noise of the wind and the constant sapping effects of the cold, we might be able to communicate better.

Negotiation is totally immersive: the outside world vanishes from your awareness and it's easy to lose all track of time. So when Karl taps me on the shoulder and pulls me out, it's a bit of a shock. I glance at my watch and realise half an hour's gone by. I can't believe it. And I really want to stay.

'Come on, Nick. Time for you to come and have your debrief.'

We walk into a room in one of the nearby buildings. It feels so good to get inside where it's warmer. He sits me down and asks me: 'So, how did it go, do you reckon?' and I run through it. Some of it went okay – I think. The four of us in the cell are working well together. We've started to engage him. But now

I also start to see – just like you always do when you're not in a stressful situation any more – all the ways I could have dealt with it better.

'The mobile was a problem,' I tell Karl. 'We could have anticipated that. What's he likely to ask for? A way to communicate, obviously. We should have had a contingency. And once he started asking, I should have been more pro-active. The best response would have been "I'll get you a mobile," or "I hear you have something important to communicate so you're frustrated about that" – not just "I haven't got one."'

'What else?'

'I worked well with my Number Two, and when I was Two I think I supported One effectively,' I say.

Next, I go on my break. It takes place in the room where the assessors are livestreaming the scenario on a screen, so I can keep up with what's happening for when I'll be rotated back in. I need to stay switched on. While I'm sitting there, I watch the situation develop: it turns out that balaclava guy has robbed a bank but it's gone wrong and he's crashed his car while he was trying to escape. Now he and a mate are surrounded by police. Then he joins his mate in a house where the two of them have taken a family hostage.

I go back in as Number Four and this time I'm pleased with how it goes. Our Number One succeeds in persuading the bank robbers to release their hostages and give themselves up, and we work with the firearms team to make sure this happens safely. That must be good. If we'd mishandled it, the role players could have enacted several different endings: a shoot-out, or police storming the building because of an imminent threat to the lives

*of the family being held. In the worst-case scenario, if they felt
backed into a corner, the gunmen might start killing hostages.*

*So the outcome for the group has been optimal – but how did
I personally perform? During the last two weeks, I've walked away
from some situations reasonably confident about how they've gone,
but I can't feel that way about this one. It was just so hard. And
I wanted so much to do the very best I could. My debrief's given
me some reassurance – it wasn't a disaster. But I'm uncertain, and
emotionally and physically drained, as well as frozen right through.*

*Please, please . . . let it be a positive outcome. But – I just
don't know. Gonna have to wait.*

*

If you've not done very well in a final assessment, an instructor
will usually pull you aside and break the bad news quietly. All
the way back to the training centre on the bus, I was slightly tense
in case this happened. It didn't, so I started to feel a bit better.
But I had to hang on until we'd all walked back to one of our
classrooms for the real relief to come. 'Congratulations to you
all. Everyone in the room has passed the course and you are now
all qualified hostage and crisis negotiators.' There's nothing like
succeeding at the thing that matters to you most. It felt good.

I'd learned a lot of things these last two weeks, but most
of all I'd learned about myself. I knew without a shadow of
a doubt that I didn't just want to do this job in the usual way,
as a volunteer, on a part-time basis. I was happy to start off like
that, and of course I knew I needed experience first, but my goal
was to negotiate full-time.

There was only one way I could do it – to join the dedicated permanent Hostage and Crisis Negotiation Unit at Scotland Yard. That team is small – it has just six people in it. I knew it was one hell of a target, but in that moment I thought to myself: *it's a long shot, but it's possible. Those six jobs exist and someone has to do them. I want to be one of those people, and I'm going to do everything I can to get there.*

*

We all went out for a drink to celebrate our success, and then a meal. I'd made good friends on the course and our group had really bonded. We knew we'd truly earned our certificates and the whole evening was a huge release of pressure, but by the end of it I was flagging from a very long day and an overdose of adrenaline, ready to collapse in a heap. I headed home, where even a proper night's sleep in a room with its air temperature above freezing wasn't enough to fully recuperate. Still, tomorrow was Friday and I wasn't due back at my desk at the Directorate of Professional Standards until the start of next week.

And then my phone rang.

'Hey, Nick. It's Karl. Do you know how many on your negotiation course were from the Met?'

'Um – three of us, I think.'

'Thought so. Right, that's great. We need cover this weekend, so all three of you are going to be on call. Is that okay?'

Wow. This is the deep end, and I've just been thrown in.

Chapter 5

HI, MY NAME IS NICKY
SPRING 2009

11 p.m. and I could hear my mobile ringing. Too late in the evening for a friend to call. It won't be family because I had a catch-up with Mum yesterday. *It has to be work.* The phone hadn't rung during the first weekend on call after I'd qualified, and although I'd received several calls since, I'd eventually either not been needed, or the incident had been resolved before I got there. *But this might be my first negotiation.*

'Nick? Hi there. Grant.'

The second I heard his voice, my heart started pounding.

'You okay to go and do a job?' he asked me.

Right then. This is it.

'Yes,' I said. 'Definitely.'

'Good. So there's a hostage situation – a baby. Guy was released from prison earlier today, done a stretch for GBH. Went round to his ex's where he's got a kid he's never seen. Three months old. There's been an altercation, the ex is alleging assault, this guy grabbed the baby and drove off. We used a stinger to stop him' – he meant the police threw down spikes across the road to puncture his tyres – 'so now he's immobilised and surrounded but he won't get out of the car. He's behind the wheel using the kid as a shield.'

'Baby boy or baby girl?'

'Little girl.'

'Where exactly is he now?'

'About ten minutes from you.'

As I drove through the dark streets, running the scenario through in my head, I felt tense but excited. I was confident that I could resolve this. I pictured myself arriving: *it's okay – the negotiator's here*. Then I'd intervene, execute my strategy and bring this crisis to an end. I was already a hero.

As I got there, it was starting to rain. Very hard. I spotted Grant standing under a large golfing umbrella. A guy called Kevin who'd trained with me was next to him, also well prepared for bad weather in a heavy-duty parka with his rain hood pulled right forward. All I had with me was a not-very-waterproof coat.

The guy's car was at an angle on a bend in a main road lined with shops. The area had been cordoned off, with police cars and an ambulance close by, and Grant gave Kevin and me a quick update. 'He's not speaking. Won't even wind down the window. We can see the baby and she seems to be asleep. The ex-girlfriend's here and she's very distressed, of course. We're talking to her now. She's saying it's a while since the baby had a bottle, so that's a big concern.'

'Have we got bottles?' I asked.

'Yes. And nappies. It's all over there with the paramedics.'

'How about you be Number One and I'll support you?' Kevin said to me.

'Yep. That would be great.' *To take the leading role was definitely what I wanted.*

The two of us walked over to the car, which was quite close to a streetlight. The silent man behind the wheel was enormous – his bulk filled the vehicle. I peered into its shadowy interior and saw the baby – so tiny that he was holding her in his two hands.

'Hi,' I said to him. 'My name is Nicky.' No response. The icy rain came hissing down. Bits of my wet hair started dripping on my nose.

'I'm here to chat to you about what's happened tonight. I can see that you care very much about your daughter. I want to keep both you and her safe.'

A siren sounded somewhere as another police car or ambulance passed by along a nearby street. No response. *Can this guy even hear what I'm saying?*

'You clearly love her,' I said. 'It's important that we get her some food, and she probably needs a nappy change.'

Nothing. He didn't move at all. *I'm worried he can't hear me.* I raised my voice slightly.

'I don't know if you can hear me properly. I wonder if you can wind the window down?'

He didn't budge. The gust of wind blew heavy rain directly into my back. I could feel a patch of damp getting all the way through to my skin. My feet were sodden and I was colder every second. *I'm never at my best when I get cold.*

'If you could wind the window down, we could talk about how to get your daughter what she needs. It's been a while since she was fed.'

There was a very long silence, apart from the banging of the rain on the car roof.

'It's important that your daughter has her milk,' I said. 'She needs a feed every four hours. If you wind down the window, we could talk about how you can get her some.'

Two hours later, he'd lowered it three centimetres. I could see his eyes now, darting suspiciously around as he tried to work out what was happening. The constant downpour must be making it hard for him to tell what the police were doing. I knew there'd be a whole operation going on around us – a tactical plan to wrap this up as quickly as possible because of the risk to the baby. If he wouldn't get out of the car, they'd be looking for a way to taser him – but as long as he was holding his daughter, that wouldn't be a safe course of action.

At least we had a name for him now – we'd found out that he was called Cam. Kevin took over as Number One while I went on a break and walked over to speak to Grant. Grant was staying dry under his umbrella, but I was so soaked through and frozen by now that there didn't seem much point trying to shelter with him.

'How's it going over there?' he asked me.

'It's hard to engage,' I told him.

'The medics are pretty worried about the little girl. We need to focus on getting something for her to eat.'

Kevin struggled too, and when he took his break I switched back in. The guy in the car still hadn't spoken a word.

'Cam, your daughter needs her bottle,' I told him. 'The paramedics have got one ready for her. I can bring it over here and put it down on the ground, so you can unlock the door and pick it up.'

I managed to catch his eye through the open slit of the car

window. Perhaps that small connection between us would help. He gave me a cold, angry glare, but at least now he'd progressed beyond ignoring me.

'Right. So I'll go and fetch you the bottle,' I went on, 'then I'll put it down next to the car and I'll go back over there while you open the door.' I caught his eye again. This approach was working. We were starting to get somewhere at last.

'How does that sound to you?' I asked encouragingly.

'Why don't you lot just fuck off?' said Cam.

*

The wintry morning sky was slowly turning streaky pink. Pretty soon it would be light. The rain seemed to be easing as well and in an hour or so this area would be getting busier, adding to the complications of managing the stand-off. The baby hadn't made a sound for hours, which the paramedics didn't think was good, and I knew from Grant that her mother was frantic. But Cam had finally agreed he'd try to feed her, so the paramedics warmed up a bottle and I carried it over to the car. As the light got stronger, I could see that his eyes were rimmed with red – he looked totally exhausted. *They'll taser him the first chance they get*, I thought. *They've got no choice. We've tried everything we can. Nothing's worked.*

'Okay,' I said. 'I'll do this really slowly. I'll put it down here – that's all I'm going to do. Then you can open the door and pick it up.'

He didn't respond.

'I know you want to look after her. I've got a nappy for her too.' I bent down and put the bottle on the ground on its side with the disposable nappy balanced on top of it so that it didn't touch the wet tarmac. 'Here you go. Let's make sure she's okay.'

'You don't understand,' he said to me suddenly. His reddened eyes flickered up to my face.

'Perhaps you could tell me?' I answered. 'How about you pick up the bottle for your daughter and once she's having her feed we can talk about what's been happening to you?'

I stepped back. To get the bottle, Cam would have to put the baby down and unlock the car door. The second he'd lowered her onto the passenger seat, as he turned to open the car, two figures in uniform ran forward in a pincer movement, one each side with bright yellow taser guns in their hands. The officer on my side yanked open the door and gave him 10,000 volts.

*

When I was in the firearms squad, I went on a training day to learn how to taser. Once a taser's been fired, the cartridge needs to be removed and replaced, and the weapon's activation switch must be in the 'off' position to do this safely. But I didn't turn mine off and as I slotted the new cartridge into position, I got the full shock up my arm. '*Shit!*' I said sharply and dropped the gun. My colleagues tried not to fall about laughing but I could see their shoulders shaking as they kept it in. When police officers taser someone, the result is to immobilise them for a short time – a nasty feeling, but then the affected area goes numb and it wears off pretty quickly. What lasted longer that day was the discomfort of knowing I'd been careless and not met the professional standards I expected of myself.

I felt just the same now. I was frustrated, disappointed and horribly deflated. I hadn't wanted my first negotiation to end with the use of force – all it meant was that an already hostile and distrustful man now had yet another reason to hate the police. The only good thing about the outcome was getting the little girl back to her desperate mother safe and well – an incredible relief to everyone. *But why did the stand-off end like this? Because I failed. But why? What was it that I hadn't done?* We'd had to get the baby away from him – her welfare was paramount – but did the crisis need to reach that point? No, I thought, *it didn't. It should have ended sooner. And if I'd handled it differently, it might have.*

I'd thought that I was going to be his rescuer, I realised, coming in with my negotiating tactics, knowing just how to sort the whole thing out. My whole approach had been all about me: how I saw the situation, what I wanted to happen. But Cam, who was Black, had seen a rather different 'me': not a hero or a helper but a middle-aged white lady who wanted to arrest him. I'd never managed to get beyond that.

My God, I thought. *That negotiation course. I learned a lot, but how much do I really know? The course was only the beginning.*

*

Summer 2009

'She's climbed pretty high up in the tree,' Liz told me. My mentor had called me in to deal with this negotiation late one afternoon that spring. 'Twenty feet at least, so if she falls we're worried she'll be seriously injured. She's put a rope round her neck but it's impossible to see if it's secured to a branch. But if it is and she falls, or if she jumps . . . '

'Do we know how old she is?' I asked.

'Not yet. She looks young. Early teens, I'd say. She won't tell us her name and we're trying to find out.'

'How long has she been up there?'

'Unclear. We got a call from a member of the public about forty-five minutes ago. Dog walker in the park. The officer who got here first tried to talk her down, but she isn't responding. Grant's on his way, Nick, but if you could engage with her now.'

It was evening in a park in south-west London, quiet and still. As I walked over to the tree, I could see a girl with her back against the trunk, thin with long blonde hair and high cheekbones, dressed in jeans and hi-top trainers. I could clearly make out the rope she'd looped around her neck. The branch she was balanced on was narrow and as I watched her, she kept fidgeting to try to get more comfortable. *Christ – she could so easily slip. And if she does – her head is in a noose.*

There were lots of people nearby – far more officers on the scene than I'd normally expect. It's normal for negotiators to be given private space to work, and I wasn't sure why they were all so close. New in the role and not very confident, knowing they were all listening made me even more nervous, as if I was standing in a spotlight. *Everybody thinks they can negotiate*, I thought. *The minute I open my mouth, they'll be judging me. Mind you, I'd have been the same myself – back before I knew anything about it.*

'Hi, my name is Nicky. I can see you have a rope around

your neck. I'm wondering if you could lift it off you, so that you're safer.'

The girl in the tree didn't answer, but she fidgeted again. My stomach clenched. I was horribly afraid she'd lose her seating on the branch.

'Can you please put the rope to one side?' I repeated. 'I'm worried about you.'

Very slowly, she lifted the noose up over her head and tossed it over another branch just above her.

'Thank you for doing that,' I said. 'I don't know what's happened to you today, but it seems like you're distressed.'

She peered down at me for a second or two, then switched her attention back to the tree. Her sad, pinched-in expression reminded me suddenly of another unhappy teenager I'd dealt with back in Walworth. Becky was the daughter of a heroin addict who had – as you'd imagine – a very difficult life at home. She'd nick small items from Boots the chemist and end up in the station which was loud and crazy busy, but we'd still managed to have several long chats about life while she was there. She loved the hot chocolate from the police canteen with extra spoonfuls of sugar stirred into it – the sweetness seemed to comfort her, and she opened up to me quite a lot in our talks and told me how she wanted to live with her grandma. I'd always felt glad that I could find a way to reach her. As I looked up into the tree, I wondered if I'd be able to offer this other desperate child anything that might make a difference. It was going to take more than a sugary drink this time.

'I'd like to find a way to help you,' I told her. 'What can I do, do you think?'

*

By the time my former trainer Grant arrived, it was very nearly dark. We'd started using torches while the fire brigade set up better lighting in the area.

'We've got ID for her now,' Liz told us. 'She's called Sarah, she's sixteen and she's in foster care – her foster mum's reported her missing and we matched up the description. Apparently they've not been getting on.'

I'm surprised that she's sixteen. She looks younger. That child-like, vulnerable face.

'So she's cared for? She has a social worker, then?' Grant enquired.

'Yes – she just got here. Her name's Gabby.'

'Maybe Sarah trusts her,' he said. 'We could ask. Shall I have a go at talking to her, Nick?' As he walked towards the tree, she glanced down at him and then looked away.

'Hi,' he said. 'My name's Grant. I think your name's Sarah – is that right?'

The big lights had come on now. I could see her very clearly, still balancing uncomfortably and silently on her branch.

'Gabby's here,' he went on. 'She's worried about you too, and she'd like to speak to you.'

I was taken aback by Sarah's answer. '*No!*' she said forcefully. At least she was engaging now.

'It sounds like you don't like Gabby much,' Grant said.

'No, I don't.'

'She's not much help?'

'No. She's rubbish.'

'Okay. So we won't bother with her, then.'

There was a pause. Grant was looking up at Sarah thoughtfully. 'So,' he said, 'I bet I can tell you what you're thinking right now. Who's this guy? What's he doing here? Middle-aged. Got a beard. What do I know, right? How could I have a clue what you're feeling?'

She didn't answer.

'My 16-year-old son would say the same.'

Her head turned the second that he'd said it. She looked directly at him and I saw the shift and change in her before she even spoke. Once a negotiator's made a connection you just get out of their way, and as Grant gently chatted, I knew I had a chance to really learn from him. As they talked, he was looking for the way she saw the world. Some problems she'd been having at school. How her foster mum would always tell her what to do. How she loved horses and would really like to have one. It never emerged exactly what had led her to climb up the tree, or tie a noose around her neck, but somehow, she'd reached a point where she'd wondered if for her, dying might be better than living. Her life didn't feel like hers, so why bother with it? She'd had no control over anything or anyone – until she'd knotted that rope. Then suddenly, everyone was paying her attention.

'Sarah?' said Grant. It had started to get light. 'We're going to have to go now, me and Nicky. Our boss says it's the end of our shift. There's another team coming who can talk to you, but we really don't want to leave you up here. How about if you come down and we can walk to the ambulance together?'

'Ambulance?'

'Yes. They're waiting to check you over, just to see if you're okay.'

He was telling her the truth. After twelve hours, negotiators have to be replaced by another team. But we didn't want to hand her over to somebody else at this stage, to have to get to know her all over again.

'I'm not in trouble?' she said anxiously.

'Not at all. I've been here all night with you and I don't want to go home knowing that you're still up here. It would be great if you came down while we're still around.'

My neck was stiff and throbbing from hours standing with my head tilted back, but the feeling of relief once Sarah was on the ground was amazing. As negotiators, we'd reached the best ending that we could, but it was hard to get the image of her forlorn little figure stuck up there on a branch out of my mind. I hoped she could be helped and supported now by someone who really understood her. I also knew that it was going to take me days, weeks, longer, to process all I'd learned about exactly how Grant did what I had just watched him do.

So – what works, then? I thought. *Not hero negotiators, obviously. Not me setting out to save the world. This job is all about the team. Sure, saving a life is kind of cool – but these are skills you have to learn. And then you must keep practising and never underestimate how hard it can be to use them. It's about caring and it's about listening actively. Finding the perspective of the person who's in crisis – how they feel, what they need. Making a connection. Being open – vulnerable, even. It's about kindness, and not letting ego get in the way. It's about walking in someone else's shoes.*

It's quite a skill set, this, really, isn't it?

*

I was deeply absorbed by my career and I knew I was lucky to have the support of a kind, caring girlfriend. Our relationship was stable and loving and my parents and family were pleased for me. As time went by, though, I had to admit to myself that something wasn't quite right.

The problem was that I was still a secret in her life. My girlfriend was really, deeply scared of coming out, and I'd tried to be understanding about this. That wasn't hard, because I truly did get it. But secrets are exhausting and they also send a message. *I'm ashamed*, they whisper. *Ashamed of myself. Ashamed of you. Ashamed to be who I am.* Secrets also stop a relationship growing in the healthy way it needs to do: I'd never met her family or friends and as far as they all knew, she was single. The more time went by, and the happier the two of us were together in private, the more being hidden from the outside world began to bother me. I didn't want to be invisible, and I knew that I deserved better.

In the end, it was too painful to go on. I couldn't force my girlfriend to change the way she felt: coming out is a life-altering decision and of course it was hers to make. But we didn't have a future together if secrecy was the condition. So I told her that we had to break up and it was horrible and difficult and sad. I was grateful to be surrounded by others who loved me unconditionally: my parents, my sister, my friends. There were so many people I could count on and they helped me to get through the heartbreak.

I'd just not met the right girl for me, I reminded myself. Or rather – I hadn't met her yet.

*

'What d'you think this guy's going to do?' I asked my colleague Jo.

I looked across the gap between the office building we were standing on, to where the man in crisis was – ten metres away at least. He wasn't moving at all. It's unusual to try to negotiate with someone at a distance like this, but there was no way to get any nearer. Jo was a more experienced negotiator than I was, and I could see that she was watching him closely.

'Hmm. Hard to say,' she said to me. 'Let's get these ropes sorted out and then we can engage. I feel like a mountaineer. Or perhaps a mountain goat.'

She wasn't kidding. The two of us had climbed six flights of stairs to get up here and it was very windy, so a decision had been made that we needed safety ropes to secure us before we could work. We'd had to carry them all the way up from the ground floor with us and my arms were still throbbing from the effort. Two firemen had made the climb with us, and they quickly started fixing the ropes to the contact points the window cleaners used for their cage. We were east of the City of London and London's stunning cityscape was right in front of us: St Paul's Cathedral, the Shard, the oddly shaped office building that everyone calls the Gherkin.

The man in crisis was quite young, dark-haired, wearing jeans and a hoodie. He'd not moved a muscle since we'd been there, just standing at the corner of the building opposite, staring down at his feet.

'Okay – you're secured,' one of the firemen said to us.

'Cheers. D'you want to be Number One, Nicky?' Jo asked me.

'Sure.' I knew I didn't have all the answers when I was negotiating, but I was always up for gaining the experience.

'Let's get started,' Jo said. 'You're going to have to shout.'

'Sure,' I said. 'Will do.' I gathered my thoughts.

Right then. So we know this guy has mental health problems. He's possibly an absconder from a treatment centre, but that's still being checked. They'll let us have more background when they can. We're not sure about his English language skills, either. They might not be too good, so that's going to be another challenge.

I cleared my throat. 'Hi!' I called across to him. 'My name is Nicky!' The wind carried my voice away. It was going to be tricky to make contact like this. *Gotta speak louder.*

'I'm worried about you!' I shouted to him. 'I'd like to see if –' His head jerked up and he looked towards me. He'd obviously heard. But there was something really wrong about his movement. In a second of instinct, I knew what he would do before he did it. He stepped forward to the edge of the building and leapt into space. His jump looked utterly unreal, like a sequence in a movie. It was as though it was happening in slow motion. We'd be able to rewind it if we wanted. As he fell, he twisted in the air, dropping with his face towards the building and grabbing at the edges of the windows. Two seconds later, I heard him hit the ground.

Jo and I both stood there frozen – hard to say how long

because the shock of what just happened had knocked out our perceptions of time. These words went through my head as though I'd spoken them out loud: *so that happened really quickly*. We'd been trained not to look over the edge if a jump was ever the outcome, but for both of us it was impossible not to. I stared down as the little ant-figures below in their hi-vis jackets ran towards where he was lying.

'Are you okay?' Jo asked me.

'Yes,' I said. I didn't really know. *I might be. Or possibly I'm not.* I felt stunned and disbelieving. 'You?'

'Yes.'

At this height, I thought, he couldn't have survived. And if by any chance he had, the fight to save him wasn't ours any more. It was time to place our trust in others – the medical team down there who would do everything they could. We gathered up our ropes and trudged back down the stairs.

*

A detailed debrief always follows when a person in crisis jumps. In this case there were two very unusual things about the outcome: one was that the man wasn't killed despite the height, although both his legs were broken: the way he'd grabbed the windows might have slowed his fall just enough. Because he was alive, Jo and I didn't have to stay on duty until we'd given statements and both of us were sent straight home. The second strange thing was the timing and speed of his decision. He'd jumped within a second of me speaking to him – so something set him off, but nobody knew what it might have been.

I spent that evening at home watching shit TV, trying to get back to some kind of normality. The image of the moment of the jump was the hardest thing for me to deal with: it was like a mental imprint. *Did I cause that? Did something I said, or perhaps the way I said it, trigger him off?* Pretty quickly, I felt clear: the answer had to be no. This was so evidently true that it didn't take too long to reconcile it in my brain. *We'd not engaged him. It was nothing that I did.* But it was a very limited comfort. I was deeply shocked and frightened to have witnessed such an act of desperate self-destruction.

A negotiator friend of mine called Mark once spent hours on a building, talking to a man in suicidal despair. Their conversation was difficult, but Mark used all his skills and seemed to have established a connection. Then the guy suddenly said to him, absolutely calmly, 'Mark, I appreciate what you've tried to do here. Thank you. I respect you enough to ask you to turn away now and not see what's going to happen.' Before Mark could say another word, he stepped over the edge to his death.

I got to know Mark well – he taught negotiation and came down often to help out on the national training course. What happened on the roof that day upset him very deeply and he shared it with his students. 'A person standing at the edge of a building is asking a question,' he told them. 'And the question is: *should I end my life? Is that what I want?* We try to influence that decision – and many times we can succeed, but not always. So we need to be prepared for that.' He was right, and all I'd add is this: when the very worst happens – and sometimes it will – negotiators need to know that we can ring each other and talk about how we feel with someone who understands.

Next morning was Saturday. My phone rang just after 9. It was Grant.

'You okay, Nick? I've been getting up to speed on what happened yesterday.'

On a Saturday morning, the first person he'd thought of was me. He knew how I was feeling. I was part of a team – such a close one, it was starting to feel more like a family. 'I'm fine,' I said, and it was true. I could box this experience, I realised – it's how you learn to survive when you're dealing with such high-stakes situations. When your work brings trauma upon trauma upon trauma, you have to park what happens. You do everything you can but sometimes what you've done was not enough. A life has been lost and you have to live with that.

There are times when we have to live with something even harder. I've heard people shouting 'Jump!' to a desperate individual on a rooftop. Once there's a crowd and one person does this, others will then copy: it's a pack instinct in humans, I think, and a very dark side to our nature. I remember a man on the roof of a row of terraced houses in east London who walked right down the ridge of the roofs to the end of the street where a crowd of local residents who'd been evacuated from their houses during the emergency was watching him from behind a cordon. As he stood there, one of the spectators yelled out, 'Just do it, mate, go on! Then we can get back home!' How can anybody act this way towards another human being?

That man didn't jump – but another negotiator I know once talked to a 16-year-old lad who felt he had no place on this earth. My friend listened to him for a very long time. He hoped that he was getting somewhere, that the boy was becoming less despairing, more willing to believe there might be someone, somewhere who could help him. Then a voice in the crowd yelled out, 'Jump, son! Go on! Let's see you do it!' and someone else laughed.

The boy looked at the negotiator. 'See?' was all he said, and then he jumped. The building had anti-suicide nets around it, but they failed and he was killed.

*

Negotiation training runs four times a year at Hendon, and as soon as I was qualified, I started volunteering to help with these courses. Just a few months after I'd passed, I found myself back there playing the role of a lady who'd taken her doctor hostage. I enjoyed it immensely and got right into my part: it was fascinating to find out what went on on the other side of the door, while nervous negotiation trainees were trying to keep talking in front of their assessors. I learned even more about the power of words, noticing that I reacted very strongly to what each trainee said. When one told me to 'calm down', I was immediately much less calm. If they were heavy and controlling, I grew angry and resistant. I was becoming more and more fascinated by psychology and motivation. Revision had never been my thing but now I was reading up on these subjects, feeling I just couldn't learn enough.

I went back to help the next course as well – and the one after that. When I rang up to put my name down yet again, the woman in the office gave a chuckle.

'Blimey, Nicky! It's like you're a member of the department!'

I chuckled back. *I'm not a member yet*, I thought to myself
– *but I'm working on it.*

*

December 2009

'Jesus – this guy's walking on his hands!'

It was night-time in the middle of December, and I'd been
called to a north London hospital along with Jackie, another
negotiator. A member of the public had reported a man on the
roof. The hospital was a sprawling Victorian pile with a narrow
ledge running along the front just below its first-floor windows,
and by the time I arrived the man had clambered down the front
of the building – a tremendous acrobatic feat – and was perched
on this ledge. He looked fairly safe, at least for now.

Getting details about him was fairly quick and easy: our urban
acrobat's name was Alex, he suffered from bipolar disorder and
he was a regular patient at this hospital. But it was late in the
evening by now, and nobody was sure why he'd turned up. Then
he took us all by surprise: he suddenly flipped himself upside
down in a handstand and set off along the ledge, walking on his
hands. His strength and balance were so amazing that I stared
at him in wonder – *how can he not fall? But he's in terrible
danger – just one slip and he'll dive head-first to the ground.*

Your overriding instinct when you see someone at acute risk
is to yell in their direction: *stop doing that! Get away from the
edge!* But Alex clearly wasn't going to listen. In the next ten
minutes he did some more astonishing balances, then clambered

all the way back up to the roof using only the edges of the windows, and disappeared among the chimneys. The first challenge for the negotiation would be getting him to stay still long enough to talk to him.

'So we don't think he wants to harm himself?' I said to the inspector in command of the incident.

'As far as anyone who's been caring for him is aware, no. I'm being told there haven't been red flags that he's suicidal or could deliberately self-harm –' He broke off as Alex shouted something from the shadows up above. No one could make out what he was saying.

We don't really know what's going on with him, I thought. *I don't think anyone foresaw that he was going to act like this. Sometimes people are in trouble and it just goes under the radar. I've seen this so many times. A mental health crisis like this one isn't always signalled in advance.*

The incident commander carried on with his briefing. 'Jackie already tried to talk to him,' he told me, 'but Alex was asking her "What do you know about me?" She told him "Not very much – why don't you tell me?" but he kept insisting that she didn't care enough about him to find out, so they got into a logjam. Now he won't talk to her at all.'

Okay, I thought. *So there's something very important to him that he wants us to understand. I'll have to make sure I meet his need for acknowledgement.*

'I'll go up there,' I said. I was Number One now, but working on my own since Alex wouldn't talk to Jackie. My only support was a uniformed PC who was not a trained negotiator, and I quickly gave him directions: 'Come up with me. If I need you to go back down and take a message, I'll let you know.' He nodded and we climbed up the fire escape together. That high-speed briefing of mine was the first mistake I made.

When we reached the top, I saw just what a warren this place was. The old building was forty-or-so metres long and surrounded by a sprawl of more modern ones, all the roofs linked up by gangways used by the hospital's maintenance staff. There were little pre-fab units dotted round – they probably held air-conditioning machinery or heating vents or safety equipment, I thought, and I could hear what sounded like an extractor fan humming somewhere. Alex could be hiding behind any of these buildings or anywhere across the roof. The PC and I cautiously set out along the central gangway. I was surprised when we spotted Alex quickly, sitting on the edge of one of the smaller gangways and swinging his legs in the air.

'Hi, Alex,' I said. 'My name is Nicky. I'm worried about you up here. I think there are things you want to tell me and I wonder if we could talk somewhere that's safer.'

He put his head on one side for a moment or two as though he was considering what I'd said, then slid under the railing and dropped down onto the shadowy roof below. By the time I'd got to where he'd been sitting, he'd vanished among the chimneys.

'Come on,' I said to the PC, and again we started looking. What I should have said to him at this point was: *stay with me. This is for my safety. If you see me stepping too close to this guy, pull me away.* Not to spell this out was my second mistake of the night.

Again we located Alex on the far side of the roof. 'Hi, Alex,' I said to him. 'I'm Nicky. I'm wondering if you can tell me what's

happened to you today?' He gave that quick sideways duck of his
head – and again he shot away from us into the dark. Chasing
him around this chilly rooftop wasn't getting us far. I wrapped
my heavy coat and scarf more tightly around me. It was looking
like a long old night ahead.

*

'Alex? Hi.'

Yet again we'd found him, on the main gangway this time.
The light here was brighter. Alex stared back at us in silence.

*He won't engage or say anything about himself, but he
wouldn't talk to Jackie because he said she didn't know enough
about him. He won't tell us, then he's angry because we don't
know. It's hard to know how to resolve this one.*

'I'd like to find out more about you,' I said carefully, 'but you
keep disappearing. I just wondered why that is?'

Alex backed away. This section of the gangway ran around
the edge of the building. To our left side, attached to the wall,
was the huge air-extraction system making its constant hum. This
close, the sound was much louder. To our right was a sheer drop
into the dark. We must be sixty feet above the ground up here,
and I felt my stomach tighten with unease. Alex was a very strong
and agile man – strong enough to push me off this gangway,
perhaps even to throw me off. Even with the PC just behind me
as backup, I thought, I'd better not get too close to him.

'Alex,' I said. 'I'd like to find out what's been going on for you
today. Can you tell me?' I took a few steps forward to make sure
that I'd be able to hear him reply. He looked extremely jumpy

and the whirr of the fan was loud and grating, putting stress on us both. All at once, he started speaking very fast – but I couldn't make out what he was saying.

'Hang on, Alex,' I said, 'I can't hear you.' I took several more steps forward until I was standing by a door in the wall. It had a green fire escape sign on it, with a drawing of a figure running from flames. Alex was still talking rapidly, waving his arms as though he wanted to make a very important point.

'Please hold on!' I called.' I can't hear! We need to be closer.'

Later on, as I went over what had happened on the gangway, I realised I'd experienced 'negotiation creep' – which was something I'd learned about on my very first training course. When you take part in an intense conversation, you naturally edge forward. It's hard not to. Then you edge some more. Bit by bit you move out of your safety zone, away from your backup – and then you realise you're exposed.

All of a sudden, Alex bolted right at me. He covered the length of the gangway in seconds, and we were nose to nose. I felt his rapid breaths on my face. He was wide-eyed and I thought he looked quite frightened, but the way he'd rushed towards me also seemed quite aggressive, and he wasn't in a stable state of mind. I gave a quick glance behind me, expecting to see the uniformed PC – but he wasn't there. He'd not moved forward when I did. Now I was alone. No backup. No stab vest. My heart began to pound.

I'd not felt this vulnerable in my work for a long time, but I could be seriously hurt here. I could die. And Alex knew it too – I could tell from his expression. Our eyes locked. The best thing, I thought, was not to spook him – not to move at all.

'I'm not going to hurt you,' he said softly.

'I trust you,' I answered, even though I didn't. He took two slow, careful steps away from me. The knot of fear in my stomach untied itself a little.

'Alex,' I asked him, 'what happened here tonight? Why did you come to the hospital?'

'To bring the Christmas presents!' he burst out. 'I was sectioned on Christmas Eve three years ago – four years ago – maybe it was five years ago – anyway – they didn't give us any presents! So I thought that anybody who's in this hospital now won't have any presents either so they should have some!' He seemed relieved to have a chance to explain all of this.

'I see. That was nice of you,' I said. I'd no idea if he'd really brought any presents.

'But the security guy at the door wouldn't let me take them in!' Now Alex seemed frustrated and upset. 'He said it wasn't visiting time, but I wanted to get inside so they could all have their presents! That was all I wanted to do, but he got angry! They don't give the patients any presents at all here – do you know that? Even on Christmas Day. Did you know that I'm bipolar? A lady doctor told me. Did you know?'

He's not well, but he seems like an intelligent person. Not quite in the same world as the rest of us and what he's doing isn't reasonable of course, but in his take on reality, everything he's done today is making sense. He has a kind of logic of his own behind his thoughts.

'And how do you feel now?' I asked him.

'Security guy wouldn't let me in!'

'So I can see that you're frustrated about that.'

'I just wanted to give them their presents!'

He suddenly moved towards me again, but this time he grabbed the fire escape door and pulled it open. Right behind it was a uniformed PC with a bright yellow taser. I was as startled to see her standing there as he was. *Shit. I was trying to build trust – but now he's seen an officer with a weapon.*

'Stand still!' she shouted. 'Taser!' Alex instantly slammed the door. His eyes were very wide and he was panting.

'Honest to God, Alex,' I said, 'I'd no idea she was there.'

'Is she going to arrest me?'

'She wants to take you where you can get some help.'

'But does she know I'm bipolar?'

'If we open the door very slowly, you can tell her.'

'But she'll taser me! She said!'

'That was just a warning,' I told him. 'She won't taser you if you move slowly. We could both walk down the fire escape together.'

'She will! She'll taser me! She will!' His panic was increasing.

'If you move slowly, I promise you she won't.'

I wanted to keep talking to him calmly, but we'd lost that moment now. Alex roughly grabbed the fire escape door and threw it open with a crash. The officer shouted, 'Stop!' but instead he took a big stride towards her. Perhaps he was just frightened. 'Stand still!' she yelled again. He took another step, she fired her taser, and he dropped to the ground.

How had this come to the ending I'd most wanted to avoid? As I went over what had happened later on, I saw the mistakes that I had made. At a number of key points, I'd got things wrong. *No use blaming the PC for not staying close to me – I'd not told him to do so. I said that he might need to take a message, and later on I told him to come with me, but I never stated, 'I need you right alongside me.'* He also didn't have negotiation training and I was the senior officer, so if he didn't quite understand my orders he might be reluctant to tell me. What I should have said to him was specific: *please do this.* After that I should have added: *let me check: is it clear to you?* As well as not protecting Alex, my failures in communication had put me in real danger too.

He was okay, and getting help now – a big relief to know. But I needed to learn from all this, so there could be a different outcome next time.

*

1 a.m. I looked up and saw a pair of thin legs in skinny jeans dangling over the edge of the multi-storey car park's top level. As I made my way quickly to the fifth storey, I heard a woman's voice echoing down its bare concrete stairwell. 'You just stay back! Stay right back! If you don't, I'll jump!'

'Emma's her name,' the incident commander told me. 'She's a well-known local character, has problems with alcohol, then there was a row with her boyfriend this evening and he left and she thinks it might be final. She's lowered herself right over the outer barrier so she's only supported on her arms. She's very drunk, and we're worried she might not be able to pull herself up again.'

When a crisis is this urgent, everyone around picks up the tension. We had an ambulance in the street below, but Emma was on the fifth floor and if she jumped or fell from this height, it was just about certain she would die. As I walked across the tarmacked space towards her, I could only see her forearms and the top of her head. I felt my heart beating faster.

'Hi, my name is Nicky. I think yours is Emma, is that right?'

'Get me another beer!' she shouted.

'Emma – I'm concerned about you hanging over the edge like that. I don't know what's happened to you today, but I'd like you to tell me about it. Can you pull yourself back up first so we can talk?'

'Get me a fucking beer or I'll jump!' Emma yelled.

'Emma, I'm really worried about you. I'd like to help you, but it's difficult until you're in a safer position.'

'I'll get back up if I can have a beer!' Her voice was very slurred. Her dark hair blew across her face and into her eyes, but if she tried to push it away, I was scared she'd lose her grip. She sounded so young, so very lost. How much longer could she hold on to the bricks in her intoxicated state? I felt the sweat on my palms.

'We don't have any beer right now,' I said. 'It's the middle of the night and all the pubs are shut. Please can you pull yourself back up? Everyone is worried you'll fall.'

'You don't care,' she mumbled. 'Nobody cares.'

'Emma – please pull yourself up. Then I'd like to find out what's happened.'

'Rob!' she said. 'Rob's leaving me!'

'Is Rob your boyfriend?'

'He's leaving!' She started to sob. 'And no one cares! No one!'

'Emma, all these people are here because they're concerned about you. I think it would be helpful to talk about Rob, but please get back up first so that you're safe.'

As she started to struggle back over the edge, I found that I was holding my breath. I couldn't let it out until she'd managed to swing one of her legs up to the edge of the barrier. A minute or so later, she was sitting upright though her back was still hunched in despair. Her feet swung down into the darkness.

'That's great, Emma. Thank you. Now can you tell me what's been going on?'

It was a very sad story: her mum had died, and she said that was why she'd started drinking. Then she'd met Rob who understood how she was feeling – he'd made her feel so safe that she'd even tried to cut down on the booze. But now they'd had an argument and this had triggered her off into a wave of despair. We talked quite rationally about this for a few minutes, but then a fresh burst of anger seemed to rise – I sensed it gathering like a wave, completely overwhelming her. She lurched forward once again, shouting abuse at everyone and twisting around as she lowered herself back over the edge of the car park. Once again she was at grave risk of falling and for a moment I was overcome with anxiety and dread.

'Emma,' I said, 'I understand you're desperate and that you think no one gets how bad you feel.'

'No one!' she blurted out.

'I've got as much time as you need. I'm here to listen. Please can you pull yourself back up so that you won't fall? Then we can keep on talking.' Again she slowly, painfully hauled herself back over the parapet and I could breathe again.

As time went by, she began to sober up. But our breakthrough came when Rob arrived and said that he'd speak to her. We told her he was there but that she'd have to come away from the edge if she wanted to see him. She agreed. Gradually her logical brain was coming back on line, and the waves of her intense despair began to fade. A little while later, she walked down to the ambulance crew who took her to hospital for her own safety. Rob agreed that he'd go with her. I don't know what happened to the two of them, but I was glad he cared enough to help her through the crisis. She'd not been left totally alone.

I thought about my training at Hendon. *It's the negotiator's job to do your best to save her life today. Just in this moment – to be here and listen. You can't solve her problems or fix her feelings or take away the reasons she feels bad. You can only hear a fraction of the story, and all you can do is act right now.* In that draughty car park, I felt I'd really started to get it.

*

In early 2011 a chance came up to go on the Met's kidnap negotiation course and I very much wanted to do it. But the timing was awful. My role at the Directorate of Professional Standards required me to be regularly on call out of hours, and my ongoing work as a volunteer negotiator meant even more weekends and evenings on call. I was using the gym as a refuge, finding that exercise was a much-needed break from the mental and emotional demands of my work. Gaining physical strength and fitness gave me a vital edge, I found. But could I take on even more? Right now, I realised, I just couldn't.

However much I loved my career, I saw the dangers of driving myself too hard and reaching burn-out. I'd come back from serious injury once before, and I didn't want to run that kind of risk. Very reluctantly indeed, I decided that this time, I had to turn the kidnap course down.

*

June 2011

'Hey, Duncan!' I was shouting very loudly to get my voice to carry up four storeys. 'I'm Nicky! I can see you standing there and I'm a bit worried about that drainpipe. I don't want you to fall!'

'Fuck off!' he yelled. 'I'm fine!'

Duncan was on a balcony, wearing only shorts, and standing on the wrong side of the railing. His scrawny figure kept on swinging out, away from the balcony, and he was supporting his weight so far as I could see on a drainpipe up the side of the building. How securely it was fastened to the bricks I couldn't tell. His dad had rung 999 that afternoon, explaining that his son had been diagnosed with schizophrenia, that they'd been talking on the phone and that what Duncan said had scared him so much that he'd rushed round to his flat. One minute his son was very aggressive, he told us, and then he was acutely depressed. He'd obviously been drinking. He'd only just broken up with his girlfriend.

As I watched from below, Duncan vaulted back over the railing and ducked into his flat. A few seconds later he re-appeared, but this time, he was carrying a very large machete. He clambered back over the railing and leaned out once more, swinging it backwards and forwards and shouting words I couldn't make out. I could see the blade flashing in the sun as he waved his skinny arm.

'Duncan!' I called again. 'I'm worried that you'll fall! And you're a long way away, so I can't hear you. I think you've got your phone with you, so can we talk on that?' There were more shouts from Duncan, but still nothing I could understand. His dad stood by the ambulance staring up, his face haggard.

'Mr Williams,' I said to him, 'would you mind calling Duncan's phone?'

'Uh – yeah – s-sure.' He pressed the speed dial, but his son wasn't picking up. 'Maybe try again in a few minutes,' I advised. On the third attempt Duncan answered. When he heard his voice, his dad just pushed the phone towards me, shaking his head and close to tears.

'Duncan?' I said. 'Hi – my name is Nicky. Would it be okay if we just talk –?' But he'd hung up.

It was encouraging that he'd even answered, and we kept trying. Gradually he stayed on the line for longer, and I started to chat with him. 'I don't know what's happened today, Duncan,' I said. 'But you seem to be distressed. I'd like to help.'

He stared down from the balcony with the phone to his ear.

'Your dad's here with me,' I told him. 'He's worried about you. How about you step away from the balcony to somewhere safer?'

'You're scared I'll go over, aren't you?' Duncan whispered.

'We want you to be safe,' I said.

'You're scared I'll die if I go over.' His voice was so soft that I could barely hear him.

'Well, yes. We don't want that to happen.'

'But I do,' he said. 'I don't want to live any more.'

*

'He's not well,' his dad told me. 'He hears voices. He s-says the voices t-tell him he should die.'

'Does he take medication?' I asked.

'He has it. I don't know if he takes it. We try to check up on him, but . . . ' His eyes filled with tears and he tried to wipe them away. Up above, Duncan still sat balanced on the balcony railing. He was gripping the machete, only holding the railing with one hand.

'What kind of support does he have?' I asked gently.

'We do our best. The family, you know. It's a big strain on us. Sometimes he'll accept our help, but other times . . . '

'Sure,' I say. 'It must be really hard.'

'And – um,' he went on, choking but trying to go on speaking to me, wanting so much to help his son. 'He's meant to be getting a – a p-package of care. From social services, you know. But I d-don't think anybody's seen him yet. And Marie left him.'

'His girlfriend?'

'Nice girl. I don't blame her. Duncan's not easy.'

As the afternoon wore on, I could see Duncan growing more tired. His voice on the phone was slow and sleepy. He didn't seem aggressive – but he was still holding the machete. I kept on talking, trying to persuade him to put it down and open the front door. Duncan was carrying a dangerous weapon, so the Territorial Support Group had been called to the incident. This is the uniformed team that deals with public order, and as I watched them filing into the building, fully kitted up and carrying shields, I felt worried about how this might work out. I really didn't want them to have to end this crisis by grabbing Duncan and maybe handling him quite roughly. Not only for his own sake; I also didn't want his dad to have to see that.

'Duncan?' I said into the phone. 'Can I come upstairs and talk to you at your front door?'

There was a silence, then a very low 'okay'. This response seemed like a bit of a breakthrough. When I got upstairs, the TSG and their equipment were taking up quite a lot of space in the passage by his flat. All of them were listening to us, but negotiation experience had given me more confidence by now and I called to Duncan over the row of shields.

'Duncan – hi again. It's Nicky. I just came up the stairs. We know you've been trying to get some help from social services. It must be so frustrating to have to wait.'

Duncan muttered something back from the other side. The only word I heard clearly was 'Marie'.

'Marie's your girlfriend, isn't she?' I said. 'Yes, I heard what happened. I can imagine how upsetting that must be.' More low mumbling from inside.

'So we need you to put the machete down and come out,' I went on. 'Nothing bad will happen to you. If you open the door slowly, you can walk downstairs with me.'

Not a sound.

'There's an ambulance here. They'd like to check that you're okay. How about you put the machete down and open the door?'

'Okay, Nicky,' I heard Duncan say at last. 'Okay.' I felt

a surge of relief. We were going to have a peaceful resolution and then he could get some help.

'Great,' I said. 'That's really great. Please put the machete down and open the door carefully.'

'I'm going to do that, Nicky.' The door began to open very slowly.

'Terrific, Duncan, terrific. Just face your palms forwards with your arms by your sides? That way, we know that you're not armed.'

'Yes, Nicky. I understand.'

'Remember the officers might handcuff you outside but that's only to make sure they stay safe, because you had a machete.'

'Sure, Nicky. Okay.'

The door swung fully open. But instead of stepping calmly towards us, Duncan stood there waving his machete wildly in his outstretched hand.

'Put the weapon down!' yelled the sergeant in command of the TSG unit. 'Put it down!'

'Come on then!' Duncan screamed at her. He swung the machete. She fired her taser and he fell to the ground.

I'd no idea why he acted as he did, just as I couldn't understand why Alex suddenly slammed open the fire escape door that night on the hospital roof. But I recognised a pattern we'd been warned about in training at Hendon – that the moment when you think that it's all nearly over and the person in crisis is co-operating well – that's the point to be most careful. *You think your negotiation's going great and you'll be off home in time for tea – but think again. It's when they know it's nearly over that someone who feels desperate will try to grab that*

*last bit of control. The most dangerous time is when you think
you're winning.*

So when you start to get the feeling that someone's going to
come down from the roof or off the ledge, I thought, that's the
moment things will alter. It can happen in an instant. The subject
changes their mind. Or they do something absolutely random.
The ending of the crisis is the time to take the very greatest
care – and always to expect the unexpected.

*

February 2012

I want to do this job full-time.

It was four years now since my first training course at Hendon.
I'd developed new skills and been challenged in every possible
way. I'd discovered new strengths and faced up to my weak-
nesses. But that certainty about my future had never left me,
even at the most difficult moments of my negotiating career.
Still – I knew the odds were stacked against my landing a full-
time role. There were only six positions on New Scotland Yard's
national Hostage and Crisis Negotiation Unit.

And then, unbelievably, my dream job came up: full-time
hostage and crisis negotiator. This vacancy occurred in the most
tragic circumstances, when a member suffered a bereavement
and decided to leave. Like many other colleagues I was deeply
distressed for her. But the opening was there – and suddenly the
pressure was on. As I typed my application, I was massively aware
that this was probably the only shot I was ever going to get.

First step: I was shortlisted. *Okay – so far, so good.* The night before the interview I barely slept at all. I'd done a huge amount of preparation – the days when I'd struggled to motivate myself to read and revise were far behind me. This was the greatest opportunity I'd ever have to become the best negotiator I could be and to help train the negotiators of the future. I was fortunate to have help and support: Murray, my boss at the DPS who'd been so pleased back when I was first selected for my own negotiation training, even ran a mock board for me so that I could feel completely ready. I couldn't have done more to prepare, and I made my way to New Scotland Yard for my interview fired up with determination and absolutely at my wits' end with nerves.

It seemed to go okay – but how can you ever tell? One of my panel was Jack – the same Jack who'd negotiated with Captain America and Thor on the roof of Alison Elliott's house, and was now deputy head of the unit here. He asked me searching questions but I felt I had the answers. Afterwards, however, my thoughts raced round and round as I went over and over what I'd said. Had I been clear enough? Had I been detailed enough? Had I demonstrated what they were looking for? If I'd blown this – well, that would be it.

And then the phone rang – and the answer was yes. My dream was mine. Nothing else will ever feel quite like it. Pretty soon there were more calls from other members of my new team congratulating me. My parents were also overjoyed and very proud: telling all her friends that I worked at New Scotland Yard was a real highlight for Mum in particular.

It was April by now, and London was gearing up for the

coming summer's Olympic Games. There were banners every-where and a real feeling of excitement in the streets as I made my way to Westminster on my first day in the new job. But I wasn't there for long – then it was straight back to Hendon for more training. By now the poor old place was looking even more run-down and I stayed in yet another former police house long overdue for TLC with peeling paint, dodgy heating (sometimes) and ropey-looking kitchens from the Eighties. I couldn't have cared less. I barely noticed. From first thing in the morning until getting on for midnight, I was gripped by all there was to learn.

First we trained in kidnap negotiation: how to use the com-munication and negotiation skills we already had to build rela-tionships quickly, in often very challenging and life-threatening circumstances. Then came negotiator coordination, preparing us to set strategies, work with incident commanders as their advisor, and be responsible for deploying the negotiation team to all calls where they were needed. Next was Gold negotiation adviser training, teaching the skills required to liaise with and advise Gold command – the highest level of police leadership. After that, international kidnap negotiation training, required by the Foreign and Commonwealth Office, is compulsory before negotiators can be deployed in any operation overseas. The last course was Hostile Environment Awareness Training – also known as HEAT. Once again it's essential prior to overseas deployment and it prepares you for being kidnapped, making sure you know what to do if – just to take one example – your hotel was occupied by terrorists.

Now I'd been trained to the hilt to do the job I'd always dreamed of. I felt ready at last.

Chapter 6

THE FEAR OF THE DRAGON
August 2012

As I started my new role, I took a difficult personal decision: for now, at least, I wasn't going to date. Since the break-up of my last serious relationship, I'd reflected on the reasons why nothing romantic had worked out for me in quite the way I'd wished. I wanted to be with a woman at ease with who she was, and I hoped that being older – I was in my early forties – I'd have the experience and the sense to know her when I saw her. But what did I really have to offer?

My work consumed all my energy and time, now more than ever. Negotiation was my passion, a way of life I'd chosen and to which I was completely committed. It didn't leave enough of me to give to someone else. Unless I was a good partner myself, how on earth could I expect to find one?

*

'Ginger nut or custard cream, Nick?' my colleague Connor asked me.

I stood in our little office kitchen at New Scotland Yard,

making myself yet another cup of tea. The Hostage and Crisis Negotiation Unit (HCNU) was on permanent standby during the London Olympic Games – if a terrorist attack took place, we'd immediately be called into action. It's happened before, at the Munich Olympics in the Seventies and Atlanta in the Eighties. But right now the threat of violence seemed pretty remote from the party atmosphere in London.

'Crikey, there's not much going on round here,' Connor said. 'Where have all the criminals gone?'

I laughed. 'Perhaps they're too busy trying to get tickets to the Olympics. I think you can still see the beach volleyball.'

I gazed out of the kitchen window. It was a grey, slightly humid summer day. An aircraft passed slowly overhead. The office was quiet – no ringing phones, no buzz of activity. Around us, the city was so still that I could hear a passenger ferry on the Thames sounding its horn. *Right. Well. Better get back to my desk, then.*

There were six full-time members of the team at HCNU apart from our boss Harry: Connor, Jack, Will, Grant, Charlie, and me. Along with us, there was also Mick who, though he wasn't full-time, had lots of experience and would often give support when we were very busy. He had a strong background of international knowledge and I knew I had a lot to learn from him.

I entered the new full-time role with the rank of inspector and four years of UK negotiation experience. To begin with, the plan was for me to focus on London responsibilities and help out with training. There would also be overseas work and cases with political dimensions, and I knew I'd need to learn a lot very quickly so that I could deal with these. It was agreed from the start that my job would then expand. I'm ambitious, I like to push myself to find my personal limits, and I relish decision-making under pressure. I was absolutely up for the challenge of all this, ready to do whatever it would take.

Except – this latest challenge wasn't living up to expectations. The hot new job I'd been so excited about was becoming a bit of an anticlimax. There wasn't enough to do – and it had been like this for weeks. I was even a tiny bit, well – bored. As I slowly stirred my latest cuppa, I could feel the question forming in my mind: *did I make the right call when I joined this department?*

My boss Harry was pretty shrewd, and he could see what I was thinking. 'This is downtime, Nick, right?' he said to me. 'The whole Olympic thing, it's not normal – so relax and enjoy it. You'll look back and kick yourself if you don't. Because I promise you – when all this goes, it's going to go.' He turned out to be absolutely right. Very soon, those peaceful Olympic summer days would seem like another world.

*

The Syrian hostage crisis began back in 2004. The kidnappings of Westerners – the nationals of many continental European countries along with Australians, British, Japanese, and Americans – were carried out by militias which had formed in the chaos after the 2003 invasion of Iraq by the US, Britain, and others. Their goal was often ransom money – but not always. Other aims were prisoner exchange with Western countries, or simply to put pressure on the occupying countries to pull their troops out of Iraq.

From 2011 onwards the unstable situation in Syria grew even worse, when a crackdown by the government against protestors angry at high unemployment, government corruption, and lack of political freedom, escalated into civil war. Foreign powers began to send money, weapons, and fighters into the country, and as the chaos worsened, jihadist (militant Islamist) organisations also became involved in the violence.

Al Qaeda, a group which had been founded in the late 1980s, was one of them. It had been behind some of the early kidnappings of Westerners, but its structure had been badly damaged by the 2003 Allied invasion. A more extreme group called ISIS – also known as Islamic State or Daesh – arrived to fill the vacuum left as AQ declined, and by 2012 it was growing more powerful. It seized Mosul, Iraq's second-largest city, and declared the northern Syrian city of Raqqa to be its capital. ISIS wanted to form an Islamic caliphate, or zone of political control, in Syria and Iraq. It funded its expansion, among other ways, by holding Western hostages for ransom.

Some ISIS prisoners were freed but others were killed and their murders, often by beheading, were made into videos and publicised to ramp up the pressure on Western governments to pay for the release of their citizens. After YouTube started in 2005, it became the terrorists' favoured site for publishing these videos. As fast as each one could be taken down by the authorities, another would replace it. My first taste of this horror came with the kidnapping of British journalist John Cantlie.

In July 2012, just as I was beginning my new job, John was reporting from Syria on the expansion of ISIS. Along with his friend, Dutch photographer Jeroen Oerlemans, they crossed over the border where they accidentally stumbled into a jihadi training camp and were captured. The fighters in the camp, a number of whom were British recruits, interrogated Cantlie and Oerlemans, and the Britons were especially insistent that they must both be spies. Realising that their lives were in danger, the two decided to make a run for it, but they were barefoot and in handcuffs and were rapidly pursued and recaptured. In the chaos, John was also shot in the upper arm although he was not seriously hurt. Once he'd been forcibly returned to the camp, his wounds were dressed by a mild-mannered young English doctor from east London who had made his way to Syria to work for ISIS.

The men's position was now terrifying: at one point John heard knives being sharpened and thought the fighters might be planning to behead him and Jeroen. But ISIS didn't yet have a secure hold of the area, and members of the Syrian Free Army suddenly charged into the camp and demanded that the journalist and photographer should be released. They'd had a really lucky escape.

*

'Hi, Nicky,' said John Cantlie. He raised a hand in greeting. I could see him on the big screen from our operations room at New Scotland Yard.

'Hi, John – how are you feeling?'

'Okay,' he said. 'Okay.' His face was very pale and his shoulder and arm were still bandaged. I was sitting in remotely on his debrief, which was being carried out in his living room at home by a detective sergeant in the Yard's anti-terrorism unit. Its aim was to find out as much as possible about what Cantlie had seen during his short time as a prisoner of ISIS: where the camp was, who was there, and what the fighters' future intentions might be. Also present and listening carefully to all of this were representatives of the British army and the security service, SO15, and the kidnap unit. My reasons for being on the call were slightly different from theirs: I wanted to hear as much as I could about what John had been through as a hostage, and to gain as full an understanding as possible of how an ISIS unit actually worked. We hoped that it would help us to deal more effectively with future kidnap crises. This international dimension to my work was like nothing I had dealt with before, and as I nervously joined the debrief, I felt like a small cog in an extremely large machine. But I wanted to expand my knowledge, and with experts all around me, this was an amazing chance to learn.

The detective sergeant talked John slowly and carefully through everything that had happened to him after he was kidnapped. Any detail he remembered, however small, might turn out to be significant. John understood this and was calm and factual throughout, trying to assist in any way he could. He'd been extremely surprised to come across the terrorist camp, he said: he and Jeroen Oerlemans had blundered into it in the dark. The detective sergeant was particularly interested in the British doctor who'd dressed John's bullet wound, and gathered a detailed description of him drawing on all John's journalistic skills of observation. If and when this man returned to London, if he could be identified it might be possible to arrest him on terrorism and kidnapping charges.

The debrief took three days, and after listening to John and watching him closely – even on a screen – for that length of time, I really felt we'd made a connection. I respected him: he seemed to be a person of integrity and also to have real strength of being. He was deeply committed to his role as a journalist, believing that the world needed to know about the developing crisis as ISIS widened its area of occupation, and that it was worth taking personal risks to get the story. The pressure and fear of his kidnapping ordeal must have been huge, but he'd survived them and stayed focused on the job in hand. Over the next few weeks, I spotted him in the media, telling the story of what he had been through and explaining the deteriorating situation in Syria.

This sense of living my life behind the headlines was strange at first – exciting for sure, but I was becoming more and more aware of exactly how much was at risk. It wasn't just one person's life that might hang on a negotiation now: this was a rapidly evolving international crisis with many lives potentially at stake. But at least I felt incredible relief that John Cantlie was safe.

*

In late 2012 and the early months of 2013, against the background of the growing crisis in Syria and Iraq and a rising number of hostage-takings there, I was also getting to grips with my new position at Scotland Yard. Then – earlier than I'd expected, following Will's retirement – I stepped up into the role of director of UK negotiation training, and Adam joined the team in my place. I was immensely proud to be doing this work, and also incredibly busy. Each year I had a minimum of seven courses to run at Hendon, plus two international trainings to prepare and supervise. I wrote guidance, updated material, and read the latest research to inform my thinking and keep me up-to-date. I was also a working negotiator coordinator, called in to direct crisis situations at least every two to three weeks.

We gave airline staff training on the best way to react to keep themselves safe on hijacked planes, and I'll never forget a presentation at one of our events by Michael Thexton, who'd been on board Pan Am Flight 73 in Karachi when it was seized by terrorists in 1986, and later wrote a book describing his terrifying experiences, *What Happened to the Hippy Man?* Another unforgettable visitor to one of our trainings was PC Trevor Lock who'd been on duty outside the Iranian embassy in London on the day back in 1980 when it was seized by terrorists, and ended up in a life-or-death struggle with one of them as the building was stormed by special forces, using the service pistol he'd kept concealed inside his uniform for days during the siege. 'I still think about what happened every day,' Trevor said. 'It's the classic symptom of post-traumatic stress, isn't it? It never goes.'

I met other inspiring people too, some of whom were the survivors of extremely traumatic events. The Amenas gas plant in Algeria was subjected to an attack by Islamist militants in which forty hostages were killed; six were British and a seventh was a Colombian living in the UK. I met one of the survivors, who'd had a suicide chain put around his neck and suicide vest placed on him by the militants. He told me that he thought he was going to die a dozen times, and seemed to find it cathartic to share his story with our trainees. I also met the widow of one of the men who was tragically killed in the same incident: she had received phone messages from her husband as he hid in the roof space. We were very much aware that all these people had been left with deep trauma.

We worked with charities, teaching staff the best way to respond if they were kidnapped. We gave NHS staff who looked after patients with mental health problems instruction in how the police work, so they could collaborate more easily when crises occurred. It was deeply absorbing and fascinating, and along the way, I found out a lot about how I should personally respond if I were ever to find myself in a kidnapping or terror-related incident. The first thing I do now when I'm staying in any hotel is walk the floor I'm on, noticing the layout and the exits, because I know that those who do this have a better chance of escape if an incident occurs.

I smile wryly at myself while I'm doing it, but it's become a deeply ingrained habit. I can't unsee what I've seen in my career, or unlearn what I've learned, and one result has been to give me a heightened sense of danger. It would take many years before I'd fully understand just how deeply I'd been affected.

*

I sensed a shadow rising: the growth of ISIS. The extremist group was gaining in both territory and power. The whole HCNU team knew it, and so did anyone who watched the news or read the papers. I'd joined this unit because I was committed to both being the best negotiator I could be and to training the negotiators of the future, but I'd not really understood how international my role was going to be. And I'd certainly not grasped just how high the stakes would get. Now, however, it was about to be shockingly brought home to me.

In November, before he'd even fully recovered from the gunshot injuries to his shoulder and arm, John Cantlie decided to return to Syria to report on the continuing expansion of ISIS. This time he travelled with the US journalist James Foley. For three and half weeks, the two men moved around in pursuit of the behind-the-lines stories that other journalists were too cautious – or maybe just too sensible – to get close to. When they'd gathered enough material, they headed for the border between Turkey and Syria, but with less than thirty kilometres to go until they reached safety, their taxi was chased by a jeep containing three armed men. Cantlie and Foley screamed at the driver not to unlock the car doors – but the terrified man did and both of them were captured. Once again, Cantlie was a hostage.

When a British citizen is abducted abroad, a member of the police kidnap team goes to the family home to learn more about the person who's been taken. How do those closest to them think that they will cope with acute fear and stress? How might they behave in captivity? Any family in this situation is under dreadful strain and extremely upset, and the cauldron of emotions tests negotiators' relationship-building skills to the limit. I hadn't yet fully completed my international hostage negotiation training when I went along with Mick, who had years of experience, to talk to John Cantlie's next-of-kin, Veronica, in her flat on the evening of the same day that John had been snatched for the second time. I was part of the police and Foreign and Commonwealth Office's support for hostages' families. As well as giving Veronica support as a close family member, it was vital to prepare her in case she was contacted by ISIS.

'We knew already he'd been taken,' she told us rapidly. She was far too tense to stay still for more than a few seconds, and her fingers kept on moving, restlessly drumming on the table in front of her, pushing back her long hair. 'We found out this afternoon – we didn't have to wait for the police. We understand what's going on out there.'

'Sure,' said Mick calmly. 'I appreciate that. I wonder if you can give us a sense of what you know.'

'What I know?' She seemed puzzled by his question. 'I know they've taken John. I don't suppose there's much difference from last time.'

'Last time when John was kidnapped and then escaped, you mean?'

'Yeah. Yeah – he's – John's very tough. He'll take any opportunity he can to get away. He's smart. And these guys holding him – come on, they're not the SAS. They're not Who Dares Bloody Wins. I mean – are they?'

Neither of us answered. I didn't feel knowledgeable enough to do so, and when I glanced across at Mick, it was hard to read his feelings in his face. I noticed that our silence bothered Veronica.

'Oh, for fuck's sake,' she said irritably. 'They're not. Everybody knows they're a bunch of amateurs. John said that. He wrote that.'

'I understand what a difficult time this is for you,' I told her, 'but we need to think about how John is likely to respond in this situation. We'd really appreciate any help you can give us.'

'How he'll respond? Obviously he'll escape if there's a chance. He's done it before.'

'How did he feel about going back to Syria?' Mick asked.

'Well – he didn't bloody think it through, did he?' She pressed her hand to her forehead, then ran it back through her hair. 'But it's so John – this whole thing. I told him not to go back – we all did. But he wanted to do the story and that's – just what he's like.'

What seemed to trouble Veronica the most as we were talking that evening was whether John had his medicine with him: he was still taking antibiotics as a result of the gunshot wound he'd received when he'd tried to escape back in September. She was focusing on this because it was specific, I thought: a small and practical thing to worry about in her bewildering fog of fear and uncertainty. Perhaps it gave her a sense of control. I made sure that I had her mobile number and she had mine and I told her that I would keep in daily contact. If she heard anything from John's kidnappers, or received any information from Syria, she should call me at once.

'Look – thanks,' she said as we were leaving. 'I know I probably sound – I'm pretty stressed right now, okay? I appreciate your time. But he'll be back soon. This is John, so – you know. He just – will.'

*

11.30 p.m., three weeks later. I saw Veronica's number come up on my phone.

'Nicky?' said her rapid-fire voice. 'So sorry I missed your call earlier. I was on the other line.' I was checking in with her every day to find out how she was doing. Sometimes we had a very brief chat, on other days we'd speak for longer.

'That's not a problem,' I said.

'So. What's going on?' she demanded abruptly.

People in deep fear are ready to do anything to get their loved ones back. They'll talk of selling all they have to meet a ransom demand, and in some cases individuals or companies may even have taken out private ransom insurance. Hostage families look for interventions – for soldiers to go in and mount dramatic rescues, whether or not that's realistic, and the longer a crisis drags on, the higher the tension on everyone involved ratchets up. I felt for Veronica deeply – she was terrified and helpless, longing for something to be done. I was becoming both her sounding board and her place to vent as the days went by.

And right now she sounded even more keyed up than usual. 'Look,' she went on, 'I don't want your how-are-you-today spiel. I've heard that already. I have a friend here with me and we've been talking all this through, and we think there's something you're not saying. So tell me. What's really going on?'

The British government's policy is not to pay or to negotiate with terrorists, but it can still be worth talking to them: there have been cases, for example, where kidnappers have agreed with requests to allow care packages to be sent to a hostage in need of medical treatment. But in John's case there had been no contact, so far as I was aware.

'I'm not keeping anything from the family, Veronica,' I said.

She sighed. 'There must be something in the background. Some – government *thing* going on. I don't know. Otherwise – this shit would be over by now.'

I could guess what she was thinking. John's kidnapping was all over the news, with rumours and unsubstantiated stories flying around, but the British police don't release information that hasn't been clarified and fact-checked. If every time you turn on the TV, a reporter is giving lots of details you don't have and talking about things the police haven't mentioned, it's easy to start to think that important facts are being kept from you. Today, ten years on, it's even worse: as well as Sky and CNN and Al Jazeera, hostages' families now face a constant stream of social media posts made by anyone, anywhere in the world, alleging all sorts of things that may or may not be true. Who and what should they believe? All this builds a vortex of uncertainty and fear.

'You mean that John would already have been released?' I asked her.

'Of course he would! It's been three weeks! *Three weeks*. There's some hold-up behind the scenes – that's the only explanation. Other reporters have been taken and set free out there, right? So what is it? What the hell's going on?' She let out her breath in a sharp, exasperated puff.

I paused, giving myself time to decide what to do. Negotiators are trained to be courageous in our conversations. There are times when difficult things must be said and painful realities must be expressed, because if something stays unsaid, it can't be dealt with. *Are you thinking of ending your life?* a crisis negotiator must ask. *Do you feel there's no point going on?* In a hostage situation, where feelings are different but equally intense, the fear of naming the truth can be the same – but it has to be named. *This nightmare could continue for a very long time.* For Veronica and her family, that thought must be overwhelming, but I needed to help them to be realistic. Along with that, I wanted to allow them to have hope and to support them emotionally, but it was also vital to see the situation as it really was. So I must lead with courage and truth, even if she didn't want to hear me.

'Veronica,' I said carefully, 'there's something you need to understand. This might not be like the last time John was captured. In fact, I don't think it will be.'

'What?' she said coldly.

'Last time, John was held for a very short period. I think this time – it might not be like that.'

'But – *why*?' Now she sounded angry. 'What's different now? For fuck's sake – the first time was only a few weeks ago!'

'So – I think it's because the situation in Syria is changing very quickly. Things feel different now to the way it felt back in September. Unfortunately, ISIS is much stronger.'

Another silence, then her tension and fury crackled around me.

'Look,' she burst out, 'you don't know John! He's not a passive guy. Jesus! He won't just sit and –' Her voice was close to breaking and she couldn't go on.

'Veronica, we need to be realistic. This is a different set of circumstances.'

'Oh for fuck's sake!' She cut off the call and I sat there, unsure what I should do next. A few minutes later, my mobile rang again.

'Hello?' said a voice. 'Is that Nicky?'

'Yes – who is this?'

'My name's Anita. I'm a friend of Veronica's. I'm with her right now.'

'Hi, Anita – thanks for calling,' I said. 'I'm happy to speak to her.'

'I think – look. Ronnie's upset. I'm not sure what you said.'

'I'm sorry if I caused offence,' I said, and it was true. The pressure and anxiety that Veronica was going through were beyond my experience and I certainly didn't want to make her feel worse. But at the same time, what I was telling her was so important.

'Could you stay over with her tonight, Anita?' I asked. 'She needs support. I have to help her be realistic about John's situation, even if it's hard.'

Anita paused before she answered, taking in what I was saying.

'Okay, then – I can stay tonight. Just so she's not on her own.'

I couldn't sleep at all after that. I'd have to log these calls with the office as I did every time, but that could wait until morning and right now, morning was hours away. The terror of John Cantlie's situation, along with the knowledge that his family faced months of wretched anxiety without any idea of how or even whether it might end, made my stomach sink. I'm a resilient person, but suddenly my sofa felt like a very lonely place.

It was more than a year now since I'd dated, and longer since I'd felt a sense of hope around love and romance. Too long, I thought. Taking this space and time had been good for me, but I felt such a sense of isolation. I made myself a comforting hot drink and sat there with my German Shepherd dog, Cora, rubbing her head and appreciating her unconditional loving support.

*

Lesbian, 34, loves sport, adventure and the outdoors. The photo showed a woman who'd just taken part in an Ironman

Triathlon competition. She was grinning triumphantly and she had the most amazing hair ever, with tumbling auburn curls.

Okay, I thought to myself as I looked at the website. *She sounds cool. Nice smile. Likes training. She might be worth a try.*

I hesitated with my hand hovering over the keyboard.

Oh God. Is this desperate, though? Can I really cope with online dating? What if she's a bunny-boiler? What if –?

Woah. Just stop a minute here. I made a really big effort to stop over-analysing.

It's just an online chat. If we get on, we'll go for coffee. One coffee. How bad can that be? Come on, Nicky – she looks nice. Give it a try. If you spot any bunny-boiling tendencies – you can just get up and leave.

There's such deep darkness in the world. In my work I was seeing so much pain, so much loneliness – the agony of people kept apart by force from those they held the dearest. Another way of seeing this was that these cruelties were a testament – again and again – to love's worth. So I had to believe – I did believe – that there was someone right for me. Although I was nervous, I felt ready to test the dating waters again.

She's out there somewhere, I said to myself. *You just need to keep looking.*

I took a deep breath and hit Reply.

*

The Syrian hostages were always on our minds, and John Cantlie became a constant part of my thoughts as the weeks went by and gradually turned into months with no news from his kidnappers.

A skilled Foreign and Commonwealth Office family liaison team took over the relationship with the Cantlie family because John's case was terror-related, which meant that I needed to find a box in my mind for the time that I'd spent working with them and pack it away. I'd had to do this before in my career: if I let all the things I'd heard and seen overwhelm me, I couldn't do my job. I'd given as much support as I could, and now I must trust others to continue to provide it.

The situation out there in Syria – people missing, lives in constant danger, loved ones in torment, daily suspense as we waited for information – became the new backdrop to my life. The tension rose as each new development unfolded, then fell back with the stories on the news. It felt like living by the mouth of a cave where deep inside, you know that there's a dragon. Right now, the dragon might be sleeping. Life is normal, and everyone gets on with normal things, but you never quite forget that it's there. At quiet moments, you can hear the monster softly breathing. And tomorrow, or the next day, or next week – you can never know exactly when – it's going to wake and appear with a terrifying roar, pouring out its breath of fire. So there's no normal life, not really, though it looks that way sometimes. You're always living with the fear of the dragon.

Whenever I met the FCO family liaison team for an update at their office in Whitehall, I saw photos of the hostages. They were everywhere – propped on people's desks and pinned up on noticeboards in offices – a constant reminder that those held captive were living human beings, not just names on a list for a newsreader to sombrely read out. I found it deeply moving to see images of these missing men and women smiling or hugging their children or graduating from college, happy and carefree as they'd once been, knowing nothing about what was to come. Back then, they'd just been living their lives, but now ISIS was robbing them of years of those lives – taking precious time from them that they would never get back.

Those photos made the hostages real – and I know that they stayed real in the minds of everyone who tried their best to free them. Their families were suffering intensely – more than anyone who's not lived through their nightmare could ever truly understand. But I hope they realised how much those of us who were working with them and for them cared, and that this helped them to feel less alone.

Our whole team was carrying the weight of these events and all of us had to find our own ways to deal with it. For me, as it had often been before, this was fitness. A new team member, Tony, had just joined the HCNU and the two of us started working out together every day. Tony pushed me hard, encouraging me to get more into weight training and building strength. It was something I had always enjoyed, but this was different – it was a chance to sweat off the tension and strain, leaving me lighter and more peaceful after I was done. The gym became a space where I could escape from the relentless pressure, shut down my thoughts, and just be in my body for a while. It grew more and more vital to help me keep my mental health intact.

But for John Cantlie's friends and family, for the family of James Foley – the pressure never let up. Some relatives dealt with this very privately while others went public with Facebook pages and updates and campaigns about their loved ones to keep them in the public mind. For them, the greatest dread was that the person they cherished would be forgotten as the news cycle moved on. I respected them for that, while for me those brief moments of forgetting brought relief. I felt it each time I let the crisis slip out of my thoughts just for a while. The families had no respite at all.

*

One afternoon, the whole team received a briefing from a member of the British Army about hostage rescue planning. For me it was inspiring, super-interesting, and absolutely shocking all at the same time, and I took away from it one cold and unforgettable fact: that when military commanders plan a rescue, they calculate the number of lives they believe their operation will cost. This doesn't just mean that hostages might be killed. So might the personnel who will be sent to get them out.

Hostage rescue is an extremely uncertain business. There have been amazing successes, but there have been failures too. Missions have been aborted at the last minute because of sudden changes in intelligence. Boots-on-the-ground operations, planned with great precision, have begun well, but then something has gone wrong and lives have been lost. There are always unknowns so before any decision is made to go ahead, a calculation is made. What are the odds of achieving a good outcome? What are the risks? The people who are making these decisions know that rescuers may die.

So how do I feel about that? I wondered. Many Western hostages were charity workers bringing education, health care, clean water, and vital support to the people of Syria, and their work had high humanitarian value. John Cantlie and James Foley were journalists, committed to revealing the truth as they saw it. But the decisions they had taken were risky – and the lives of others who might be sent to help them were also being placed on the line. Up to now, I hadn't deeply considered this dilemma.

I couldn't find a tidy moral answer to all this, and I'm not sure I can now. It's part of living life behind the headlines – that there's sometimes not one simple conclusion. All you have is the best you can come up with at the time.

*

February 2013

'Nick – come in here and have a look at this.'

It was late afternoon in New Scotland Yard, quite early on in the New Year. As I was leaving work, I stuck my head around the big operations room door to say goodnight to my colleagues and saw a group of people sitting at the big oval table in front of a laptop with our head of unit, Harry, and Jack. I recognised our visitors as psychologists and FCO advisers. The screen on the wall was showing a report from Tehran on Sky TV. Harry beckoned me in.

'We've got an email,' he said. 'Came in today. It's from ISIS. It's about John Cantlie.'

Who the hell gets emails from ISIS? This seemed surreal – impossible, even. As I stared at the screen, I felt the dragon waking.

'It was sent to a family member and they forwarded it to the security services,' Harry went on. 'It's a demand for money. We need to analyse it first, then there are two decisions: whether we reply, and if we do, what we say. So what do you think? All ideas are better than no ideas.'

He must have seen me hesitate. Of course I was ready to help in any way I could, but I wasn't yet confident that my knowledge was anything like that of the others – after all, they were experts on the countries in question, the history of the terror groups, and the psychology of kidnapping. I still felt very new.

'Nothing's off limits, Nick,' he said. 'This is a first direct contact with them. It's never happened before. We're all finding our way. So you might have an idea we haven't thought about.'

The British government doesn't negotiate with terrorists, and nobody did so that day. But governments do talk to them and try to understand the way they think and act. We don't pay them and we don't give them concessions, but you have to open up dialogue wherever you can because it's only by talking that matters will ever get resolved. A few hours later, the negotiation team sent our advice on how we should reply to the Foreign and Commonwealth Office. The final call on what the British government should say to ISIS was theirs to make.

*

Kidnapping in Britain can be a bit of a shambles. This might sound surprising but it's certainly been my experience. That's because it's often done on impulse by a person who's angry. Perhaps a deal's been done – often about the sale of drugs – but someone hasn't paid what they'd agreed and a hostage is grabbed to apply some pressure. But if the kidnapper hasn't thought things through, holding someone can turn into a headache quite quickly. Where should they keep them? Who will feed them? Who will guard them? Can their guards be trusted and how should they be paid? When the kidnapper tries demanding a ransom, it often turns out that the family can't get hold of cash quickly enough. Now the police are closing in and the whole thing's a mess – and sometimes the result can be a quick release.

The terrorist group ISIS had none of these problems. When it started seizing Westerners, it had its infrastructure solidly in place: a network of camps and safe houses to move prisoners around, and guards who felt themselves to be soldiers in a cause and who would see the mission through. The organisation was also prepared to use extreme violence and to commit acts of torture and even murder, which made it highly challenging for those who opposed them to hold their nerve. Al Qaeda, the older terror group with the longer history, had stepped back from the use of violence during the last few years. Its leaders felt that these methods had backfired and increased opposition from some countries, particularly in the Middle East, who might otherwise support its anti-Western aims. But ISIS was completely committed to its bloodthirsty path, and this was driving a wedge between the two groups.

One group of ISIS members took the lead in its brutality, and I was starting to find out more about them: the four young British men who became known to the world as the Beatles. The Beatles were the ISIS head jailers – the ones who dished out the most extreme punishments to their captives. They held at least twenty-seven foreign nationals for ransom between 2012 and 2015, and one of them, Mohammed Emwazi, was identified quite early as the likely kidnapper of John Cantlie. The driver of Cantlie and Foley's taxi, when it was chased by three armed men, had given a description, and this member of the Beatles was a distinctive, muscular figure who'd been seen in several previous hostage-taking and execution videos. The British press had even given him a nickname: 'Jihadi John'.

Like everyone on our team, by now I felt more and more compelled to follow every new development in Syria. I constantly checked the news and set alerts so that any breaking story about the crisis would come straight to my email. I also had a growing need to understand these kidnappers better. The cruelty of the actions of men like Jihadi John was hard to comprehend, but they must have motivation: to try to understand what this might be doesn't mean excusing it, but it would help us make better decisions on how to respond. Who exactly were we dealing with? How did these individuals think and react?

When a group of Italian and French journalists who'd been held by the Beatles were released, their reports on the group were deeply disturbing. The level of violence the four men were using was so high that it seemed to come from pleasure, rather than from a colder calculation of the effect it might have. Who in their right mind would go into this horrific warzone in the first place when they didn't have to? But these guys hadn't just done that, they seemed to be enjoying themselves there. They appeared to relish inflicting pain, the journalists explained – like kids who liked to pull the wings off butterflies.

My colleague Connor had the harrowing responsibility for watching the videos that ISIS would regularly upload to YouTube, some involving executions by beheading. He would sit in the ops room and go through these forensically, looking for evidence – sometimes at great emotional cost to himself. I knew from my own experiences in policing that something that's been seen can never be unseen, and how certain images stay with you. But Connor was doing vital work: were there clues about where the videos had been filmed? Could any ISIS members be identified? In some of the videos, the killers openly showed their faces, and governments were able to identify their own citizens. As he watched, Connor grew familiar with the Beatles, and in particular with Jihadi John.

'Can I ask you something?' I said to him one morning.

'Sure, Nick.'

'This latest video you're looking at – it has Emwazi in it, right?'

'Yep. Pretty sure it's him.'

'Can I watch it? Not as far as the point where he kills the hostage, but the preparation that he does. His process. Because right now, I'm working in the dark. I don't know how he thinks. It would help if I understood better.'

Connor looked at me. 'I think it would,' was all he said.

'I mean – how would someone hate someone else so much that they would be willing to behead another human being? Maybe I can work out his belief system. How he sees the world. Try to make some sense of it.'

'Nick – you can come in with me tomorrow. See what you think.'

I sat down with him in the ops room in front of the screen.

'I don't want to see the moment when he actually beheads the guy,' I explained. 'If you can tell me when it's coming, I'll look away.' Connor understood without my needing to explain any further.

'Sure,' he replied.

The video began. I kept my eyes on the figure of Jihadi John standing behind the kneeling prisoner, finding that I was breathing more shallowly. It had been shot in the desert – a pale, dusty landscape under a bright blue sky with clouds racing along in the wind. *What must it be like to be out in all this space after months locked in a cell?*, I wondered. It's impossible to watch something like this without a feeling of dizziness coming over you – a kind of disbelief as the moment of death approaches. My purpose here was narrow and specific – to learn about the murderer, and I knew that if I let myself get flooded with emotional responses then the part of my brain that I needed to keep on line, the deductive, analytical part, wouldn't function so well and I might miss what I was looking for. So as a cold twist of fear ground its way into my stomach, I focused on remaining detached. The hostage's face was ashen. He knew what was just about to happen but made no attempt to move or resist. *This is the past,* I reminded myself. *He can't be saved.* But the sense that I should find a way to stop a helpless man from dying was intense.

'Look away now, Nick,' Connor said. 'I'll tell you when it's done.' I faced the wall, keeping my mind a careful blank. When several minutes had gone by, I turned back. I don't know why I didn't wait until Connor told me I could do so – perhaps it was my effort at detachment that confused my sense of time. I looked back too soon and I saw the hostage die – a lonely figure in an orange jumpsuit, his body contorted in pain. To see this was a serious mistake and I immediately knew it. I felt the image snap into my memory, cold, compact, and clear. From now on, it would always be with me.

*

The dragon in the Middle East was awake and spreading terror, but the job I had to do still went on. There were other hostage dramas going on around the world and in Britain. The suffering of the Khatun family was one such situation, although every time I went to visit them, I was moved by the way they tried to carry on with normal life during their ordeal. I could often tell that Mrs Khatun had been crying, but each time I arrived she made an effort to pull herself together.

The first time I met her, she was sitting in the kitchen with her elder daughter Tanvi, tightly holding each other's hands. Behind them, her son Lakhan restlessly paced the room.

'How much money are your husband's kidnappers demanding?' I asked her.

Tanvi and her mother consulted together. Mrs Khatun's English was poor and her daughter had to act as her translator.

'$400,000,' Tanvi told me nervously.

The Khatuns were comfortably off: they had a lovely house in Finchley with two cars parked outside in their driveway and another in the garage. Mr Khatun was a businessman who owned a number of companies in Dhaka and London and also had some involvement in Bangladeshi politics. He regularly travelled between the two countries, and it was on one of those trips that he had been snatched.

Mrs Khatun said something anxiously to Tanvi in Bengali.

'My mother says,' Tanvi told me, 'that she is very worried about my father. He has some medical problems – pains in his chest, a bad back – and she thinks that the stress will be hard for him. She hopes that this will end quickly.'

It's a human instinct to want to offer reassurance, but there was no way to know when Mr Khatun's kidnappers would next get in touch, nor how long this situation might take to be resolved. As their liaison, my role was to integrate with the frightened family, build a supportive relationship with them, and prepare them for the kidnappers' calls. I had no sense of the political background to the case nor of what might be happening in Dhaka, and I did not need to know: too much information can make it harder to be present and it helps if the relatives have confidence that their liaison isn't keeping secrets from them. Even the reasons why Mr Khatun had been targeted by these criminals weren't clear to me: was it a purely financial operation, or could there also be some political grudge?

Whatever the reason, the whole family was in turmoil. Mrs Khatun was frantic about her husband, while Tanvi's main concern was for her mother's well-being. She stayed constantly at her side and was open with me about her fears. 'My mother,' she would say, 'she won't tell us how's she's feeling. But at night I hear her crying.' The Khatuns' younger daughter Bhaijanti was still at secondary school and was also deeply distressed, and Tanvi, who was only a teenager herself and studying for her A levels, was trying to act as a parent to her while their mother was struggling. We arranged for a Bengali translator to help us talk to Mrs Khatun more easily when Tanvi wasn't around, but he just seemed to slow things down. The tense, unhappy atmosphere in the house affected everyone and I was never confident that the true sense of what was being said on either side was coming across.

But the girls' older brother Lakhan was our most challenging character, and as the weeks went on I had a growing sense that he didn't trust the police. Two months into the crisis, the latest demand from Dhaka was for half a million dollars, and the family responded that they would try to pay. I encouraged them to try to negotiate with the kidnappers for the times of these calls to be easier for them – Dhaka was six hours ahead of London, and the phone tended to ring in the small hours of the morning, which would throw Mrs Khatun into a panic and leave everyone more exhausted. Even a small change in timing might help the family to feel more in control.

'You know that Lakhan's got a second mobile, don't you?' Tom from the kidnap team warned me. I updated the team carefully after every contact I had with the Khatuns, letting them know how the family was doing or making them aware if anything unusual had happened. 'He's making lots of calls on it when he's away from the house. He's being very careful you don't see it. I just don't trust that guy. I think he could be planning something on his own.'

'You think he could be in touch with the kidnappers?' I asked.

'Possibly, yes. Or trying to get hold of them.'

'His mum will lose her mind if she finds out.'

'Can you talk to him, Nick? Don't reveal that you know about the second phone, but see if you can find out what he's up to.'

But it was almost impossible to have a proper conversation

with Lakhan. He was a student at a college in London, and came and went from the house at irregular times without keeping his mother and sisters informed of his whereabouts. And when I did try to speak to him, he was evasive.

'How's it going, Lakhan?'

'I'm okay,' he'd always say. 'I'm okay.'

'We've not spoken for a few days, and I was wond–'

'So what?' he interrupted. 'I don't have to report to the police!'

'Of course not. And I'm glad you've been able to have some time away from the house – it's so tense.'

'Are you trying to find out where I've been?' he asked me suspiciously.

I took a deep breath.

'I'm not, Lakhan, no.'

'I'm a victim here!' said Lakhan angrily. 'Why are the police spying on me?'

'I don't want to spy on you. I just know you've got a lot of stress right now and I'd like to help. I've been chatting to Tanvi and she's worried about you too.'

'Tanvi doesn't need to worry,' Lakhan muttered.

'I think she's taking on quite a lot right now, looking after your mum and Bhaijanti.'

'She's just a child. I can look after my family,' he snapped.

'If you'd like to talk things through, you can ring me or anyone else on the kidnap team,' I said to him. 'Any time, day or night. We're always here for you.'

The problem, I thought, was how overwhelmed and out of control he felt, but how impossible it was for him to admit it. He wanted to step up, to be the strong man who could fill his father's place and care for his mother and his sisters, but the pressure of all this was a crushing burden for him. He loved his father deeply and he was very scared, and to watch him push away our help and isolate himself at such a difficult time was very hard.

As the crisis dragged on, I was placed on 24/7 family liaison duty one week in three, available at any time of the day or night during that time if the kidnappers contacted the Khatuns, and they needed advice, or just if someone wanted to talk. Then for the following two weeks, I would be officially off duty – but it didn't quite work out that way. To start with, Lakhan never rang any of us, but then he decided he would only speak to me, whether or not it was my turn to be on duty, and his refusal to communicate with the other two liaison officers began to cause tension and bad feeling. I was never sure exactly why he did this, but I did wonder if it was because I was a woman. Lakhan was insecure and brittle, longing to take charge in this crisis but unable to do so. Perhaps it was too hard for him to share his sense of weakness or his feelings of failure as a man with other men.

*

'Nicky! He is found! He is free!'

It was the middle of the morning and I was in the gym when I saw a call from the Khatuns' landline number. Mrs Khatun was sobbing so much that at first I could hardly make out what she was saying.

'That's wonderful news, Mrs Khatun! I'm so happy for you all. Is your husband okay?'

'I think!' In the background I could hear both the girls also crying. I wondered whether Lakhan had heard the news of his father's release yet.

It appeared that the kidnappers in Dhaka had simply changed their minds. Things might have got too hot for them as police forces in two countries tried to track them down. Possibly the ransom payment was taking too long. Or – who knows? – perhaps in some mysterious way Lakhan's behind-the-scenes manoeuvres had paid off. Mr Khatun hadn't been well looked-after over the last few months and was in a battered, weary state – but at least he was alive and it was over.

The Khatuns' joy and relief was wonderful – hearing how happy they were made everything we'd tried to do worthwhile. In the middle of the Syrian nightmare of helplessness and fear, one family at least was re-united.

*

I met Jules, my wife-to-be – the triathlon woman with the long auburn hair – in 2013. Up to then, all my girlfriends had been policewomen – I guess it's because I've always spent a lot of time at work – but to start with I didn't know what she did for a living. I decided that this didn't matter: her online profile sounded funny and cool and we had plenty in common. Perhaps it would be good to do things differently this time. For a while we just chatted, taking it slowly and starting to share information and then photos.

The first picture of Jules I ever saw was the one which showed her competing in an Ironman competition. I noticed that what she was wearing seemed familiar, and peered at it more closely.

Yep – definitely a Met Police triathlon suit. It was a bit of a give-away. *Um – are you a policewoman?* I asked her in the chat. *Yes!* she typed back. *How did you guess? Is that okay?*

I had to laugh. I know people tend to have a type, but some-how I'd been drawn to a policewoman even when I hadn't known she was one. We still joke about the way she left a clue for me right there. 'Not exactly Hercule Poirot, was it, Jules?' We met up for coffee and then met again for dinner. Then we decided that we'd go to a concert. It was lovely, and quite early on, I think I knew. I'd found someone special at last.

*

On 19 August 2014, the American hostage James Foley, the fellow journalist captured with John Cantlie, was beheaded by ISIS. Within days, a video showing his murder was uploaded to social media. The dragon had breathed flame.

The next few months were filled with horror. Four more ISIS hostages were murdered: American Steven Sotloff, British aid worker David Haines, former British taxi driver Alan Henning, who had gone out to Syria to help deliver humanitarian supplies, then another aid worker, American Peter Kassig. Their killings piled up pressure on governments and on the other countries whose citizens were hostages in Syria.

The burden of the crisis hung oppressively on everyone at HCNU. Weirdly, perhaps, the one thing we never did in our office while all this was going on was communicate our feelings to each other. Each time footage was released of another beheading, we would come into work, say something like 'Have you heard the news?' acknowledge it and then just carry on. Everyone was dealing with the horror in their own way, and we were too busy to stop and think, so we put our heads down and got on with it. We were police officers, after all, accustomed to trauma after trauma; in our job, you find your own mechanisms for coping. Or perhaps there was another reason. Maybe this nightmare was so huge that to open the door and let it in risked us becoming overwhelmed. To survive, we had to keep it locked away.

I took the decision to use some of the ISIS videos in training at Hendon. The terror group, after all, was using this same material for its recruitment.

'You are about to see shockingly violent things,' I told my students. 'But you might have to negotiate with someone who's been radicalised by this content. You could find yourself talking to a person who's watched this video and instead of seeing a sadist cutting the throat of a helpless victim, they see a hero or a martyr to their cause. If your job is to try to understand them, it's important that you see what they have seen.'

The trainees were stunned by what they watched. But the negotiation skills I was teaching still remained the same: to listen and to try to relate. Finding out how a radicalised young terrorist recruit has made the decisions that he has is the first step in understanding him, and then connecting with him, and then persuading him to change his mind.

*

November 2014

By late 2014 the only Western hostage still surviving, so far as we knew, was John Cantlie. For months there'd been no news of him at all, then suddenly more videos began to appear. This time, they weren't beheadings but news reports, seven in total, presented to camera by John himself, still alive but now speaking as a mouthpiece for ISIS. His series was entitled *Lend me your ears: letters from a British detainee*, and he reported that the terror group was successfully expanding, winning battles, coming to dominate the region. By now, what he was saying wasn't true: ISIS was declining and would eventually lose 95 per cent of the territory it had taken.

It was impossible to know the full story behind John's reports for ISIS. Were they the result of coercion? Conversion? A desperate tactic for survival? Perhaps he'd made a judgement that working in this way was his best chance to be of value to his captors and therefore to stay alive. Who can really understand what it's like to be held hostage for months and years on end – the pressure, the loneliness, the ever-present dread of violent death? What does that do to someone's mind?

I watched him talking on the screen, remembering the calm, reflective man I'd heard speaking when I first took part in his debrief, and trying to work out what was happening with him now. He'd grown much thinner, gaunt and sunken-cheeked with blackened, rotten teeth. But his voice remained strong, and although his delivery was professional, unemotional, I caught an occasional flash of the sense of humour I'd seen back then. I hoped that some essential part of John had stayed intact through all of this, but it was very hard to tell. Whatever the truth might be – this man was a remarkable survivor.

*

'We don't have suicidal people here, Nicky! Nobody. Nobody at all.'

'But,' I said carefully, 'surely you must have? There are always people who are struggling.'

'No! Because you see, if you climb a bridge here and you say you're going to jump, we will shoot you!'

That was the moment when I realised that my colleague from the Philippines police didn't quite mean what he was saying.

While the Syrian crisis was still raging, Mick and I were getting on with a very different part of our job, training the Philippines hostage and crisis negotiation team. It was hard work, but I loved it. The Philippines has a massive problem with gang-related kidnaps and the local police force faces challenges with endemic corruption, but the individual officers I met filled me with admiration: they didn't have even half the equipment they needed to do their work, but still tried their best. Their amazing 'can-do (somehow)' attitude was obvious from the very first morning of teaching, when a line-up of trainees turned up for firearms instruction. I'd expected to see them kitted out in full protective clothing, boots and helmets, but they were dressed in shorts and flip-flops. But they were still resilient, good-humoured and positive – as well as unbelievably addicted to karaoke – and worked impressively hard in every lesson that I gave them.

The centre of Manila is a completely Westernised two square

miles, a world of bright lights, high-rise buildings, bars, and burger joints, for tourists and rich citizens. But it's surrounded by the intimidating poverty and slums of a developing country. All the big hotels there had guard dogs on duty – except that the dogs were golden retrievers, a breed that's well known for being gentle and playful. *That's weird*, I thought. *How effective can they really be?* As I looked more closely, as a dog lover I also noticed that these boys and girls weren't exactly in the first flush of youth.

'Where on earth did the hotels get their dogs?' I asked a local police colleague. He explained they were retired hearing and seeing-eye dogs: they must have been eleven or twelve years old. The hope seemed to be that once these good-natured seniors were wearing bright yellow bibs with the words 'Security Dog', they'd somehow be able to terrify local criminals.

Perhaps it was being so far away from home that made it possible for Mick and me to really talk for the first time while we were in Manila. We went out after work one evening for dinner in Harbour Square and sat in a bar afterwards chatting. Around the harbour, lights were coming on and we gazed at their reflections in the water. As the cool night breeze reduced the sticky heat of the day, we both began to relax for the first time in a while. New Scotland Yard seemed a million miles away. And then Mick suddenly said to me, 'Nicky – how do you feel about Syria?'

There was no time to ponder. I just gave him the truth, as simply and directly as he'd asked.

'Awful,' I said. 'Absolutely terrible.'

He nodded. 'Do you find that you're thinking about it? I mean

– all the time? Like it goes round and round in your head and you keep seeing the faces of the hostages and people who've been killed and you can't stop going over what's happened to them?'

I thought about the video I'd watched in the ops room when I was there with Connor. That helpless man being butchered by a terrorist. I'd stored the horror in a tightly sealed place in my mind, but just for a second, reflected in the dark waters of Manila Bay, I caught the orange flash of a jumpsuit. I quickly closed my eyes to push the image away.

'Yep. All the time, Mick,' I said. 'Every single day.'

We talked until late that night, and we listened to each other. We realised that we both felt the same. We'd coped with the pressure of the hostage crisis by closing off our reactions and emotions, but our mental storage boxes were getting full to bursting. There was so much shut inside there – so much fear and stress and grief.

'When I get back home,' I said, 'I might talk to Harry about getting some counselling about it.'

'I reckon we all should have it, to be honest,' Mick said. 'I mean today it's just a normal thing, counselling, isn't it? People understand that it affects you when you deal with stuff like this. At the start of my career, no one realised. You couldn't really ask.'

'Same here. That's 'cos we're old school, right? We're heritage police.'

Mick laughed.

'Should we have flagged this up earlier, do you think?' I asked him. 'Did we need more help all along?'

He sighed. 'You know what? I think we did. So – yeah. When we get home – we'll ask.'

*

In 2014, an Italian hostage named Federico Motka was freed by ISIS following the payment of a multi-million dollar ransom. Motka smuggled out with him a letter from John Cantlie. The existence of this letter was concealed until April 2022.

For the six British and American prisoners, Cantlie had written to his family, *the group is demanding a total of $100 million*. The prisoners he was referring to, along with himself, were James Foley, Steven Sotloff, David Haines, Alan Henning and Peter Kassig. They were the last of twenty-four hostages taken by ISIS, nineteen men and five women.

The British and American Governments are the most hated and therefore they are demanding the most for us, John's letter went on. *The amount of ransom is extremely high, but it is the only way the rest of us here will ever be released. If the money is not found we will remain prisoners here until we die, either by natural causes or executions.*

A total of €40 million had been paid by European governments for the others but the final six had felt completely abandoned, according to media reports years later. I read about this in a magazine after I'd retired, and thought of how John Cantlie must have believed these words and despaired. The sorrow this brought up was so raw that I burst into tears. I wished I could have told him that it simply wasn't true. He had never been forgotten, not by any of us. But he was beyond any help that we could give.

We love our families, John's letter concluded, *and we pray you are holding up under this situation.* A few weeks later, the Beatles began their beheadings.

There's no evidence that John himself was murdered by ISIS. No video of his killing was ever released. But in July 2017, eight months after his final TV report from Mosul, the city suffered a devastating bombardment and was re-taken by Iraqi forces. No one knows if he was still being held there at the time. He has never been found. He's the only one of those last six Syrian hostages whose fate is still unknown today.

*

When Mick and I returned to London from the Philippines, we talked to our boss Harry just as we'd agreed, and requested some counselling for the whole team to deal with the stress of the ongoing situation in Syria. My first session was the only time I'd ever spoken about what I'd been dealing with to anyone beyond my closest colleagues.

It was the start of our team receiving proper help. Each year from that point on, all of us filled out a questionnaire, and if we were identified as needing additional support, we got it. I know I'm lucky that throughout my hostage and crisis negotiation career, awareness of the impacts of trauma has been growing and help's been put in place.

'My chest feels tight all the time,' I told the counsellor. 'It's just – a weird feeling. Like I can't quite take in a full breath.'

'Any other physical symptoms?'

'I'm really tired. The last few months I can sleep for eight hours and I still wake up exhausted.'

'And how about in yourself – your emotions?'

'Well – I keep on thinking about the hostages. I have to make an effort to *stop* thinking about them. If I let myself drift – if I'm dozing in bed on a morning when I don't have to get up, say – I find I'm seeing their faces.'

'And how does that make you feel?'

'Scared,' I said.

'Scared of what, exactly?'

'I don't know. Just scared. But . . . '

I hesitated.

'But what?'

'I was going to say – what about the others? The rest of the team. The people who've been more involved in all of this. What about Connor? He's seen terrible stuff – far worse than I have. It seems stupid for me to be saying that I'm affected by talking to someone online in a debrief, when he – I mean –'

The image of a man in an orange jumpsuit flicked up in front of me. A shadowy figure with a knife stood just behind him. I quickly pushed the mental snapshot away.

'None of these things happened to me,' I said to the counsellor. 'I didn't actually go through this. Do I have a right to an emotional response when – they weren't my experiences at all?'

'But you've seen videos,' she said. 'You've done trainings, talked to hostages' relatives. All the negative emotions of the crisis – this drip-drip-drip of trauma and fear – have been around you non-stop. You don't have to compare yourself to other people. What you've seen and what you've done have had a very real impact on you.'

It's hard to get my head round that at first. But yes. It does make sense.

'There's something else as well,' I told the counsellor.

'What's that?'

'I have a really strong need to keep things separate. At work I deal with all this – stuff. This darkness, I suppose. That's quite a dramatic word, but I think that's what it is. And the people in my life that I care about – I feel that I must keep the darkness away from them.'

'Because you want to protect them?' she asked me.

'Yes. Very much so. My parents, obviously. My sister. And now my new partner and her daughter.'

Jules told me straight away she had a 6-year-old girl. I knew that the level of trust involved was huge: if Jules was ready to introduce us to each other, it must mean that she was serious about me. By now, I really hoped that she was, and it was an honour to meet her daughter. I'd never expected something like this to happen to me but as time went by, I was feeling more and more sure that the three of us had a future together as a family.

'The bad stuff,' I told the counsellor, 'I don't want it around us. I don't even want to speak about it when they're there. It's not that I can't talk to my partner – of course I can, she gives me loads of support – but I'm keeping this away. These awful things – murder, torture – they're like a shadow. The most important thing to me is that it never falls on them. Does that make sense?'

'Yes,' said the counsellor. 'Oh yes. I think it really does.'

Chapter 7

LOVE AND MONEY

'How much have the kidnappers demanded?' I asked the young man in front of me.

'25k,' he mumbled.

'Does your family have 25k?'

'No.'

It was 1 a.m. and we were sitting in a cramped little office in a police station in north London. Even if this guy did have 25k in the bank, there'd be no way for him to get hold of it in the middle of the night. Kidnappers tend to forget that even if you have the money in your account, it's tricky for most people to quickly get their hands on lots of cash.

'So when they call you back, Kieron,' I said, 'you're going to have to tell them.'

'That I don't have it?'

'Yes.'

'But they'll hurt Ashley! That's what they said!'

It wasn't hot in the tiny room, but he was sweating. He obviously in a state of terror. Then his mobile rang.

'It's them!' he cried wildly.

'Okay. Take the call. Put this guy on speaker.' He did as I told him and we both heard the kidnapper's voice. It was absolutely calm and controlled.

'If you want to see your brother again,' he said, 'I want 25k.'

'Uh – uh – I don't have 25k. I can't get hold of it!'

'Sure you can get hold of it.'

'I can't! I can't start ringing people now! It's the middle of the night!'

The kidnapper's tone didn't change. 'I want 25k.'

I mouthed: '*Ask to speak to your brother.*'

'So – so let me speak to him! Let me hear he's okay and I'll see if I can get it!'

'You're not speaking to him,' said the implacable voice. 'I want 25k. It's up to you.'

I mouthed: '*Ask again.*'

'But if you won't let me speak to him,' Kieron said, 'how do I know you've really got him?'

There was a pause. Then the kidnapper said: 'We'll call you back.' The line went dead.

*

My time with Kieron hadn't started well.

'It's a shit idea getting cops involved in this,' he'd told me flatly. At that point it was only a few hours since he'd had the first phone call telling him that his younger brother Ashley was being held hostage. He started off by trying to sort it out himself, asking mates for leads and working out who might be behind it, but as the phone calls kept on coming and the threats of violence kept on getting worse, he'd lost his nerve and dialled 999. Now we were supporting the family as they waited for the kidnappers' next move.

'My brother's been stupid, right?' Kieron muttered. 'He thought he was a big man. Tried to do some deals and now he owes some people money. Bad people. There's nothing you can do.'

'The kidnap team has lots of experience,' I said. 'We've dealt with hundreds of situations like this. We can help you.'

Kieron was terrified the kidnappers had him under surveillance and that they'd know he was working with the police, but he finally agreed to let me pick him up in my car in an isolated spot. He was a stocky young man with closely cropped hair, dressed in expensive sportswear and obviously very much on edge. It was after midnight as I drove him along the North Circular Road in north London, trying to gather as much information from him as I could.

'What exactly did the man on the phone say to you?'

'They've got Ashley. And if we don't give them money, they'll mess him up.'

'Is it always the same man who calls?'

'Yeah. Yeah – I think so.'

'D'you have any idea who he is?'

'No.'

'Are you sure? No suspicions? Why would he pick on Ashley?'

'Not got a clue, mate.' Glancing at him in the passenger seat next to me, I could see the distrust in his face.

'Kieron,' I said, 'it's really important that you don't leave anything out. People in situations like this don't always tell the truth to the police. But right now, my only concern is helping your brother. You've no idea at all why this is happening?'

'Nope,' he muttered.

He obviously didn't want me involved, so how could I build a relationship with him? I needed to find a way to get past his mistrust. But fear was all around – not just Kieron's fear for Ashley's life, but also his fear of my judgement – and it was clouding his thinking.

'You've probably had bad experiences with the police before,' I said. 'I get that. But I'm not interested in what Ashley might have done. Just tell me – was he dealing drugs?'

Kieron didn't reply, but I was pretty sure that this kidnapping was the result of a drug trade that had gone wrong. It's a fairly regular occurrence, and individuals who are held hostage quite often end up later on as hostage-takers themselves as part of ongoing gang-on-gang conflict. Kieron was right about one thing: Ashley had got himself involved with some pretty scary people.

'Police don't help us,' he growled at me. Then he clammed up. We arrived at the police station and were given a small office to use. We sat on opposite sides of the overcrowded desk while I prepped him for the kidnappers' next contact.

By 3 a.m., we'd taken six more calls and the amount of money they were demanding had risen to 35k. The kidnapper sounded businesslike and matter-of-fact as he threatened to shoot Ashley and throw his body in the Thames. I listened in to all the calls, trying to assess just how real the danger was, who the hostage-takers might be, and if they'd really do what they were saying they would. Kieron himself clearly believed everything they were saying. He thought that his brother's life was in imminent danger, and panicked more and more as the demands kept escalating.

'If he doesn't clear his debt to me,' the kidnapper told him flatly, 'that's my reputation screwed. And I can't let that happen, see? It ain't personal. It's business. Your brother has my money.'

'Can't you just wait until morning?' Kieron pleaded.

'No. I'll call you back in fifteen minutes.'

By now Kieron was too agitated to stay in his seat. He jumped up to pace the room but it was too tiny for him to take more than three steps without bumping into a filing cabinet.

'For fuck's sake!' he muttered. 'What's the point of calling the fucking cops? You're no bloody use!'

'How much money could you find when the banks open, Kieron?' I asked him.

'I dunno.' He ran his hands through his hair. '5k, maybe.'

'So next time he calls, make him an offer. Say it's a deposit. Try to keep him talking.'

Ten more minutes of suspense. I fetched Kieron yet another coffee from the machine down the hall. We went over what he should say before the phone rang again.

'We've got your brother here,' the kidnapper announced. 'He'd like a word.' Kieron gasped with relief.

'Hey, mate! You okay?' Then Ashley's voice came through. He was trying to talk tough but he sounded really young and very scared.

'Yeah, 'course. Yeah, man. I'm doing okay.'

'They hurting you?' his brother demanded.

'N-no. I'm not hurt. J-just get the money. Get the money, bro, then they'll release me. C-can you do that?'

The kidnapper's voice cut in coldly. 'Yes. He can do that. And he'd better. If he doesn't, the next thing you'll be getting is a bit of your brother in the mail.' Again the line went dead.

'For fuck's sake!' Kieron yelled, and he banged his fist down on the desk in front of us. I thought it was better to let him vent for a minute, so I didn't react to this. Then my own phone rang and I stepped outside for a moment to answer.

'Nick? It's Tom from the kidnap unit – we worked together on the Khatun kidnapping, remember?'

'Yeah – hi, Tom.'

'So intelligence has been gained that Kieron's still trying to sort this out himself. He made some phone calls last night and there's a gang of his mates looking all over. They seem to think they can track down the kidnappers themselves.'

I was aware there was a big police operation underway all around me, with highly skilled people gathering information and questioning and watching. I trusted that bigger process: I would be told what I needed to know and as the negotiator, my attention must stay here in this room and on the relationship I was trying to build with Kieron. Too much input from the outside would distract me. Kieron, however, didn't feel the same way and it was no surprise to learn that he hadn't been telling me everything. I went back into the room.

'Is there something going on that you've not told me?' I asked him.

'No way, man.'

'I think there is, though.'

'Nah. Why you police so suspicious?'

'Your brother owes someone money, doesn't he? I think it's

a drug-related debt. You do understand that if any of your friends try to confront people like that, you might be putting Ashley in danger?'

Kieron wouldn't look at me directly.

'You know that, Kieron – don't you?' I repeated.

He went on staring at the floor. 'Dunno what you're talking about, Nick.'

'I don't care what Ashley's been doing,' I said. 'This is about saving his life. I'm not here to judge – I'm here to help him. The best way to do that is to trust me.'

Just after 4 a.m., we got another call. It was a woman's voice, sobbing hysterically.

'Debs!' Kieron shouted. Debs? 'What is it, sis? What's happened?'

'Speaker, Kieron,' I reminded him quickly, but I didn't think he'd heard. He was gripping the phone, ashen-faced. Then he let out a scream.

'What d'you mean? What body part, sis? What you sayin'?'

Shit, I thought. *These kidnappers are using actual violence. If they're prepared to do that, it's more serious than just someone making threats and talking gangster.*

'Kieron!' I said. 'Is that your sister Deborah? Please put the phone on speaker!' But Kieron was too frantic to take in what I was telling him.

'Debs says they've cut off a body part and put it through the letterbox!' he shrieked.

'Kieron!' I said urgently. 'I need to hear what she's saying!' His hands were shaking so much that he could barely hold his mobile. Finally he put the speaker on and I could hear Debs's voice.

'There's a n-note!' she was stuttering. 'Somebody b-brought it to the house. "If you don't pay, you'll get a body part next."'

Kieron threw the phone down on the desk. It skidded across to me and I grabbed it. 'Fucking police!' he yelled. 'This is what happens when you trust you lot!'

'It's just a letter that's arrived?' I said urgently to Debs on the other end. 'There's nothing else in there?'

'No, no!'

Kieron was losing it. 'That's it! I'm done with this!' he shouted, and flung the office door open.

'Kieron,' I told him, 'if you walk out of here, you're on your own.'

'Too fucking right! I'll deal with it myself!'

'The Met is putting all its resources into trying to save your brother. We've done this before many times. I already told you – we're your best chance here. Please sit down.'

The phone rang yet again and he snatched it in a panic, but then as he listened, his face changed. It was Debs again, shouting loudly enough for me to hear.

'– big chain mark round his neck! And he can't walk, Kier! They've beat him up!'

'Ashley's just got home!' Kieron cried. 'They dropped him off!' He burst into tears of relief.

'Is he alright?' I asked.

The ending of the crisis seemed quite sudden, but I wasn't surprised. In my experience, a criminal kidnapping can quickly become pretty messy and complicated for the hostage-takers, and these guys had decided to bail. But they still wanted to teach Ashley and his family a lesson so they'd kicked the shit out of him: he was covered in cuts and bruises and later on it turned out that his arm and leg were broken. But at least he was alive and no ransom had been paid.

As Kieron tried to pull himself together to go home and I handed him his jacket, he gave me a clumsy but surprising hug.

'Yeah,' he said. 'Uh – Nick. Thanks, yeah?'

'That's okay, Kieron. I'm glad you've got Ashley back safe.'

My phone rang again. It was the negotiation liaison officer from the kidnap team.

'Is Kieron still with you?' she asked.

'Yes.'

'There's a warrant out for his arrest. Can you detain him?'

I looked across at Kieron. He was crumpled and tear-stained and still trembling, gulping what was left of a cup of cold coffee.

'Detain him for what?' I asked. 'What did he do?'

'Road rage incident a few weeks ago. He slapped another motorist and kicked a car.'

I paused. This had probably been the most traumatic experience of Kieron's life, and I'd been through it with him. He'd given me some aggro and he clearly didn't trust the police, but he'd co-operated and done what I'd asked him all through this harrowing night. I really didn't think that I could end our time together by arresting him. I was the senior officer here, and this was my call.

'I'm not prepared to detain him for minor criminal damage right now,' I said. 'I'll take responsibility.' Kieron caught some of what I'd said and his head turned sharply towards me.

'Kieron?' I said. 'I've just been told there's a warrant out for you.'

'So what you gonna do?'

'I'm not going to arrest you. I think right now you need to get home to your family. When you've seen Ashley and things are a bit calmer, can you get yourself round to your local station and deal with this warrant, please?'

'Er – right,' he said gruffly. 'Right. Okay, Nick. I'll do that.' After that he couldn't get out fast enough – perhaps he thought I was going to change my mind. But I wasn't. This was simply not the moment to throw Kieron in a cell. Letting him go home was the human, decent call and I was good with making it.

A few weeks later I was speaking to an officer from that local area and she asked me for Kieron's address. I didn't question her about it, but that probably meant he'd not done as he said he would and reported to the station. That was disappointing, but I still felt the call I'd made was right. I remembered the trauma he'd gone through that night, and the brutal attack his brother has suffered at the hands of the kidnappers. Kieron's priority afterwards must have been to stay around Ashley and Debs to protect them – not to follow police procedure. I had compassion for that.

I'll never know how long it took the family to get over their trauma – and their ordeal had lasted only hours. Months later, I hoped they reached some closure when Ashley's kidnappers came to trial following a lengthy police investigation. The gang was found guilty and its members were sentenced to nineteen years.

*

'Por Dios!' Agustina looked exhausted. She'd been up all night getting phone calls and messages on WhatsApp from a gang that had kidnapped her brother. The two of us were sitting in a hotel room close to Queensway in west London, waiting for the next time they would call. I'd arranged to meet her there because the kidnappers might be watching her home.

It was a warm, sunny Saturday morning; outside in the busy street I could hear people laughing and chattering in cafes. But Agustina's face was drawn and she looked dreadful, hunched in a chair with both her hands gripped in front of her in anxiety. She was in her mid-thirties, fashionably dressed with long dark hair, but she'd been up the whole night and her clothes were crumpled now, with dark sweat stains under the arms and lines of smudged mascara running down her cheeks. She was finding it difficult to hold herself together.

'Matias has been so stupid!' she said to me, struggling not to cry. 'He's got involved with these people – really dangerous people. People who sell drugs. He – he wouldn't want me to tell the police, but –'

'Right now it doesn't matter what he's done,' I reassured her. 'What matters is his safety.'

'He's just a really stupid boy. He was working as a runner for this gang. He thought it would be like *Breaking Bad* – you know, that he could start a criminal empire and be cool and make millions of dollars!'

Unfortunately, it was a familiar story. A person who starts working for a gang can sometimes think they're being clever, making easy money, staying in control. But the gangs so often turn out to be far more dangerous than they've realised.

Agustina jumped as her phone alert went off.

'Oh Dios! Nicky – it's them.'

'What does the message say?' I asked her.

'15k this time.' Her lips began to tremble as she read the message. 'Last night they said 10, then they said 12, and now they want 15. The longer I wait, they said, the higher it will be.'

'Ask for proof they really have him,' I told her.

'But I have to get the money!' Agustina cried. She was very close to panic.

'Please wait just a moment. Before you do anything – let's make sure they're really holding him.'

'What shall I say?' She looked up at me desperately.

'Just ask for proof. Ask for a photo with a date on. Or maybe they'd let Matias ring you if you ask.'

'I asked that! Last night and this morning I asked if I could speak to him. They'll only use messages on WhatsApp.'

Her mobile pinged again.

'Dios!' She held the phone out to me, pointing at the screen.

'What are they saying now?'

But before I could look at the message, her phone pinged yet again and she burst out crying, completely at the end of her tether.

'Pay or we will kill him, it says now! What should I do?'

I felt my own phone vibrate in my pocket. 'Agustina, just sit here for a moment,' I said to her. 'I need to take this call.' I stepped out into the corridor, relieved to be away for a moment from her infectious, overwhelming panic.

'Nick?' said the voice of my kidnap liaison officer. 'Got an update for you here. We've found Matias.'

'He's been released?' I asked.

'No. He was never a hostage. This whole thing's a scam.'

Did I really hear that right?

'Repeat, please.'

'Repeat – he's scamming her, the brother. He's not been taken hostage.'

'All these messages she's getting are from him?'

'Yep.'

'Shit,' I said. 'The poor woman. She's in a terrible state.'

'Yeah. It's a bastard thing to do.'

No wonder there've been no phone calls, I thought. *To pull a sadistic stunt like this if you were speaking to someone would be much harder. But sending messages on a screen is nice and easy. This guy wants to scare his sister half to death and WhatsApp chat's the simplest way to do it.*

There was no way I could soften what I had to say next. Slowly I stepped back into the room.

'Agustina,' I said. 'There's something I have to tell you. I'm so sorry, but Matias is fine. He's hasn't been kidnapped. He's trying to get money from you by pretending that he has.'

For several seconds she couldn't speak a word. I could see her brain trying to push the meaning of my words away. Then she just said, 'Sorry? Sorry – what?'

'He's not really been kidnapped,' I repeated. 'He's pretend-ing.'

'*What?*' Her face was full of bewilderment and disbelief.

'I know this is difficult for you to hear.'

'But – but – why? Why would Mattie do that? Our family has always supported him. Are you sure?'

'I'm sorry, but yes. We are sure.' Agustina buried her face in her hands.

We stayed another half an hour in the room while she struggled to take in what I was saying. She kept asking me to check, and was I sure, and how I knew. The sight of her misery was awful.

'He'll be charged,' I explained to her. 'This is an offence that he's committed against you.' But I knew that didn't help. In the end I drove her home to get some sleep. There would be follow-up for her – victim support and advice from the police – but her terrible betrayal by her brother would be part of her now. This was life-changing – something that would take her a long time to come to terms with.

It wasn't the cruellest stunt I ever saw. A few months later came an even nastier kidnapping hoax. This time the trickster was a woman named Varvara who persuaded her new boyfriend Isaak that she'd been taken hostage with a series of terrifying phone calls. She even came on the line herself, crying and pleading for the ransom to be paid while the supposed kidnapper shouted threats in the background. Isaak was in bits. He was a businessman who owned a cleaning company in Surrey, and he was blaming himself for her terrible ordeal and making frantic phone calls to put the 30k ransom together.

'Here she is!' he cried, pushing his phone into my face. 'My beautiful Varvara! I can't believe she's mine!' I took a look at his photos – and straightaway I felt suspicious because I couldn't believe it either. Varvara was in her early twenties and she looked like a supermodel – so why was she with Isaak? Love might be blind, but he was a short guy at least twenty years older than she was. His cleaning business was doing quite well, but he wasn't Jeff Bezos either. You have to be cynical sometimes.

'Er – how did you meet Varvara?' I asked him.

'On a website,' he explained. 'These girls – they are so beautiful, so kind. Often they have problems in their countries. Varvara, she has many responsibilities at home looking after her family. It's her mother, you see. She is very ill.'

'And how exactly do you help her?'

'I give her lots of love and support. And I send money for medicine for her mother. It's so expensive! And twice I've bought her plane tickets to London so that we can spend time together.'

'You've only met her twice?'

Varvara, of course, was scamming him. She didn't have a sick mother and the kidnap plot was faked, cooked up with her real boyfriend. A police investigation tracked the pair of them down pretty quickly and when I had to tell Isaak what was going on, I don't think I've ever seen a person look more crushed. He'd planned his whole future with this woman and now she had broken his heart into bits.

We offered him support as a victim, but Isaak wouldn't take it: he didn't want to admit what had happened and see Varvara as she really was, or how far she'd been prepared to go for money. He felt deeply humiliated and blamed himself for being a fool. But all the poor man had really done was to love the wrong person.

*

It was a Saturday, late morning. It was hot. Jules was driving and ahead of us, the bumpers and brake lights of the cars in the traffic jam on the M25 stretched as far as we could see. London's orbital motorway is famous for its hold-ups but driving through the centre of the city takes even longer and for us, making the journey from where I lived in the suburbs to the south up to Jules's house in the north was becoming a regular weekend nightmare. Behind me, in the back seat, her daughter Megan squirmed impatiently.

'Are we there yet? Mummy? Are we there yet?'

'No, sweetie, we're not there yet,' Jules said.

'Duuuuh! How much longer? How much longer are we going to be stuck?'

Jules and I exchanged glances.

'I'm not sure,' Jules said soothingly. 'There are so many cars, aren't there!'

'This is s-o-o bo-o-o–o-r-ing,' Megan moaned, kicking her feet into the back of my seat for the twentieth time this morning.

'She's not wrong, hon,' I muttered to Jules. 'It is pretty boring.'

'No, she's not,' Jules muttered back.

'It's not a very fun way to spend a Saturday, is it, Megs?' I said.

'We get stuck here every week when we come to pick up Nicky!' Megan pointed out. 'It's always all jammed.'

She was right. I looked sideways at Jules, and found that she was looking sideways back at me. I realised we were thinking the same thing.

'Um – so – perhaps we shouldn't be spending hours every weekend driving to get Nicky,' Jules said. 'Perhaps it would be easier if we lived in one place. What do we all think?'

'That's a great idea,' I said, 'but Megs still needs to be close to her dad's house, so I think I should be the one to move.'

'So then we wouldn't have to get stuck here any more?' Megan asked us.

'Nope! We could do much better stuff instead!'

'Yaaaay!' said Megan. She gave me another accidental kick in the back, but at least this time it was a happy one.

'Would you mind that, Nick?' Jules asked me. 'Being the one to move? I know it would be a big hassle.'

It's amazing how happy you can feel all of a sudden in the middle of an ordinary day, just doing ordinary things – even when you're stuck in a boiling hot car at Junction 10. I smiled at Jules, and she smiled back.

'No, honey,' I told her. 'I wouldn't mind at all.'

*

My phone rang at 2 a.m. Next to me, Jules stirred.

'Nick?' said the voice of the pan-London supervisor. This is the officer responsible, twenty-four hours a day, for calling out any additional support that's required for policing: firearms units, negotiators, working-at-height teams. 'We need negotiators. There's a guy up a tree following a chase after police tried to arrest him. But the tree is hanging over one of the main railway lines into central London – if he falls, he'll be electrocuted. The rail people have had to turn the power off, so until this guy comes down we'll have no trains.'

'Nick?' Jules mumbled. 'Is that work?'

'Yeah. Gotta go. Guy up a tree.'

'Good luck, honey.' She'd quickly grown used to me disappearing to crisis negotiations in the small hours. She rolled over and fell back to sleep.

I needed to select my team. Downstairs in the living room, I opened my laptop and brought up the list of those on call, considering their personalities and strengths. I'd taught quite a few of them on the course at Hendon, and worked with nearly all. Getting the right people was vital, but time was a huge factor here: it was already fifteen minutes since the phone rang and in just under three hours, the rail networks running from the central London terminus should be starting a new day. It was a Wednesday morning in August – fortunately not the busiest time of year, but tens of thousands of commuters still needed to travel on hundreds of trains and a stoppage was going to cause chaos. I decided to call in two Londoners, Chris and Evan, who could both be there in under forty-five minutes.

By the time I reached the scene, it was almost 3 a.m. The summer night had been quite cold and the street was already cordoned off. The area was part industrial and part residential, with a few small new-build houses alongside some commercial sheds, all backing onto a high fence next to an expanse of railway lines. Many tracks converged there, a couple of miles down from the terminus, which was one of the capital's largest stations. The whole track area was lit by powerful lamps high above.

Two hours left before the trains should start running. The safety of the man up the tree was my central concern but as the incident commander got me up to speed, I could already feel a different kind of tension. If those trains weren't on time, someone would start losing money. Lots of money. *And power-ful, important people who lose money aren't going to be happy.*

The incident commander went on with his briefing. 'This guy tried to rob a branch of Currys at the shopping precinct down the road, but he set off the alarms. He was still at the scene when the first unit got there, and there was a dog unit nearby so they were sent round too. The guy legged it and then climbed up this tree. No response from him since then.'

I was watching the man high above us, a thin figure dressed in black motorcycle leathers sitting on a branch. He must be quite a climber: he'd managed to clamber at least thirty feet. I wondered briefly how he'd made it up there – the tree didn't have many lower branches he could have used. Perhaps he'd jumped across from a fence at the end of the garden next door. It's amazing what people will do to try to escape from the police – I've seen some remarkable feats.

'Does he have a mobile with him?' I asked.

'Yep. And he's sending texts to someone.'

'Do we know who?'

'No information yet. Local intelligence is trying to work out who he is.'

Chris went in as our Number One to try to talk to him. 'Sounds like you've had a rough time tonight . . . ' I heard her saying. She worked hard, but it was very slow going. He wouldn't respond to her at all.

By now it was after 5 a.m. and just starting to get light. I've watched the dawn break many times after a stand-off through the night, and it often changes things for the better. Morning makes people realise how much time has passed and that this can't go on much longer, and as a new day begins, they sometimes begin to think more clearly. But this sunrise was only bringing us more headaches.

6 a.m. Chris took a break and Evan went in to try to talk. It was still surprisingly chilly and the man in the tree must be frozen, but even an offer of a hot drink and some food was met with silence. The wide expanse of empty rails gleamed in the early-morning sun. By now, these tracks should be active and the trains should all be moving.

7 a.m. Rush hour should be well underway. On a normal morning, trains would be rattling past every few minutes. I pictured the hundreds of message boards at hundreds of stations: *Service has been suspended due to a police incident.* Right now, thousands of people couldn't get to their offices or job interviews or hospital appointments or colleges or schools. They'd stand on the platforms for a while to see if things improved, trying to decide when to give up and find another way to make their journey. After that, they'd start piling onto buses or getting in their cars and jamming up the roads, bringing London to a standstill.

7.30 a.m. The growing warmth was a relief after the chill of the night as I stood with one of the PCs on the cordon.

'How's it going talking to that guy?' the PC asked me.

'Right now, we're not getting very far,' I admitted. He gave me a sympathetic nod.

'He's pretty strong. Be careful.'

I was struck by this remark. How could he know?

'How d'you know he's strong?' I asked curiously.

'We grabbed him last night, but then he got away. The dog

caught him and Rob hit him with the asp.' An asp is a retractable baton used by the police.

'Are you saying this was before he climbed the tree?' I asked. I knew nothing about any of this – and I definitely should have been told. The PC looked surprised at my question.

'Um – yeah. Hasn't anyone briefed you about it?'

'Would you mind telling me exactly what happened?' I said.

'Right – um – so when Rob and me arrived at Currys to respond to the alarm, we saw him and gave chase. The dog van headed him off and when we got there, the dog had him cornered and was holding him. We went to cuff him but he lashed out – Rob got hold of his arm but he was bloody strong so I hit him with the asp on the leg. But he managed to break free and just leapt up the tree.'

I needed to know about all this the first moment I arrived. Not telling me was a serious oversight. No wonder this man won't engage with us. Up to now we've been negotiating with our hands tied behind our backs.

'Thanks for that,' was all I said. I immediately updated the team.

'Guys – I'm afraid there's been some missing information. We've got a man here who's been hit with an asp in a pursuit and unfortunately was also held by a police dog. So he doesn't trust us and he's very fearful – I'd say he was in fight or flight and now he's gone into freeze. Also he knows that the minute he comes down, he'll be arrested. We need to address his trust issues first – show some empathy about what happened with the dog biting him, and really try to build a connection that way.'

*

8 a.m. I looked across the silent rails in the bright morning sunshine. Rush hour should be at its peak by now, but swathes of the region were completely shut down and I knew it must be carnage out there. The stand-off with the man in the tree was starting to make the local news headlines, and reporters with cameras were setting up by the cordon at the end of the street. Any minute now, the railway's bosses and London's civic leaders would start arriving at their desks and deciding what action they should take.

My phone vibrated in my pocket. I took the call, and found myself speaking to the chief superintendent of the local police station.

'Chief Superintendent Brown speaking,' he said. 'Can you give us an update, please? We're starting to come under some pressure from the rail company over the stoppage.'

'Right now, sir, there's been no progress. The man in the tree won't engage with the negotiators.'

'Do you have the working-at-height team with you yet?'

'Not arrived yet, sir.'

'What's the plan for now?'

'He's in a precarious position and he must be getting tired. He's extremely distrustful and our first priority is to get him to talk and to try to persuade him to come down without physical intervention.'

'Physical intervention is too risky, in your view?'

'Yes, sir. There's no trust between this man and the police. There's already been physical contact during the pursuit and if anyone tries to get close to him, I think he'll fight. If that happens and he falls, he could be seriously hurt or killed – even with the power to the lines switched off.'

'Right. Understood. Our big problem is the bean counters at the rail network. A stoppage like this costs them thousands an hour – more than that, according to them – not to mention the huge disruption to passengers and the traffic problems and the costs of that as well. Their boss has been in touch with the London Mayor's office about it. I'm starting to get phone calls from the top.'

'Understood, sir,' I said. Although I had no doubt where my priority lay – ending this incident without injury or even death for the man in the tree – it was impossible not to be affected by the rising political tension. A knot of anxiety was growing in my stomach. I found myself glancing at my watch.

'Do we have an ID for the guy yet, Nick?' Chief Superintendent Brown asked me. 'Or any idea who he's been texting?'

'I'm afraid I've not been given that information yet, sir.'

Once I'd taken his call, I walked over to Chris and Evan to check their progress. Nothing had changed. I didn't mention my conversation with the chief superintendent or the mounting financial implications of the stand-off, but I knew they were both very much aware of the wider situation. Then I sent a PC to McDonald's up the road for coffee and bacon rolls for them. First things first – the whole team must be famished. They'd been working for five hours and so far, there was still no end in sight.

*

Just before 9 a.m., the cherry picker arrived. I watched as it was carefully manoeuvred into place and Evan climbed onto its platform. Having him up there on the same level as the man in the tree would hopefully be helpful: no more craning necks, which gets painful for the team on the ground, no more psychological sense of disadvantage for the negotiators, and it would give them a much better look at him. He was still refusing to engage in any way.

A short while later, the working-at-height team arrived to give their assessment of the chances of physically removing him. Pretty quickly, they said no – too many risks involved. The branch he was sitting on might break. It would be difficult to reach him, the drop onto the railway below was too far and their biggest concern was that he would resist. The outcome we all feared was for this man to be seriously injured or killed in a fall following a fight with police. At a quarter to ten, my phone rang again.

'Nick,' said Chief Superintendent Brown, 'I'm going to patch you through to the head office of the train company.' The call was brief and all I could do was give the same information. Their tone was pretty terse. It couldn't have been clearer that no one was happy.

Ten minutes later, I took another call.

'Nick – I've got Gold on the line. He wants a briefing. Commander Jenkins is also on this call.' *Wow*, I thought. *Someone's gone right to the top on this one.* The police Gold commander was the senior officer in overall strategic control, and all information and developments were immediately fed in to him or her. Commander Jenkins was another very senior officer – one rank above a chief superintendent.

'Good morning, sir,' I said. 'I'm Inspector Perfect, the negotiator coordinator.'

'Who is this man in the tree – do we know?'

'Not yet, sir. All we know is that he came from a burglary so he's aware that when the stand-off ends, he'll be arrested.'

'He won't talk?'

'He's not engaging. sir. No progress yet. I would have expected more by now, and his silence is concerning. But he must be close to exhaustion and his position is hopeless. At some point he must realise that he's got to come down.'

'What contingency do you have if the branch breaks or if he jumps?' Gold enquired.

'That's a problem, sir, because the railway line that he's hanging over is on the far side of a very high security fence. We'd have to climb over to retrieve him. It's another reason why the electricity needs to stay switched off.'

'He's been up there for nearly eight hours. Surely there's a risk that he could slip from exhaustion?'

'Definitely, sir. He could just fall asleep. But if he loses consciousness even for a second . . . '

'Understood. Let's keep trying to get this concluded as quickly and as safely as possible.'

*

At 11 a.m., I was patched in on another call with Gold. This time, I was told, several senior rail executives would also be present. The situation was becoming even more nerve-wracking.

'The network has been paralysed for six hours, Inspector,'

one of the rail team began. 'We've no trains running across the region, and there's widespread disruption beyond due to trains not being in their proper locations. We need to know what's going to be done about this.'

He'd not yet mentioned numbers – the actual cost of the disruption in pounds and pence – but he didn't need to. I knew that's what everyone was thinking about.

'I appreciate your concerns,' I said. 'I think my team is –'

A woman's voice cut in.

'Look – we need a resolution to this, Inspector. Can someone not climb up there and grab him?'

'There's already been an assessment carried out by our working-at-height people,' I told her, 'and their advice is no.'

There was a very tense pause. I could hear a murmured consultation going on.

'So,' the first executive went on, 'what you're saying here, Inspector, is that one man – a burglar who's escaped from the police – can create this kind of stand-off situation and your people can't resolve it?'

'Right now,' I said firmly, 'my opinion is that the negotiators need to be given more time. This man must be nearing exhaustion.'

The first executive sighed. 'But surely, Inspector – as my colleague has suggested – there must be an option for the police to use force to end this? It's not pleasant, I know, but you could taser him, perhaps? Something needs to happen. The optics here are dreadful.'

I believe that I am quite a centred person. Remaining calm in tense situations is vital for the work that I do and it takes quite a lot to wind me up. But now I felt a surge of annoyance. I paused for a second, weighing up whether to go ahead and say what I was thinking. I decided that I would.

'You should probably bear in mind that the optics of him being killed are pretty dreadful too,' I told them.

The pause that followed what I'd said was more than tense – it was electric.

'Right – so what about sending somebody up via the cherry picker?' a third voice cut in. 'Can't someone jump on him from there?'

Negotiators have to be trained in working at heights every six months by the ropes team. As part of my most recent training, I'd ended up hanging from a harness halfway up the side of a building by the Thames in a practice rescue. Below me was a slipway running down into the river where a company called London Duck Tours rolled its bright yellow amphibious vehicles into the water so that the tourists on board could enjoy a trip around the city sights and a river cruise all in one go. As I waited for the rescue team to clamber down the side of the building towards me, I couldn't help but wonder darkly what would happen if my harness gave way and I landed splat in the middle of somebody's Duck Tour.

I have so much respect for this team. Heights work is difficult and dangerous. The ropes team can't get everywhere and the risks they take must be carefully calculated. Grabbing hold of a person who's likely to violently resist you, thirty feet above the ground in a tree that might give way with a railway line below – it must all sound so straightforward when it won't be you who's trying to do it.

*

I didn't doubt my assessment of the situation, or that the team was doing our best possible work in this fraught situation, but as midday approached, the pressure was really building up. I was about to take another group call from the network company with the office of the London Mayor also patched in. But before the call began, I spoke again to Gold.

'I'm taking calls from the assistant commissioner,' he explained. 'There's maximum pressure on to get this resolved.'

'I appreciate that, sir.'

'The rail company is answerable to its shareholders, and they are not happy. All they keep asking is how long, how long, how long? They're telling us that their losses are in the hundreds of thousands.'

'I'm afraid it's impossible to say how long, sir.'

'They're demanding other options. All I can do is explain that there aren't any.'

'That's correct, sir. The negotiators haven't made progress yet. We'll keep going until we get him down safely.'

'Okay. Understood. So we need to join the call. We'll let them say their piece and then we repeat that we're doing all we can.'

*

'We've had another idea,' piped up the train exec hopefully a few minutes later. 'We think one way out of the situation would be to use a helicopter.'

This remark was followed by silence. *Someone's been watching too much* Die Hard, I thought. It was difficult to know how to reply.

'We think the helicopter could lower an officer into the tree to remove the man,' the exec went on.

'Inspector,' said Gold to me calmly, 'are you able to – um – give a response to that?'

'Certainly, sir. In my view there would be – ah – issues with this idea,' I replied carefully. 'The helicopter would be very expensive. It would take time. And then we'd need an officer who's trained to – er – extract a subject in this way. If that's even possible.'

'I wonder if you grasp just how much this situation is costing us?' The exec sounded extremely exasperated. He stated the figure and it was eye-watering – definitely at the upper end of what I'd been thinking. But it was also the most helpful thing he could have said. Quite suddenly, after all the mounting pressure and anxiety of the morning, hearing that number gave me absolute clarity.

It doesn't matter, I thought. *Money's not the most important thing. Even if the cost was ten times higher, or a hundred times – it still wouldn't be. A man's life is at stake here.*

'I hear what it's costing you,' I told him. 'But what is the price of a life? Because – that's what you're talking about.' I noticed that the conference call had suddenly gone quiet.

'Thank you for your update,' the executive said tersely. 'We'll come back to you if we need more information.'

2.30 p.m. *We've been here almost twelve hours. We're not getting anywhere.* We needed a change of shift: new negotiators to replace the knackered team on duty. Apart from one bacon roll, they'd not eaten all day and they had to take a break. I took another phone call from the chief inspector. 'Nick,' he said, 'I think you've been here long enough as well.' I didn't want to leave but I knew that he was right. Then one of the PCs came hurrying towards me.

'There's a woman just arrived at the cordon,' he told me. 'She says she's this guy's girlfriend. His name is Jayden. Her friend told her she'd seen him on the news.'

Getting a name can be a big breakthrough moment. It makes it easier for the negotiators to establish a connection, and it starts to shift psychological control. It's easier for someone whose identity is unknown to feel powerful, or that they have one over on the police. I hurried over to speak to Jayden's girlfriend, and she agreed to go up on the cherry picker to talk to him.

'He won't come down,' she told me anxiously afterwards. 'He's too scared. He thinks the police will beat him up.'

'Could you please reassure him? Could you tell him all we want is to end this situation safely?' But even after she'd had another try, he wasn't budging. We were running out of options. It was deeply discouraging for all of us, and definitely time to change shift.

'Nick? There's someone else here now. She says she's his granny.'

*

'Him a good boy,' she said to me emphatically, 'but he gone off de rails.'

Jayden's granny was a tiny little lady – less than five feet tall.

I got the feeling that quite a lot of what she said on any subject was going to be emphatic.

'Has he been in trouble with the police before?' I asked her.

'It not him fault,' she said firmly. 'He wit' de wrong crowd, you understan'? Him don't talk to his family no more.'

'I understand,' I said. 'It's difficult when young people don't tell you what's going on, isn't it?'

Granny nodded. 'But him a good boy,' she repeated proudly. 'Him mek mistakes, but him always like mi cookin'. Him respeck mi.'

'Do you think he'd talk to you?' I asked her. 'I mean today – now. While he's up the tree?'

'Oh yes. Him always talk to mi. I tink if we talk, he come down. Mi tell him dis no good, dis behaviour. Causin' all dese problems for people.'

'Okay,' I told the team. 'So Jayden's grandma might be able to help here. Just make sure she doesn't get too cross with him. I get a good feeling about her, I think. But it won't help us if she starts telling him off.'

I needn't have been worried. He did have a lot of respect for his grandma, and she certainly sorted him out. Within an hour they'd agreed that she would go home and fetch him some of her homemade rice and peas, which was his favourite meal. When he'd eaten that, he agreed that he'd come down from the tree, and then he'd be arrested. Making this a condition allowed him to feel he had some power: even though he had to give up, at least he'd managed to cut a deal first. The only problem, at least as far as Chris and Evan and I were all concerned, was that it all happened only minutes after the second negotiation shift had taken over, which led to a lot of ribbing among the team. 'How long were your lot there, Nick? More than twelve hours? As soon as we arrived it got sorted in less than forty minutes!'

We put up with this as graciously as we could manage, muttering under our breaths that it was really *our* shift that had done all the hard work. I was proud of us all – we had done a good job and showed great resilience in keeping going when Jayden wouldn't talk to us. Chris and Evan had stayed on it for hours – throughout a very tough day they had never even thought of giving up.

Rice and peas were the answer. Not tasers or helicopters or violence. If someone ends a stand-off after an ear-bashing from their granny and because they can have their favourite dinner, as far as I'm concerned that's a win. It was far better to make a deal for food which costs pennies than to carry on using many thousands of pounds' worth of resources while a man's life was at risk. For Jayden, rice and peas meant security and family and home. That meal represented love, and it was love and his trust in his grandma, not threats of violence or the thought of all the money he was costing, that brought him down from that tree. I never did find out what the railway company's accountants made of it.

Chapter 8

'Guys – we have a fast-time kidnap in Nigeria. Not much more information yet. We're going to the NCA now. Get what you need, sort a car, and I'll see you in the car park in five minutes.'

Up to the moment Harry calls my colleague Tony and me into his office, it's been a fairly peaceful morning. The day's bright and sunny, and Tony and I, who both love working out, decide to take our lunch breaks at 8 a.m. so that we can put in some time while the gym's still quiet. We go early like this whenever we can, preferring to use the energy boost it gives us to keep going through the rest of the working day. Once we're done, we head back to the office.

Now all of a sudden, our normal day has vanished. We look at each other. Aside from Harry, we're the only two members of HCNU in the office today, and both of us are still fairly new to the world of international kidnap. We're the ones who are going to have to take this on.

'Okay?' I ask him.

'Yep,' he replies. 'Let's do it.'

10.00 a.m.

The three of us are on our way across London to the offices of the NCA – the National Crime Agency. Harry's on the phone and judging from his end of the conversation, this is something big. He's deep in thought, clearly considering his options, but not yet ready to share them with us. He does give us a factual briefing: the British national who's been abducted is called Jim Judd and he's been taken with two Nigerian locals, David Haruna and Idris Isa. The three men are all very senior employees of a multinational called TransWorld Systems, working in their office in Lagos.

10.25 a.m.

We arrive and are whisked upstairs to an unremarkable briefing room – overcrowded desks, blue carpets, whiteboards covered in scrawl on the walls – where we're given the latest intelligence by Alex, the NCA's lead on kidnap. Also in the room are another senior member of NCA and a board-level representative of the victims' employer, TransWorld Systems. The presence of this high-level executive is interesting, suggesting to Tony and me that the kidnapping in Lagos has been known about for some time – could be hours, could be days – before we've been called in.

This is quickly confirmed during our briefing. 'The kidnapping happened yesterday afternoon and contact has just been made by the hostage-takers. At this stage it looks like a criminal kidnap. Jim Judd was the only non-Nigerian present at a work-related social event, a picnic for company staff held a little way outside the city. Those who attended were vulnerable in that location, and somebody spotted them. Whoever it was might just have got lucky, or they might have had their eye on their potential victims for a while. As a Westerner, Judd's certainly a valuable hostage.'

'What steps are being taken to pay the ransom?' Tony asks. It would be normal for a company like this one to have kidnap insurance in place.

'A senior member of our team out there is taking steps to gather money to meet their demands,' comes the reply from the representative of TransWorld. 'This guy's taking it badly – he seems absolutely shocked by what's happening.'

'We also have information from an intelligence source which suggests that right now, the hostages are on the move,' Alex says. 'Their change of location is concerning and we're seeking clarification on it.'

Tony and I don't ask too many questions at this stage. We bear in mind that our role here is not to understand the politics of this crisis but to take appropriate action to free the British hostage and his fellows. But I am struck – and I know Tony is too – by the speed with which events are moving, and the urgency with which everyone is behaving. It's quite normal for kidnappers not to make contact for weeks or even for months, but Jim Judd was only taken yesterday. So what's the rush? Kidnap insurance also pays out slowly – but here's a senior company executive chasing after ransom money within twenty-four hours. A fierce anxiety is driving everyone, and there must be a reason for this.

'Do you guys have enough to be getting on with?' Harry asks us.

'We need a quiet room that we can use as an office,' I say to him. 'And a phone.' A room is quickly located – very small indeed, in fact it feels more like a broom cupboard, but it's away from noise – and a phone is plugged in for us. At least there's only one hour's time difference between England and Nigeria; that will make our work simpler.

10.45 a.m.

Tony and I set ourselves up with our laptops. Then we talk each other carefully through the situation, making sure that we both understand what's going on and have the same information. The sense of urgency around this kidnapping is intense and its tension is infectious. It's vital for us to keep clarity as events rush forward.

10.55 a.m.

Harry bursts into our cramped little working space with an intel update.

'Look, guys – this is hotting up. The hostages are moving north-east towards a well-known Boko Haram controlled area. My guess is that the people who've taken them aren't liking all the attention they're getting and want to sell them on, and Boko Haram would definitely be interested in buying. It's happened before in this part of the world. We need to progress this as fast as we can before that happens.'

This is really bad news, but it certainly explains why everything is going at break-neck speed. Boko Haram is an Islamist terrorist organisation based in the north-eastern part of Nigeria. Founded in 2002, it's notorious for its brutality and has killed tens of thousands of Nigerians in attacks against the police, armed forces, and civilians. Its atrocities include mass abductions, the displacement of millions of innocent citizens from their homes, and the creation of regional food crises and famines. The group famously kidnapped 276 female students from a school in the town of Chibok, and years later many of these girls remain missing. For the three hostages to fall into the hands of this group would be disastrous. Harry heads back to his own office, leaving Tony and me on our own. We look at each other anxiously for a moment, then without needing to say a word we both get on with what needs doing.

11.15 a.m.

Alex provides us with an update from NCA.

'TransWorld has appointed a local private security company negotiator,' he tells us. 'His name is Liam and he'll be your point of contact. It's vital to have someone local on the ground to enable us to negotiate a safe release.'

'So we're working directly with this guy?' I double-check.

'Yep. The company's kidnap insurance pays for him and he's dealt with similar cases in the past. You need to speak to the NCA's representative in Lagos as well. He has contacts in the embassy there so he might have extra info. His name's Simon. You'll be needing both their numbers.' Alex gives these to us rapidly and we scribble them down. 'So – is there anything else you need from me right now?' We confirm that there isn't.

11.30 a.m.

I quickly call both Simon and Liam but don't learn much that's new, apart from that two further calls have come in from the hostage-takers with no real progress. Liam seems like a pretty switched-on guy with lots of experience, amenable and happy to work with us, but I find our rapid introduction to him slightly worrying. It seems to me that this situation is developing at lightning speed without enough clarification of what's happening on the ground.

After that, there's a lull. This is normal in international hostage negotiations and there are many reasons for it. One is simply that kidnappers are often operating in locations where there's no mobile signal. Another, of course, is that they deliberately go off-grid because they know that their devices can be located and tracked. Waiting is always the most difficult time. Tony and I take the opportunity to grab some coffee and a sandwich.

1.00 p.m.

The phone rings at last and we put the call on speaker. It's Liam.

'I've got an update,' he tells us. 'I've made direct contact with the hostage David Haruna. He's one of the directors of TransWorld and the kidnappers have allowed him to call some of his friends. One of these friends has access to cash and they've agreed he'll get the money together and pay the hostage-takers what they're asking.'

Woah. Just hold on a minute here. Tony and I look at each other in consternation. It's the first time that either of us has worked with a private security firm like Liam's and we're not sure how reliable he is. We've been worried for a while about the speed of events, and now this sudden development takes our anxiety to a whole new level.

'Just hang on, Liam,' I say to him. 'Getting the money together? We don't have a whole lot of information yet. Are all three hostages together? Are they even still alive?'

Liam clearly wants to be helpful but I'm surprised at how trusting he seems because in situations like this, people lie. Whenever there's a kidnapping anywhere in the world, word gets around on the street, everyone smells money, and randoms start to call in claiming to be holding the hostages. That's why you don't accept what anybody tells you until you've checked the facts. What a hostage says may not be true either – they could be under duress. Frankly, I'd have thought that a professional would know that.

I speak directly to Liam.

'Right now, we're getting ahead of ourselves,' I tell him. 'The picture's confused – we shouldn't just believe whatever we're being told. The first thing we need to do is confirm that the three hostages are actually all alive and safe. Until we know that, my advice would be not to progress this any further. Right now we don't even know what terms David is agreeing to. We've no details about how any release might take place.'

'Right,' Liam replies. 'Right – I can do that.' I don't spell it out to him at this stage, but it's also bothering me that everything that's happening is on the hostage-takers' terms, with no control at all from our side.

As the call ends, Tony says to me: 'I reckon Liam's under pressure from TransWorld to get this wound up fast. That's why he's jumping the gun.' It's a good point, and I nod. I think he's right.

1.25 p.m.

Liam calls us back.

'I've made a few more calls,' he says, 'and we need to streamline things here. This friend that David Haruna has been ringing – the one who's saying he can get hold of the cash – he's becoming too upset and emotional to cope. He's not really handling the pressure. The kidnappers want progress too, so they've agreed that David will speak directly to me.'

'Okay,' Tony answers, 'that sounds positive.'

'So I'm going to try to call them back and patch you guys in,' Liam continues. 'We're after proof of life.'

'Great. Yes, we are. Let's do that.'

'Also the ransom demand has come down. They'll accept 36 million naira now – that's the local currency. Sounds like a lot but it's around 75k. To start with it was quite a bit higher.'

'Someone out there can get hold of 75k in cash just like that?' I clarify.

'Apparently, yes. I think the banks are less secure so people hold on to reserves of money in case anything happens. Well, the people that can afford it do.'

1.45 p.m.

We're successfully patched in on the call. The line is very bad, but we can hear the hostage-takers speaking in the Hausa language in the background, and David Haruna translating. Most importantly, the voices of the British hostage Jim Judd, and Idris Isa, can also be identified. All three are definitely alive, and Tony and I feel considerable relief. David confirms that he has contacts in Lagos who are raising the cash for the ransom, and Tony and I don't get involved in the details of this: our assumption is that either TransWorld's kidnap insurance will pay out to cover it, or the company itself will recompense them. What's important is that both sides want this over and done with as quickly as possible.

But during the call, my concerns start to grow about the hostages' welfare. David tells Liam that they have all been walking throughout the previous night and been given very little time to rest during the day. They're exhausted, thirsty, hungry, and becoming more and more distressed.

'Try to find out exactly where they're being held,' I quickly prompt Liam. 'We need to gain as much information as we can before the kidnappers end the call.' But when he asks, the hostages don't know. They're clearly very disorientated.

'We've no idea where we are – and we were dressed for a picnic,' David Haruna cries, 'not to march for hours through rough terrain in darkness! All of us have fallen down. We're covered in bruises. We're bleeding. We must have more water.' He sounds frantic.

Then we hear the kidnappers' voices again in the background, raised this time and roughly giving orders.

'We're moving off!' David tells us urgently. 'They want us to keep going right now.'

I don't like the sound of this at all. Abruptly, the call cuts out and we're left to wait.

3.40 p.m.

Another call from Liam.

'David's just got through to me again,' he says. 'The hostage-takers want to know what's happening and what arrangements have been made to pay the ransom.'

'How do things sound now?' Tony asks.

'Well – they're still speaking through David rather than directly to me so it's hard to tell, but I'd say they're upping the pressure.'

I'm looking for a way to take this forward, knowing that everyone wants a resolution. 'Do we have anyone who can act as a go-between for the ransom payment?' I ask. 'Someone who's trusted by both sides?'

'I don't know yet. I need to speak to TransWorld about it. I'll come back to you.'

4.10 p.m.

'Right,' Liam tells us. 'The kidnappers are prepared to accept a guy who works for TransWorld as an intermediary.'

'If both sides are good with that, then fine,' I tell him. 'It's the money being available quickly that's keeping the kidnappers interested here. If it wasn't, they'd just sell these guys on. They'd probably have done it already.'

4.50 p.m.

It's Liam on the phone again, this time sounding rattled.

'Er – so, I just heard from David again and he's really scared all of a sudden. I'm not sure what's happened but he's just said to me, "Get the bloody money sorted, will you? I don't know how much more of this I can take."'

I feel my stomach turn over with anxiety.

'I tried to encourage him that everyone's doing as much as they can to arrange the payment,' Liam says, 'but these guys are having a bad time. It's really getting to them. They must be close to breaking point by now.'

4.53 p.m.

Simon brings us an update on the location of the hostages. They've moved a considerable distance to the north-east, he tells us – no wonder they're sounding so worn out, given the speed with which they're being marched cross-country. Most worryingly, they're getting close to Boko Haram's territory. We contact Liam, and the news gets even worse.

'I'm hearing rumours that the gang that grabbed them is getting spooked and wants a quick sell,' he says.

The situation is becoming more alarming and another troubling thought occurs to me. I don't think that professional criminals would panic like this. 'I think these kidnappers have bitten off more than they can chew,' I say to Liam.

'They're just opportunists, you reckon?' Liam asks. 'They saw an easy target for kidnap and thought – hey, looks like it's Christmas?'

'Yep. And amateurs are riskier. If they were pros, they'd know how this would go and they'd have done some forward planning. But I don't think these guys were expecting all the international interest. If they've lost their nerve now and want to sell the hostages fast – who will they sell to? Round there, there's only one answer.'

'Boko Haram,' Liam replies grimly. It's our worst moment since the crisis began. We all feel a chill of anxiety.

'Liam – can you call them again?' I say to him. 'Find out exactly what's going on. If the kidnappers can be reassured that there's a plan to meet their demands, they might hold on to the hostages a bit longer.'

Liam agrees that this is what he'll do. The silent wait that follows is the grimmest one yet.

5.28 p.m.

Liam calls us back. He's been trying to make contact, but the phone line that he's been using up to now is suddenly dead. This isn't a good sign.

'You need to keep on trying them,' I tell him. He agrees that he will do so every two hours.

10.30 p.m.

We've heard nothing and our nerves are in bits. We decide to move to a hotel nearby where we can try to get some rest. We call Liam to update him on our plan, and notice how exhausted he also sounds. I'm not surprised – the pressure of talking directly to the hostage-takers is immense, and Tony and I focus briefly on his welfare, asking how he's feeling and if there's anyone around him that he can call upon for support. Right now, as the company's representative, a lot seems to be falling on his shoulders. He was involved in the kidnapping before we were, and has been awake for more than twenty-four hours.

11.00 p.m.

Tony and I check into a local hotel. It's in central London so it's extremely expensive and as we're last-minute arrivals, we're lucky to get rooms that are next door to each other. However, both are tiny. After hours in the cramped broom-cupboard-style office at NCA, it feels stressful for both of us to be cooped up yet again.

11.30 p.m.

A colleague, Jake, is sent to relieve me. I've never met him before: he's an international negotiator who works for another police force. There are so few internationally qualified negotiators available in London right now that Harry has put out a call for help. I feel absolutely worn out but I don't really want to go off duty while the tension is so high and I'm so closely involved in what's going on. Reluctantly I arrange for a cab to take me home, and I get back shortly before half past midnight. I feel too fraught to be hungry but I know I need nourishment so I manage half a slice of cheese on toast. Although my mind is racing, I eventually manage to fall into a light sleep.

Thursday, 3.30 a.m.

I'm woken by my phone. It's Harry.

'The intelligence picture is changing rapidly,' he tells me. 'The kidnappers and their hostages have definitely moved into the Boko Haram-controlled area.'

'Shit,' I say. Harry agrees that this is very bad news. I don't add: *and those poor men are still walking. I hope they've had some water by now.* I know that Harry is as aware of their plight as I am.

I try to go back to sleep but this latest news is playing on my mind. Jules is away and I'm alone. As top executives at an international company, receiving briefings about the political situation in Nigeria will be part of the three hostages' jobs. That means they all understand what the stakes are and who the key players in these dreadful events are likely to be. They'll know it's likely they'll be sold on to Boko Haram. How must they be feeling? What might they do to try to cope in this awful situation? I twist and turn for quite a while, then just as I'm close to dozing off, my mobile rings again. I grab it instantly.

4.25 a.m.

'Nick? It's Harry. I'm afraid I have bad news.' He doesn't keep me in suspense or do a big build-up to try to prepare me, just tells me directly. 'We've received a report that all three hostages have been killed.'

I freeze.

'What?' This is devastating news. 'What the hell happened?' I ask him. 'How do we know?'

'The picture's still quite confused,' is all Harry says. But I know he must have got this from a reliable intelligence source since he's sharing it with me. When something so disastrous occurs, it's always followed by intense self-questioning and already I can feel my mind starting to play back the events of the last day and a half. I think of how exhausted and desperate and scared these three men must have felt in their last hours. *What could we have done differently? Was there any way we could have prevented them from dying?*

No chance of further sleep tonight. Pretty soon I'll be called back to take over again at NCA. I sit in bed with my knees drawn up under my chin, staring into the dark.

5.15 a.m.

The phone rings again.

'Nick? There's been some crossed wires here,' Harry says. 'I've just had Liam on the line and he's spoken to all three hostages in the last few minutes. They're alive, and they're okay.' I'm flooded with relief.

'Thank God for that.'

I don't comment further, as no one is to blame for the confusion. In fast-moving negotiations abroad, you're reliant on other police or military personnel giving you information. I know my colleagues will be cross-checking and verifying everything they hear to the best of their ability. The situation on the ground must be chaotic.

6.00 a.m.

Harry's outside my door in a car to take me back into central London.

'I'm sorry about the call in the night, Nick,' he says to me. 'That was good intel – right until it turned out that it wasn't.'

'No problem,' I say. 'I appreciate that. Is Tony alright?'

'Yep. We got him back to the NCA at 3.30 this morning to give support to Jake.'

6.45 a.m.

We reach New Scotland Yard where a very familiar face, that of my colleague Karl, is waiting for us to pick him up. Long ago, he was my tutor when I trained as a negotiator at Hendon. Now he's volunteered in response to Harry's request for support and it's good to see him. Harry gives us our instructions: the two of us will proceed together to NCA to take over from Jake and Tony, who will then go home to rest.

'You look knackered, mate,' Karl tells me, and I manage a grin. *I bet I do.*

7.15 a.m.

Tony's not at all keen on the 'going home to rest' instruction, and we practically have to force him out of the door. I understand the way he feels completely – it's very common to want to stay around when you are totally immersed in managing a crisis. We've also heard nothing from the hostage-takers for hours, and although we understand that there may well be reasons for this, it's difficult not to read too much into it.

9.30 a.m.

Liam calls. After a long and testing wait, the hostage-takers have made contact once again. But now they have a new demand: from this point on, we must speak to them directly in Hausa, rather than going through David Haruna's English translation. Perhaps they're suspicious that David has been giving the authorities additional information as he's been speaking. We need to find a Hausa translator, fast, and the language barrier adds even more confusion to an already very confusing incident. TransWorld Systems locates a local man who's bilingual and willing to help, but when he comes on the phone from Lagos he sounds extremely nervous. He's clearly never been involved in anything like this before. I can't help having doubts about how he'll cope under pressure.

There's no further contact during the morning, which is deeply worrying. So much could go wrong here. While we wait, Karl and I talk through possible scenarios, trying to come up with courses of action we would follow for each one. What if the kidnappers separate the hostages? What if they kill one of them and keep the others alive? What if they increase their ransom demand? We wait around, desperately trying not to overthink the situation, and checking in with Liam every hour. The hours crawl by, and midday passes. Everyone feels drained as the afternoon begins. It seems incredibly long and drawn-out.

3.00 p.m.

'This is it. Payment's been agreed,' Liam tells us. 'The ransom's being handed to the intermediary in the next few minutes.'

It's almost a shock to move from hours of torpor to action stations. We go through every detail of the plan to transfer the money to the hostage-takers with Liam. 'I won't be in contact now until it's done,' he says. 'I need to keep this line clear. I'll call you as soon as we have an outcome.'

'Okay,' I answer, and hang up.

So now we wait. This is the moment of peak risk. The money is with the intermediary and he is on his way to a spot in open countryside where the kidnappers have agreed to make contact. It's a gamble. What if they take him hostage too? What if they grab the money and kill him? What if they take the money and depart, but then don't free the hostages as they've agreed?

'This guy's taking a hell of a chance doing this,' Karl murmurs. He's right.

'Yep. But it's his call, in the end' is all I can say.

3.57 p.m.

The phone rings and it's Liam.

'Okay. The payment's been transferred,' he tells us.

'So far so good,' I say to Karl. All we can do is go on waiting.

6.25 p.m.

Our nerves are ragged. We've no idea how much longer this will take. I'm desperately tired but aware that if this suspense continues, I won't be sleeping tonight either. Then the phone rings. It's Liam.

'I've got someone here who wants to speak to you,' he says, and the voice of the Hausa interpreter comes on the line. He's crying and laughing and talking all at once. There must have been a breakthrough.

'Thank you!' the interpreter shouts. 'Thank you, thank you, to everyone in London!' The emotion of the moment is raw.

Then we hear Liam again, professional and calm. 'We have Jim and the others safely with our people,' he tells us. 'All three of them were released ten minutes ago.' They're alive. It's over. It's okay.

9.45 p.m.

I'm on the train heading home. By now I'm so deeply fatigued that I've almost passed through the tiredness, finding a kind of second wind that keeps me on my feet. The stations are still busy, but as I travel I feel completely detached from all the people around me. It's surreal to be alongside normal life and everyday activity when in my head, I'm so completely somewhere else. Right now, the everyday world makes no sense. And this normality that everyone is taking for granted – I also know how fragile it is. No one is as safe as they'd like to think they are. Any one of us could find ourselves caught up in chaos far more suddenly and quickly that we like to imagine. There can be dramas going on below the surface, invisible to everyone around.

The incredible experiences I've just shared with Tony and Karl and Jake, and with Liam and Simon and David thousands of miles away in Nigeria, feel like sliding doors which can never be closed. They're human stories intertwining for a brief moment, making an unimaginable difference to the next chapter in the lives of all those involved, creating a trust that can't be broken. How do you share that? How do you take that home? How do you go back to normality? I'm not sure. I just know those 36 hours are something that none of us will ever forget.

Chapter 9

PLAY DEAD SO THEY WON'T KILL YOU
NOVEMBER 2015

'All set for tomorrow, then, honey?' Jules asked me.

'All set.'

After twelve weeks camping in the attic at my parents' house in Ealing, with Megan downstairs in the spare bedroom, our new house was refurbished and ready for us to move in. It was a big relief. My parents had been welcoming, they loved Jules and Megan, and we got on really well – but not having your own space starts to get to you.

Moving house is always stressful but tomorrow shouldn't be too bad, I thought. We'd organised everything well in advance and arranged for our furniture to be stored nearby when we'd sold our old places two months before. We'd both booked annual leave, we'd arranged doggy day care so we didn't have to put Cora, and Jules's dog Molly, through the stress of moving day, and we'd taken my parents out to dinner to say thank you for having us to stay with them. Now it was Friday 13 November. All that was left to do was get an early night, ready for the rigours of tomorrow.

'Nick?' my dad called. 'Come and see this.' He was watching BBC News in the living room and I walked through and stood behind the sofa. The item on the screen was a breaking story from Paris – a pretty confused picture, with explosions at a football stadium but also reports of shootings in the city.

'What do you think?' he asked me. Straightaway, like everybody else in the UK who was seeing it, I thought of 7/7 – the suicide bombings ten years earlier on London's underground and buses. The MO here looked similar: multiple attacks, spreading terror and confusion.

'It could be a terrorist thing, unfortunately,' I said.

My mum walked in. 'Terrorists?' she asked.

'Not here, Mum. In Paris.'

'Paris? Not again. Like at that magazine,' she said. She was thinking of the shootings by terrorists at the offices of a satirical publication called *Charlie Hebdo*, which had taken place ten months before. I frowned at the screen, trying to pick up exactly what had happened. 'Yeah, Mum. It does sound a bit like that, actually.' The situation seemed worrying, so we all sat down to watch for a minute – then found we couldn't stop watching.

The report was being constantly updated as details from France became available: two suicide bombings outside the Stade de France, then multiple attacks on cafes and bars a few miles away in the centre of Paris. The images looked horrifying, with many people lying on the ground and emergency services heading to the scene, but no clear picture yet of just how many had died or been injured. François Hollande, the French president, had been watching the football match – an international friendly against Germany – and was now being rushed away by his security detail to take command of the situation. A map of central Paris came up on the screen showing the locations of the reported attacks. Then suddenly, there was a new one.

'We are receiving reports that the Bataclan theatre in Paris's 11th arrondissement has also been attacked, with shots reported during a concert that's taking place this evening. We'll update you as soon as we have more.'

Jules headed for the kitchen to make us all some tea and we kept on watching. By now it was quarter to ten.

'We're receiving reports that a group of armed men has entered the Bataclan theatre on the nearby Boulevard Voltaire, firing indiscriminately. It's not clear how many have been injured but the auditorium was packed for a concert this evening by a band called Eagles of Death Metal. It's been confirmed that British nationals were among those attending the concert, but we don't know yet if there are any British casualties.'

Random attacks. No regard for human life. Everything designed to cause the maximum amount of terror and chaos. 'Nick,' my mum asked, 'could this be ISIS?'

'Yes, it certainly could. There are other groups too, though,' I told her.

'We're now hearing that the terrorists have taken a number of hostages and are holding them inside the Bataclan theatre. It's not yet clear how many are being held or whether those holding them have made any demands.'

I suddenly realised that everyone in the room was looking at me. We went on watching in silence.

'The British police are reporting emergency calls from relatives of those still in the Bataclan theatre. Some of them have been texting and WhatsApping family and friends from inside the building, and we're hearing that there may be people hiding from the terrorists underneath the stage.'

'I'm pretty sure I'm going to get called into this,' I said. Jules caught my eye. 'Nice timing, terrorists,' she murmured.

For the next half an hour I expected my phone to ring, but it didn't. By now it was confirmed that the gunmen had opened up on the crowd inside the Bataclan with automatic weapons, so the number of dead and injured was going to be high. It wasn't clear yet how many hostages they were holding. I kept looking at my mobile. Still nothing. 'Ah, well. Perhaps Harry's got it covered,' I said to Jules. 'And I'm on leave, after all. And he knows we're moving house. Let's go to bed.'

As we went upstairs, Jules said suddenly, 'Remember our first proper date, Nick?'

'Of course.' I smiled. It was a great memory: we'd been to see the band The Killers in concert at Wembley. Crowds of people dancing, everybody having a great time. Both of us had known that we were falling in love.

'I mean – how could –? – I dunno.' She shook her head. 'Those people in Paris. They were having a night out. I bet they were happy just like we were. And then someone starts firing at them.'

'I know,' I said. 'I know. There are no words.' We looked at each other.

'Evil is a word,' Jules said softly.

The phone call came just before eleven. 'Nick?' Harry said. 'I know you're on leave, but we need you to get to the Yard. We're sending a car.'

'Sure,' I said. If I could help, that's what I wanted to do.

'You've been called in?' Jules asked me, looking not surprised at all.

'Yep. No idea how long.'

'Um – so – we're moving house tomorrow.' She never over-reacts, but I could see she wasn't happy.

'Don't worry!' I said. 'I'll be back.'

When I got downstairs, I found my dad was still up.

'Are you going to Scotland Yard, then?' he asked me.

'Yes, Dad. They're sending a car.'

'What will you have to do, love?'

'Not clear yet. Depends on how the situation develops.'

We heard a siren in the distance.

'That'll be for me,' I told him.

The police car cut its siren as it turned off the main road onto residential streets, but the blue light was still flashing as it drew up outside the house. As Dad pulled himself out of his chair and walked over to the window, I realised that he thought this was exciting. He was so proud of what I do, and even in the middle of a terrible crisis, seeing it gave me a little burst of happiness.

'Sounds like a busy night, love. Hope it goes okay,' was all he said.

'Thanks. I'll update you when I can,' I said to him. I hurried up the garden path and jumped into the back of the car. As we pulled away, Dad was watching round the edge of the curtain. He really was quite thrilled.

*

Blues and twos into the centre of London. As the dark streets flashed by, I thought about the horror in Paris. When I'd said to Jules that I'd be back, it wasn't a false reassurance (which wouldn't work with her anyway): I really didn't think this hostage-taking would go on for very long. But the reason was the very worst one possible: the violence was so extreme and the threat to life so great that I knew the authorities in Paris would act fast. I felt certain that preparations to storm the Bataclan theatre were already underway.

Fifteen minutes later, I arrived at New Scotland Yard. The place is quiet at night, with many of its windows unlit and just one member of staff on duty on the front desk. Most of the lights work on energy-saving sensors, only coming on as you walk by, and as I strode along the fifth floor towards the ops room, I could see its brightness spilling out into the dark corridor ahead. It felt unreal to step out of the quiet shadows into the glare and noise and chaos of an international crisis. And right now, chaos was definitely the word. I was quickly brought up to speed by Harry.

'Emergency COBRA is in session right now. Adam from kidnap is responsible for family liaison and he's talking to the relatives of the Brits inside the Bataclan. He's handling that from home and he's been able to speak to some individuals who are inside hiding under the stage. Connor and our new guy Afif are on their way to Paris. We want you to go straight to Central 3000 and provide support there. Liz is going to need all the intel you can get from the negotiators at the theatre for her reports to COBRA.'

Liz, my old mentor, was now the Counter Terrorism Assistant Commissioner and in charge of liaison with SO15, the anti-terrorism unit – which was why she would be in that COBR meeting. Central 3000 is the Met Police's central coordination unit for major incidents, and COBR stands for Cabinet Office Briefing Room, which must once have been where emergency situation meetings were held. These days it's used as shorthand for any high-level meeting where senior government leaders and their advisers, usually the military, security services, and the police, along with specialists in fields such as public health or infectious disease, decide on how to respond to national emergencies.

When I reached Central 3000, I met another colleague, Danny, a member of SO15. He was also a negotiator: I'd trained him and knew him pretty well. It felt good to be greeted by a familiar face.

'How's it going, Dan?'

'Difficult, to be honest. What do you need from me, Nick?' he asked directly.

'All the intel that you have. First of all – what are we dealing with? How many terrorists are in there? Are they rational?'

'Three men, all armed with automatic weapons. Right now, they're reported to be calm and working effectively together. When their ammo was used up, one guy covered the others while they reloaded. Now he's posted at the emergency exit, and he's killed a few who tried to make a break for it and get out that way.'

'Any idea how many are dead?'

'Not known yet. The place was full. The shooters aimed down at the stalls to begin with but when that went quiet, they fired up into the balcony as well.'

'How many British are in there?'

'We're trying to find out. Some of the Brits called the French police direct, but quite a few got hold of their families in England and then they rang 999, so right now there are multiple comms channels open and it's pretty frenetic. Adam's got a ton of names and phone numbers on Post-its stuck to his kitchen table and his wife's helping him to write it all down. He's texting and messaging as many of them as he can.'

Later on, I thought, *will come the process of identifying the dead: the horrible, vital, detailed work of going through who bought tickets for the concert, who's reported missing, who's not come home, who never will. Right now, all Adam can do is just grab names and help the ones who are living.*

'Has he got through to anyone who's hiding in there?' I asked.

'To some of them, yep.' Danny and I looked at one another, picturing for a moment the sheer terror those people must be going through. Then our training kicked in. We switched our focus to the work we had to do.

My job as a negotiator is often intimate: one-to-one with someone who's in crisis, or backed into a corner, or very, very angry or despairing. I sense their emotions all around me and it's a totally sensory thing, with sights and sounds and smells all forming part of it. But this crisis was happening entirely through screens, and screens are a barrier. There were moments that night when my sense of dislocation from the horror was acute: although I was hands-on, assisting in every way I could, I felt extremely hands-off. At other times, I was pulled in much more closely as the qualities of emotional transference – the ability to tap into someone else's feelings and work out what's going on for them – that my years of negotiation training have developed in me kicked in, allowing me to feel intensely present.

I was responsible for intel – gathering every update in the blizzard of information coming in, clarifying it as far as possible then passing what I'd learned through to Liz in COBRA. The picture was confused and we didn't know yet how many people had been murdered, but one of the survivors would describe what she saw in the auditorium as a 'colline' made out of bodies. 'Colline' is the French word for a hill and I'll never forget that word now: they had built a hill of the dead.

'What's the latest from Adam?' I asked Danny.

'Nothing from him for the last twenty minutes. He's got so many messages from families coming in, he said he's barely keeping up.'

'So if we were faced with this situation here, how would we play it, do you think?' I enquired.

My logical brain was already thinking about negotiator training. There would be so much we could all learn from this. And to have this to consider also helped to ease the helplessness Danny and I were both feeling, trained to be protectors but forced to watch and listen at a distance, providing vital backup but unable to protect the innocents caught up in this nightmare. If I'd been asked to travel on a helicopter to Paris right that moment and be directly involved, I would have done it, and I know that he would too. Now he looked thoughtful, considering my question and also understanding, I believe, the reason why I'd asked it.

'We'd need to get through to as many people inside the building as possible, obviously,' he said. 'Tell the ones under the stage or hiding elsewhere to keep calm and to be silent. Remember to put their phones on silent too. Say that help is coming. And the guys in the auditorium – the only thing to say to them is play dead. There are bodies on the floor, so hide underneath them and don't move. That way, the terrorists won't kill you. Adam will have told them that for sure. I just hope they can do it.'

Play dead. Hide yourself in a pile of corpses. This was what was happening right now to dozens of people who'd gone out to relax and have a good time on an ordinary Friday night in a concert hall in Paris.

'The team will go in there very soon, Dan,' I told him. I was thinking about my years in the firearms unit, picturing the preparations being made as the French armed officers prepared to risk their lives to end the crisis. 'But the hostages are in a bad location. Or a good one, I suppose, if you're trying to hold people at gunpoint. It's a small and narrow space. So how do special forces get in there without risking the hostages' lives?'

'I hope they find a way,' said Danny grimly.

'And what about the negotiation?' I asked him. 'The guy who's got the lead over there is talking to the terrorists by phone. There are twenty or so people being held – could be more. How would we play that?'

Danny considered my question.

'Difficult. It's gone quiet right now. It's like the terrorists hit pause. As if they're having a sit down.' He scowled. 'I mean – what the fuck, Nick? Why would they just stop what they're doing?'

'It makes sense to me, actually,' I told him.

'How come?'

'Because they'll have an energy dip right now. They've just

massacred a load of people and after that, you have to stop. Your body can't take any more adrenaline. It kind of burns you up.'

'That's an actual medical thing?' Danny wanted to know.

'Yep. I was talking to one of our psychologists about this and he said it happens because it takes a lot of energy to kill people. When you've finished, it kind of runs out. If you want to go on killing, you have to take a break first.'

'So this is the time to negotiate?'

'It might be the only chance there is,' I told him.

'We need to get that in our training, Nick,' Dan said. 'For – you know – the next time. Because that's going to happen. And then it will be us who'll have to respond.' We both held our breaths for a moment, knowing it was true. *One day, something just like this will happen in Britain – and we will be called in to deal with it.* Then my phone flashed up more intel and the crisis swept us forward once again.

'I've just received information from the French negotiators,' I reported to the assistant commissioner.

'Go ahead, Nick.' As usual, Liz was remaining unflappably calm.

'They're telling their incident commander that this will only end one way. The French negotiator says nothing will come out of this – those are his exact words. The terrorists have gone in there to die – he's sure about that. They're not going to surrender. They won't release the hostages.'

'Is that their most recent assessment?'

'That's thirty seconds ago. It ties in with intel from a hostage in the corridor. She told her boyfriend on WhatsApp before the terrorists took her phone off her that the men who are holding them only want to blow themselves up. That was the way it felt to her. Again – those are the exact words she used.'

'To blow themselves up?'

'Yes.'

'Thanks, Nick.'

I knew that the police would move in very soon. *There are too many hostages, too many lives already lost. This building has to be stormed.* But the idea of carrying out an armed assault on a narrow hallway crowded with hostages and defended by three armed men in suicide vests was terrifying. It was also the only option left. Otherwise, the bloodshed would be even worse.

At 1.20 a.m., armed police moved in to the Bataclan theatre. They charged the door into the upstairs corridor, which was partly blocked by hostages who'd been forced to sit close to it, and exchanged fire with two of the terrorists, while pulling as many hostages as they could out of the way behind their shields. One of the terrorists detonated his explosive vest. Another tried the same but was shot dead. The operation lasted three minutes, and all of the hostages survived. ISIS later claimed responsibility for the Paris attacks, in which 130 innocent people died. 90 of them were in the Bataclan.

I knew that we would learn from what had happened. That's why Danny and I had started to ask questions that night: what if this happened here in London? The siege at the Bataclan theatre would lead to new thinking, and to the creation of an entirely new terrorism negotiation unit at New Scotland Yard to deal with events on this scale: an incident with dozens, even hundreds, immediately killed or injured, and aggressively determined assailants whose intention is cause the maximum amount of death and destruction and then to die themselves. *The world is changing*, I thought, *and the negotiators' perspective needs to change too.*

But these thoughts were for another day. Right now, there was only shock and grief. As I made my way out of the building, Liz was also on her way to her car.

'Do you need anything else before I go?' I asked her.

'No, thank you.'

'It's just as well,' I said, 'because I have to get some sleep. I'm moving house in four hours.'

Liz smiled. 'Well now, how's that for ideal timing? Best of luck with the move!'

*

It was still dark when I left Central 3000. Very soon the winter sun would rise and the city would wake up. I walked to Vauxhall railway station. It was 5.30 on a cold November morning, and I found myself caught up with the last few clubbers heading home after a long Friday night of partying – tired, happy people who knew nothing at all about the drama at the Bataclan theatre. Some of them were drunk on the platform, shoving each other and stumbling and laughing. Several were slumped on benches, pretty close to nodding off. I was right alongside them, waiting for our train, but also, I wasn't. I was alone and far away in a place with gunfire and explosions, watching a monstrous, murderous bloodbath.

The impossible ordinariness of this London Saturday morning left me feeling dazed. To make that gear change – shifting from Nick who gathered intel for COBR and thought about how to talk to terrorists, to Nicky who arranged removal vans and paid doggy day carers – just seemed insane right now. It was just too big to take on board – too much for my brain to process. I sensed my self-protection kicking in, pushing reality away.

I texted Jules, who was getting up at home, packing our last few things in cases.

'I'm on my way back,' I told her. 'I'll go to bed for an hour or two, then I'll be ready for the move. It's only one day – let's just get through it.'

'Sure. How do you feel, Nick? I've seen what happened.'

'I'm okay. I'm looking forward to going home. To our proper home, I mean. To the new place.'

'Me too, honey. Me too.'

She knew I wasn't okay, not really, but I'd get through the day and get through this. I was safe, the people I loved were also safe, and when that's true, you can get through anything. I stood there, shocked and exhausted, back from outer space, waiting to make my journey home.

Chapter 10

THE WAITING GAME
2016

Matthew Harper was a charity worker in Brazil for over twenty years. He provided humanitarian support for the inhabitants of the country's notorious *favelas*, or slums, until at 5 a.m. one morning in February, three armed men burst into his hotel room in São Paolo and took him hostage. At first he thought his captors would immediately kill him – an absolutely horrific experience.

It turned out that they wanted him alive. Matthew had fallen into the hands of a criminal gang with just one simple goal: money. But international criminal negotiations can progress extremely slowly and it wasn't until May that they finally got in touch with his family. The case also involved two governments, Britain and Australia, since Matthew held dual nationality. Jules and I were at home a few days later, busy preparing a BBQ lunch for some friends, when my work phone vibrated with a message from my boss, Harry.

'Nick? Matthew Harper's kidnappers have just got in contact. They want to talk to someone close to him, but Matthew's dad is in his nineties. So they've agreed to deal with a long-term friend and colleague of his instead – the two of them worked together for years. Her name's Cheryl, and she's actually in the Middle East right now in transit from London back to Sydney. She's willing to help and she says that she'll stay there and meet you. It's the quickest way to get you face-to-face with her and bring her up to speed, so you're flying out tonight with Afif.'

I stayed for the BBQ and chatted to my friends, but my heart and head weren't in it. All I was thinking about was what I would be doing, what I needed to take with me, and what the arrangements would be. A few hours later, I was on my way to the airport to catch my flight with no known date of return. Jules gave me a hand with my packing and told me to call her when I could. I know how lucky I am that she understands the demands of my job and is always incredibly supportive.

The journey with my colleague Afif, our most recent recruit to HCNU, was an eye-opener and not at all in a good way. I was travelling through international airports with a man of Arabic appearance – and he kept getting stopped. It happened outbound at Heathrow, and again when we landed and were followed round by security guards so oppressively that I offered to go and speak to them.

'Afif,' I said to him indignantly, 'we need to tell someone that you're a policeman!'

He shrugged. 'This happens everywhere,' he said. 'It happens all the time.'

The exact same thing would be repeated heading home, with suspicious looks from every side. I was astounded and depressed by this glimpse into his world.

Afif spoke fluent Arabic, a very big advantage in getting things done here quickly. But I still felt nervous and under-prepared for the upcoming meeting with Cheryl. Not only were Afif and I both very tired after flying overnight, but our last-minute travel arrangements meant we hadn't sat together on the plane, so we'd missed valuable time to talk things through. Fortunately he was chilled and collected: he's just about the calmest person I have ever had the pleasure to work with. I also found the location rather strange – a fanciful-looking city on the Persian Gulf, built as a playground for the super-rich with dizzying highrise towers and vast, sprawling US-style shopping malls. In one of these, we saw a fish tank three storeys high – a truly surreal sight which heightened the sense of unreality. Surrounded by extremely well-heeled tourists and people relaxing on their holidays, we were both hard at work and in constant suspense, waiting for Matthew's kidnappers to get in touch.

Afif and I were staying in the same hotel as Cheryl, and I called her as soon as we arrived, agreeing to meet in the lobby in a couple of hours. Our first tricky decision was where we should set up our office: a Muslim guy working with two women in a hotel in the Middle East needs to be cautious. We didn't want to make any missteps, and decided that Afif's room should become our HQ: that way it would be clear that Cheryl and I left the place each evening. It was a smoking room so he could go out on the balcony for a puff to help him cope with the tension, and that also allowed Cheryl's room to remain apart from all the drama of the kidnap negotiations. We hoped this would let her get some rest.

'We have intelligence from London,' I explained, 'that we're expecting a call from the kidnappers pretty soon.' It was vital to prepare her properly for this high-pressure role. She was a bright woman in her fifties with lots of experience after decades of working for international agencies providing humanitarian aid. She'd worked with Matthew for a long time and had a good idea of how he might respond to the awful strain he was under, which made her an excellent source of information.

Next I spoke to another member of the international kidnapping team in Australia, because Matthew was a dual national, and to a police colleague in Brazil who was in touch with the British embassy there, seeking updates on Matthew's situation. My call to Brazil was the most reassuring. 'This will be done and dusted pretty soon,' my contact said. 'We're with the military guys now and I can tell you – it's not going to be long.'

'Good,' I said. 'Great.' I'm accustomed to being given only the information that I need as a negotiator, and I'm well aware that lots of things that I don't know about can be going on in the background. This did sound positive, though.

The three of us spent the next five intense days in Afif's hotel room waiting for the kidnappers to make contact, and over the course of them we built a close emotional relationship. First, Afif and I had to prepare Cheryl for the calls she might receive from the hostage-takers, advising and coaching her on what was best to say, and bringing all our international experience into play. We didn't know exactly how the kidnapping would develop, so we worked through different scenarios: *if they say this, then our best plan is that you respond like this . . . if the phone rings in the middle of the night while we're not with you, you could . . .* Cheryl picked it all up quickly and was obviously strong under pressure: her years in international aid work and her knowledge of the risks of working in remote locations had given her a pragmatic, logical coping style. We also tried to get a sense of why Matthew had been targeted for kidnapping: was it possible that the charity they both worked for had upset anyone, or caused some kind of offence? But there was no obvious reason that Cheryl knew. As we finished each interviewing session, we contacted London with an update and our initial impressions, then sent our recordings back for more thorough analysis.

Then around 7 p.m. each evening, after a drawn-out pressure-cooker day, the three of us would get changed and go out for dinner. At first we just chatted about ordinary life: *so what do you like to do? Where did you grow up?* But as the days passed, our talks began to range more deeply as we grew closer to each other in the super-intense atmosphere. *What did we believe? What were our hopes and dreams? How did we end up in the unusual jobs we all did?* And all the time we sipped our drinks and tried our best to relax for a while, Cheryl's mobile phone lay silently on the table, reminding us that the menace of Matthew's situation hung over everything. Our shared goal here was to save a man's life.

*

The kidnappers will be calling in the next few hours.

Three days in, that was the information we'd been given in our early-morning phone briefing with London. We didn't say anything to Cheryl, and the tension as we waited was so great that I almost wished I didn't know about it myself. Time on tenterhooks is brutal. All we could do was spend it in even more intensive prepping than usual, to make sure she was ready to talk to them.

'Cheryl,' I said carefully, 'there may be things I ask you to do today and you won't know why. Basically I'm saying "trust me" without really knowing me, and I realise that – but it's all in the interests of getting Matthew back.' She nodded. She was streetwise and she'd probably guessed there was something going on that I couldn't tell her. It was incredibly helpful that she stayed on board with us through the whole experience, sharing our belief that to remain with us and co-operate with what we were trying to do was the best way for her to help.

But by mid-afternoon my doubts were setting in that anything would happen that day. It took until late evening before we were stood down by another call from London: 'Sorry, guys. There's been a change of plan. It's not happening.' I felt crushed by disappointment, and quickly realised what the problem was: hope. I'd thought that we were winning, and that – just as my instructors back at Hendon always told me – is *definitely* the most dangerous time not just physically, but emotionally too.

I found out later on just how fast the international situation had been moving. It had emerged that Matthew was not being held where the police originally believed he was, so a developing plan to get him out by military means had been shelved at just a few hours' notice. As the negotiators on the ground we were told only what we needed to know, and as a small cog in a large international wheel, all I could do was continue to feed the best information I could gather back to London. But the assurances I'd had to begin with, that this kidnapping would soon be over, were fading further every minute.

*

Badass TV cops famously make it through the stress of their
jobs with heavy smoking and drinking, but as usual I found
that the best way to cope was to hit the hotel gym. When that
wasn't enough, I worked out a bodyweight circuit I could do
in my room. Afif puffed on cigarettes when things got really
tense, but apart from that his biggest vice was cup after cup of
English breakfast tea from the hotel room refreshments tray, and
the two of us kept joking with each other that we just weren't
sufficiently hard-bitten.

What would have helped most would have been to get some
proper sleep, but under this kind of stress rest goes out of the
window, even without the disorientating effects of long-haul
flights and changing time zones. Whenever I did drop off, I kept
on waking. I'd abruptly sit up at 3 a.m. and check my phone was
still switched on (of course it was), and it wasn't accidentally set
on silent (why would it be?), or the battery wasn't suddenly flat
(it was fine last time I checked), and it was definitely plugged in
to the charger (it's hardly going to fall out by itself), and that
I hadn't somehow missed a vital message. After that I'd lie there
thinking and thinking. *What if the kidnappers ring Cheryl right
now, in the middle of the night, and she takes the call alone?
Is she ready? Have we helped her enough? Have we prepped
her enough? Would she be okay?* In the back of my mind there
might still be hope for a quick resolution of the crisis; I couldn't
help thinking of the assurance I'd been given at the start that
Matthew's ordeal would soon be over. But then I'd begin to
worry about the rescuers and the risks they might be called upon

to run if a go-ahead was given for military action. Every single option here meant danger. In the end, I'd drop off to sleep again out of sheer exhaustion.

And then, as abruptly as this drama had started – all of a sudden it was over. My phone rang late at night. Although we'd carried out the support role we'd been assigned, Matthew's release wasn't as imminent as had been hoped. Afif and I were therefore flying back to Heathrow the following afternoon, I was told. This felt awful and wrong. We'd bonded closely with Cheryl in the last five days, and to leave her suddenly alone in a continuing crisis without explanation went against everything we had come here to do. I knocked on her hotel room door early the next morning to tell her: 'Cheryl – we're returning to London – thank you for all your help.' She just gave me a quizzical look and didn't ask me why, probably because she knew that I'd been given my instructions and wouldn't have the answers for her anyway. But leaving her like this certainly didn't fit with my values of protecting and serving as a police officer. It felt crappy.

I was still simmering with annoyance over what had happened when I got back to London – so much so that I went to express my concerns to Harry.

'Look,' I told him, 'I don't mind not having all the pieces of the puzzle, but I think we got this one badly wrong. We left Cheryl stranded.'

Harry was matter-of-fact. 'I understand that, Nick. But this was a decision based on the best use of police resources.'

'Ah, come on,' I said. It was hard to get past how uncomfortable I felt about the way we'd treated Cheryl. 'This was the most intense period of this woman's life. She was coping well but she was scared, and we'd got a connection going. Just an extra day of debriefing, winding down, preparing her for when we left and reassuring her that the operation to try to resolve the kidnapping is still ongoing . . . that's what it needed.'

'But you and Afif being out there – you were costing us a lot of money,' Harry pointed out. 'Once it became apparent that the situation had changed and you couldn't achieve what you'd been sent to do, we had to get you back home. And while you were there you weren't here, and there were resource implications for this office too.'

I was looking at what had happened from an emotional perspective, while London, the Met, and the FCO were looking from a logistics and budget perspective. No wonder what we were seeing wasn't the same. *In the end*, I thought, *accountants rule the world. They certainly make all the big decisions.*

*

The plane was seized by terrorists just before take-off at Birmingham airport in the Midlands. Now a gang of men was holding more than 200 people hostage at knifepoint. They'd not yet made any demands. The story was carried immediately by all the country's media, creating an acute sense of crisis.

Except that none of this was real. This was one of the exercises that all Britain's emergency services run several times a year, role-playing emergency scenarios: a bombing at a football match, a shooter at a school, a terrorist attack on a public building. Rehearsals on this scale mean that when events like this one do take place, the people who respond will be absolutely ready.

I was sitting at a table at New Scotland Yard, video-linked to a meeting of COBR. Right now we could see on the screen a representative of the Prime Minister, along with senior staff from the Foreign and Commonwealth Office, the Home Office, and the Ministry of Defence. The meeting room was full. At the end of the table sat the police Gold commander. Final decision-making power lay with him, with backup from the firearms unit, the security forces, bomb disposal, a senior leader from the local police station in Birmingham, a press liaison officer, the community response lead who would need to take decisions about communicating with members of the public close to the site of the hijacking, a family liaison lead responsible for contacting the families of the hostages, and someone from surveillance who was working on finding out as much as possible about what was happening on the plane. All around us, screens showed the crisis unfolding in real time: students and police cadets playing the roles of hostages on a real aircraft, actors performing as the terrorists, reporters running stories intended to go out across the world's media. This scenario was designed to test everyone, from the 999 operators who'd taken the first panicked calls reporting the hijacking, to the firearms units who'd already surrounded the plane.

Our immersion was total, and everything felt absolutely real. From now on, all staff involved in the exercise would work twelve-hour shifts twenty-four hours a day, going without sleep if need be as the drama built and built. Every member of the team would also undergo observation and assessment by an experienced peer, and their performance would later be assessed. Each word that was spoken would be recorded verbatim for the inquiry which would follow: each moment and every last detail would be scrutinised and every possible lesson learned. *Why did you say this? What was your thinking here?* The pressure on us all was very high, but on Gold it was enormous – the buck absolutely stopped with him.

But as he opened the meeting, I felt uneasy for a rather different reason. Everybody else around that table was invited – and I was a gatecrasher. I'd taken the decision that HCNU had a vital part to play – so I was going to make it happen. As the exercise began and everyone hurried into the command centre, I jumped up from my desk and headed in. Sometimes you just do what you have to, and for me this was one of those moments.

Gold went round the table, quickly making sure that everyone had been introduced. When he got to me, there was no time for etiquette.

'Why are you in this meeting?' he asked bluntly.

'I'm the Gold Negotiation Adviser and I'm here to give you advice from a negotiation perspective,' I said firmly.

I was taking a hell of a chance and I could see that Gold was thinking about it for a moment. Not every senior officer takes the role of negotiators seriously, or factors in what we can bring to the table, often because their experience of working with us during their careers has been limited. Too often – even now – we're regarded as newcomers, add-ons, 'nice to haves', soft power – not as hardcore or essential. But pretty quickly I could see that Gold got it.

'Okay,' he said to me. 'Go on.'

I quickly gave my update. 'One of our negotiators is working to establish communication with the hijackers. We've also made contact with a hostage by text and passed what she's been able to tell us to the intelligence unit. The hijackers' mood right now is clarity and logic rather than emotion and the atmosphere is calm. My recommendation is therefore that we continue to negotiate. No one understands their intentions yet, and that's critical to ascertain. We need a sense of how they might react to our actions – the better we can predict this, the stronger our decision-making will be.'

'Thank you.' Gold continued round the table. 'What's happening with the press?'

'We have holding lines going out,' the press officer reported. 'We've made a statement confirming that the plane has been seized by four men, unknown motive at present. Right now we have a Twitter storm focused on the weapons: everyone's asking how they got the knives on the plane.'

'Right. Give me a firearms update.'

'We have the plane surrounded by ARVs and the SFOs are en route,' came the reply.

'Do we have audio from the cockpit?' Gold asked.

'No, but we're working on it.'

'And who's dealing with the families?'

'Family liaison. We are currently working through the list of passengers and next of kin.'

As the scenario unfolded and Gold gathered the information he needed at each stage, he began to check with the negotiators every time. He'd grasped that our perspective formed a vital part of his decision-making. The aircraft hijack role-play ran for three days and I worked the twelve-hour night shift throughout. Twenty-four hours in, the state of calm and logic in the hijackers' group began to fall apart: one loose cannon among them was becoming more aggressive with the hostages. He dragged a pas- senger who had unwisely drawn attention to himself from his seat, pulled him roughly into another section of the aircraft and forced him to his knees. We were all acutely concerned that this man might be subjected to violence and began to discuss intervention. The hijackers' leader started ordering the others to further reinforce entry and exit points on the plane: clearly he knew what the plans of the authorities might be.

'What do the negotiators think?' Gold asked me.

'We may need to change tack,' I briefed the group. 'I'm concerned that the chances of them harming a hostage is rising. I advise continuing to talk, but in tandem with preparations for tactical intervention.' Fifty hours in, with command on board the aircraft breaking down, the hijackers became so volatile that Gold made the call to hand control over to the army. A team of special forces stormed the plane just before midnight on the third night. All the hostages were safely rescued and the hijackers were taken into custody. Everyone was exhausted but elated.

My own elation, once I'd recovered from the stress and lack of sleep, was particularly high. This exercise had been a real breakthrough for us, and I knew it. *The recognition and respect my team deserves just got a whole lot closer.* It was exactly what Harry had always told me: 'We have to show them the value we bring. We need to get into those meetings.' I knew that I'd been right to take the chance.

*

Yet another hijacking – but this time the waiting game was for real. The news came up on the screen in the ops room at New Scotland Yard: a plane had been forced to land in Larnaca, Cyprus. I was acting head of department while Harry was on holiday and therefore in charge of our response, and I briefly called the rest of the team in for an update. I spoke to Liz by phone from the ops room, and as ever, her wealth of experience made her a great sounding board.

We'll keep a watching brief, we decided. *It's a potentially serious incident but there doesn't seem to be a connection with the UK.* But forty-five minutes later, all that changed. There was a British citizen on board, we were notified: a 26-year-old man named Gavin.

'He's contacted his friend via WhatsApp,' an officer from SO15 told me.

'Hmmm. That's a chance-y thing to do,' I said. It's definitely not a great idea to be tapping away on your mobile while you're being held hostage.

'Agreed. I'll send you this friend's number.'

I spoke to the friend five minutes later. 'What's Gavin like?' I asked him. 'What's he likely to do? Is he a risk-taker? Would he try to be a hero?'

The friend didn't think so, but he wasn't really sure.

'Message Gavin back, and tell him not to try anything,' I said. 'He needs to be the grey man in a situation like this. That means don't draw attention, don't speak, don't get the hijackers' eyes on you. Once you get them watching, or they decide they don't like you, that can be dangerous. Make sure he understands that.'

'Right-oh. Yep, I'll tell him,' the friend said. We ended our call, but the conversation left me uneasy and uncertain.

A few minutes later, I was staring in amazement at a picture from WhatsApp on the ops room screen. It was taken on the plane and showed Gavin with the hijacker, grinning, his sunglasses still perched on his head. The hijacker, who appeared to be wearing a suicide vest with wires poking out of the front, looked surprised by this turn of events but quite happy to be posing for the shot.

'What the hell is that?' I asked Liz. 'What kind of terrorist poses for a selfie?!'

'Hmmm. There's something not right here,' Liz muttered. 'It's not actually a selfie, mind you, Nick. I don't think this guy took it himself.'

'Potato pot-art-o,' I said tartly, and she chuckled. 'His mates are calling it a selfie on Twitter. According to them, this guy likes his banter and getting his picture taken with a hijacker is just what they'd expect him to do!'

Liz sighed. 'The whole situation feels bizarre, if I'm honest,' she told me. 'But that doesn't mean this hijacker's not a threat. He might want to make himself a martyr, or just get in the headlines any way he can. We don't know what he might do.'

I called Gavin's mate again.

'What on earth's going on?' I asked him. 'I thought you told him to keep a low profile!'

'Um – yeah. Yeah, I did. But Gav's kind of a wild man, I guess. This is the sort of thing he'd do.'

'Look,' I said, 'just tell him he needs to take this seriously. He could get himself killed.'

The strange situation in Larnaca rolled on through the day. The hijacker turned out not to be a terrorist at all, but a psychologically unstable individual whose main request to the authorities was a plaintive demand to see his ex-wife. We briefly discussed sending over a negotiator on a military flight to support the Greek team on the ground, but then the hijacker released most of the hostages anyway. I did notice, though, that he hung on to the selfie guy right up to the end. Perhaps our wild man Gavin had made a new friend.

*

Jules and I were married at Mayfair Library on a gorgeous April day – so hot and sunny that it could have been midsummer. Megan and my niece are close in age and were our bridesmaids. I think I sobbed with happiness the entire ceremony.

Afterwards we walked through St James's Park with the family and close friends who'd attended, stopping at an ice cream van which had taken advantage of the heat and was doing a roaring trade, and went for a blessing at a little church near New Scotland Yard (seeing the place up close thrilled both my parents). My sister Dani and Jules's best friend both read lessons. Then we jumped in cabs to take us to one of the piers by the Thames to board the boat where we'd arranged to hold our larger evening celebration party.

A few months before, when we were working out the guest list, I'd told Jules that I'd like the HCNU team to come, but I didn't feel quite sure about asking them. The words just came out of my mouth – until I spoke, I'd not thought too much about exactly what I was going to say.

'Um – why?' she asked me.

'Errr . . . because . . . ' and then I realised the thought that I was having. *What if they don't want to come to a gay wedding?* Jules didn't tell me off for saying that – she just smiled.

'You should definitely ask them,' she told me.

So I did, and of course they wanted to come: they'd have been insulted *not* to be invited. They were thrilled for me. *All these years*, I thought to myself, *and here I am, still making up stories in my own head about what other people might think*.

The party on the boat was joyous – the perfect ending to the happiest day of my whole life. There was a buffet and a disco as we went sailing along and the sky began to turn pink as evening approached. A police boat went past and I thought nothing of it. A few minutes later, a lifeboat went by too. Then the boat began to slow. That was when I went out on deck to see what was happening. We were approaching Hammersmith Bridge and suddenly I saw a man up there, on the wrong side of the railings, clutching what looked like a can of beer in his hand. A figure on the deck of the police boat was standing underneath and I realised this person was trying to talk to him. It was a crisis negotiation.

'Oh my God,' said one of our guests. 'I think he's going to jump!' And two seconds later, he did.

The lifeboat was right there, and the man was pulled out of the water very fast. They must have taken him to hospital quickly, and I'm sure that the help and support he needed would be available there. There are so many people in trouble in the world, struggling in their lives, in need of care and understanding – and there was one of them, right in the middle of our amazing day of happiness. I didn't need to be reminded just how lucky I was – I knew already. I still think about that guy, and I hope he was okay.

*

Since Afif and I returned from the Middle East, Matthew Harper had remained in captivity. He'd now been held hostage for six months, and I thought of him often, painfully aware that his situation was still unresolved, and of the prolonged strain on his elderly father. Two of his cousins, with the support of other family members, had therefore taken over the role of dealing with the authorities – and potentially, of course, with the kidnappers.

Then news came through of a possible positive development. Matthew was a joint Australian/UK citizen, and I was asked to fly to Australia's capital city, Canberra, to take part in the next stage of negotiating with his kidnappers for his release. The Australian team would take the lead and I was needed to act as an adviser, taking over a watching brief from a colleague who had been working there for the last few weeks. It was a role that would require some diplomacy: the British police have more kidnapping experience than the Australian force, but our aim would be to support our colleagues in Canberra if they needed us, rather than to run the whole show, and of course to report all the details to London. If we could play a part in securing this man's freedom, I was ready to do everything I could.

*

'G'day. Good to see ya. Hope ya had a good flight.' Detective Sergeant Rukhsana Singh from the Canberra police department greeted me with a cheery smile.

'Hi,' I said blearily. 'Yes, I did, thanks.'

I was struggling with jetlag after a gruelling twenty-two-hour flight from London to Australia. We'd jumped ten time zones, my body clock was scrambled, and getting any proper sleep in cattle class is pretty much impossible, so right now I felt dead on my feet.

'Great to hear! So we'll drop you off at your hotel for a quick freshen up, then COBR meets at ten this morning.'

I peered at my watch, which I'd set to Australian time as soon as we took off from Heathrow in a hopeful attempt to orientate myself to where I was going. Already it was after 8 a.m.

'As soon as that?' I said dizzily. 'Really? Will there be some coffee?'

Rukhsana gave me a sympathetic smile. 'Sure.'

I slumped in the back of her car, taking in the city sights through a fog of exhaustion. *You'd better wake up quick*, I thought to myself. *In just under two hours, you'll be representing Her Majesty's Government.*

After a very quick shower, a change of clothes and some hastily slurped coffee, Rukhsana drove me straight to Canberra's central police station for a whirlwind round of introductions to my Australian police colleagues and the security personnel and government representatives who would become my friends and workmates over the next few weeks, in particular my liaison officer, Paul. The middle of Canberra is small so the key government buildings are close together and our hotel, the British High

Commission, and the police station, turned out to be within a twenty-minute walk of each other. As capital cities go, it's not a high-energy place, but more of an administrative centre full of offices and car parks.

I was there to take over from my British colleague, Ali. Once I was up to speed, she would be recalled to London. That meant it was critical for me to get my head around everything that was going on fast, and I spent my first two hours in Canberra with her, trying my best to focus and absorb all the details while she gave me a lightning briefing on the latest position with Matthew Harper. The coffee was kicking in by now, which helped a bit – but not as much as eight hours' sleep would have done.

Then, less than half a day since I'd touched down in the country and after more than twenty-four hours on my feet, I prepared to give my first advice face-to-face to the members of Australian COBR. No video links or phones this time: I would actually be present. It was lucky I was close to dropping off from exhaustion: if I'd been fully awake, I'd have been a lot more nervous dealing with the highest level of the country's intelligence service, the head of their armed response division, the Secretary of Homeland Security and the Secretary of Defence.

The meeting took place inside an Australian government building in a high-security meeting room. There were intense searches and checks before anyone could gain admission, even if you were a police officer, and when fifteen or so of us finally gathered around an oval table, a representative of the Australian Prime Minister Malcolm Turnbull brought the meeting to order. In the centre was a cluster of microphones in case anyone needed to call in, and screens and monitors hung on the surrounding walls. The atmosphere was businesslike but tense, and as I was introduced I was suddenly, acutely aware that I was there to represent my country. I was also aware that I was very close to falling asleep. Every time I felt my head start to droop, I dug my fingernails hard into my palms and jiggled my legs up and down under the table. *Stay awake! You cannot – you absolutely CANNOT – nod off in this situation.*

'Our strategy right now is to keep on negotiating,' the Prime Minister's representative said. 'We're keeping the channels open and maintaining dialogue. It's also what our British colleagues are advising us to do.' He went around the table, asking for everybody's input.

'Well, yes, that's fine,' the Secretary of Homeland Security replied with a frown, 'except we've pretty much got nothing else. We're just waiting on them. I'm not comfortable with that.'

'And there are concerns about Matthew Harper,' the Secretary of Defence added. 'I'd say he's at high risk. Remember he's in his sixties, he's been missing for six months now, and even if he's been treated well during that time, there's likely to have been a very large impact on his physical and mental well-being.'

'What's the likelihood that his captors will sell him if things get too hot for them? Just pass him on to another gang that makes them an offer?'

'I'd say there's a very real chance of that. It's happened before in South America.'

As I listened to their discussion, I grew more and more aware of the rising level of concern. I left the meeting with a heightened sense of urgency . . . but still not quite as urgent as my need to get some kip. I finally managed to grab a few hours – then it was straight back to the police station with Ali, and on to the British High Commission for another meeting. At least one thing was beyond a doubt: everyone was doing everything they could.

*

It takes days to fully recover from jetlag, but after forty-eight hours or so I was a little less comatose. My police colleagues in Canberra were welcoming and helpful but I was very much aware of how much other work was going on in the offices around me: just as for me back at New Scotland Yard, one kidnapping case was only a small part of this team's workload. So in between our updates and meetings, I tried to be considerate and stay out of my Australian colleagues' way, knowing that keeping an eye on me represented extra work for them.

In a few weeks' time I also had a major national negotiation training course at Hendon to run, so during the day I hot-desked around Canberra police station, opening up my laptop wherever I could, thanking heaven for technology, and getting busy with my job in London. The time difference meant that there was little action on the kidnapping until late in the evening, when I would suddenly be faced with slews of urgent emails and anxious phone calls about the Harper case. Our military contacts were telling us that there were real signs of progress. The family was wanting information – what could we tell them? There were rumours in the press – did we need to make a response? The Brazilian authorities were seeking to identify a safe person – trusted by the kidnappers – who could act as a go-between on the ground in São Paolo: could one be found

that both sides would accept? Until this could be agreed, there
was no real chance of a release.

I gave the best advice I could on the negotiations and on
what kind of communication was likely to gain the kidnappers'
cooperation – but in terms of the larger situation, I was very
much aware that I wasn't in control. I could make small decisions
about my day: going to the gym, eating healthy food, keeping
up with my own work . . . but beyond that, I had no ability to
direct the outcome. This sense of helplessness gave me a glimpse
of the horror that the victims of the kidnappers must feel. *How
long will this go on? How will it end? No one knows, because
it's not your decision and there's nothing you can do.*

Then, at the start of my third week in Australia, I felt a change
in the air. A rumour started to grow that a ransom price had
been agreed for Matthew Harper, and everyone seemed a little
more confident. If this was true, I thought – always bearing in
mind that there could be no certainty of anything – there might
be a chance of a breakthrough in this case. I so hoped that it
was: after all these months, I felt intensely committed to reaching
a resolution and bringing Matthew back to his desperate family.

And by now, I wanted this to end for another reason too. I was
longing to go home. Everyone in Canberra was friendly, and
a colleague at the station invited me to dinner one evening with
her family, which was really kind and I very much appreciated
it, but there's a kind of alone-ness that you only feel in crowds.
Everyone around you has their own life going on and their loved
ones to go home to, but there you are all by yourself, and the
thought of the people and the places that you're missing just hits
you in the face. As long as work fills every second you can stay

a step ahead of the feeling, but as soon as the next quiet moment comes, it catches up with you again.

I miss my family, I thought. *It's strange how you can travel halfway around the world and when you get there, you see your home so clearly. I'm so lucky to have these people in my life, and I very badly want to be with them.*

*

'We have a breakthrough!' Paul announced. 'There's going to be a rescue and it's happening tonight. We've been told to expect a call to finalise Matthew's release around 11 p.m. our time.'

This breaking story seemed confused, but I immediately updated London on what I was hearing – although I suspected they were already aware of these developments. We seemed to be the closest we'd yet been to a resolution, and I shared the excitement felt by everyone around me. Then another thought came too, like a shadow of the first. *What about the rescuers? What risks are they running? How many lives are in the balance?* I reassured myself that there were so many factors in play in a decision to go ahead, from the weather to the quality of the information the authorities can get: with so much at stake, if intelligence couldn't confidently support such an operation then of course it wouldn't happen.

I waited at Canberra police station that night, sitting in the conference room with four other members of the kidnap team in case my input was needed. The coffee wasn't great but we all drank it steadily. Hours went by and the tension mounted as 11 p.m. approached. Then it passed, and still we'd heard nothing. No one said much, but we knew that we were dealing with highly unpredictable people who work to their own rules. No news doesn't necessarily mean disaster when someone's far from a city – they might need to walk a long way to get a phone signal. But as the minutes limped by, it grew harder and harder to explain away the silence.

At 3 a.m., a call from Brazil came through. No details – only, 'It's not happening tonight.' No further explanation, no real intel. Just – that's it. We walked out of those offices completely deflated. Yet again we had thought that we were there. I remembered yet again what I'd been taught back at Hendon. I'd seen it with Alex who'd been tasered on the hospital roof and with Duncan and his machete, agreeing to put the weapon down and come peacefully out of his flat but then suddenly appearing with it swinging from his hand. *It's when they know it's nearly over that someone who's desperate will try to grab that last bit of control. The most dangerous time is when you think you're winning.*

Still – it was brutal to feel hope and then to have it snatched away. I called home in the early hours of the Australian morning just to hear familiar voices, and reminded myself that very soon, I'd be back with the people that I loved. I was more aware than ever of the long, drawn-out cruelty that these kidnappers were inflicting on their victims.

*

Our emotional rollercoaster ride continued over the next two days. The kidnappers made threats and different numbers were discussed. Now, finally, we seemed to be closing in once again on a deal.

'The family's agreed to pay a ransom. 250k in sterling,' Paul told us.

'Right,' I replied. This time round, I'd made up my mind that I wouldn't hope too much.

'You know the problem, don't you, Nick?' he went on thoughtfully. 'It's this idea the kidnappers have that we're all rich. I mean – sure, I know some of us are, certainly by the standards of downtown São Paolo. But these guys seem to think every single Westerner's got cash just sitting in the bank. You can see how it looks – when someone has so little themselves, how do you persuade them that a person who owns a house in London, say, or Sydney, isn't rolling in it?'

I thought this was probably right. 'I reckon they look on estate agents' websites and think we're all millionaires,' I said. 'They always seem to think the families have got more money.'

'Yeah. They can't grasp that for us to pay them, we might have to sell everything we own.' Paul shook his head angrily as he spoke. 'Perhaps they don't want to understand. They're playing a bloody cold game and if they thought of us as human beings, it would make their business harder. So they're never going to do that, now, are they?'

*

'So you're saying that this guy we're dealing with is an agent,' Paul said to me. 'He works out in São Paolo and he knows a lot of people. He's like a middle man. And if we wire him the money, he'll handle the transaction directly to the kidnappers. Well, okay. But the real question is, Nick, can we trust him?'

'He's worked with families before when successful ransom payments have been made,' I explained. That was the intel that I'd received from London. I couldn't help having private doubts that these negotiations were really being carried out in good faith, but this lead was our only hope right now for Matthew's release.

'Okay. So we can trust him sometimes. But can we trust him *this* time?' Paul wanted to know.

'That's a tricky one,' I said. 'We know this guy's corrupt. And he's working with people who are also corrupt. Let's face it – bribery's fairly endemic in Brazil. But right now, he seems like our best bet. I'm assured that he's proved reliable before. Whether he will be this time – no one can give a guarantee.'

'What will he do with the money when it's wired to him?'

'He'll convert it into cash for the kidnappers. And of course, he'll take his cut. Anyhow – it appears they trust him. So right now, we have no other option but to trust him too.'

A few hours later, I was sitting with four of my Australian colleagues in an office in Canberra police station. The room was stuffy and the tension was electric: today should be the day of Matthew's release. The main negotiation phone was on a speaker, so that everyone in the team would be able to hear what was being said, and I was acting as note-taker for the call, which was also being recorded.

'The kidnappers' money should have reached them by now,' said Paul. 'It was transferred just over an hour ago. Not much longer to wait.'

The phone in the middle of the meeting table rang. Paul pressed the button to reply.

'I am representing the kidnappers who are holding Matthew Harper,' said a man's voice.

'Right,' Paul replied. 'We have good news. This matter is settled and your money has been paid. Now we can move to –'

'Not so fast,' the representative cut in. 'We're still waiting for our £250,000.'

The line gave a very loud crackle as he spoke. It made me wonder for a second if I might have misheard. My stomach lurched. Paul and I exchanged glances.

'Can you repeat, please?' Paul asked him. 'Our line here is poor. I didn't quite get that. Just to confirm that £250,000 has been paid this afternoon.'

'Nobody has paid,' the voice said coldly. 'We are still waiting for our money.'

A ripple of confusion ran around the conference room. I looked at the others, who were staring back at me. No one spoke, but there was consternation on all our faces.

'But – we've paid you,' Paul repeated. 'We have paid you today.'

'Nobody has paid!' the man yelled. 'Do you think we're fools?' His sudden switch-up in aggression took all of us by surprise. I scrawled on a piece of paper as quickly as I could. *Reflect back. Listen!* I wrote. I pushed it in front of Paul, who glanced down and nodded. I saw him taking a deep breath.

'Okay,' he said, as calmly as he could. 'Okay. I hear what you're saying. I wonder if there's been a misunderstanding here. I can assure you that the money was paid this –'

'No it wasn't!' the man shouted. 'We haven't got the money! If you don't pay, he dies! Is that what you want?' Without any warning, the line went dead.

Where was the ransom money now? I doubted we would ever find out. The only thing we knew for sure was that it had been handed over to the middle man. After that he might have stolen it, but it would be a very risky thing for him to do. The likeliest explanation was that he had done his job and the kidnappers had received it but decided they could get a second payday by lying, denying this, and simply demanding more.

The disappointment was horrible and the loss of £250,000 was sickening. We were no further forward, but we had no choice other than to accept what had happened. The family would now have to attempt to find yet more money. As I thought of the dashed hopes and unrelenting anxiety for Matthew's father, I felt wretched. I rang Connor in London to share my disappointment and we talked the crisis through. Like me, he wasn't ever so surprised: trickery and lies are all part of the many risks of international hostage situations.

'So we carry on negotiating,' he said to me. 'How else can we respond? We just remember that they're greedy. They'll be back. It's a waiting game now.'

There was nothing more that I could do in Australia, and a few days later I was called back to London – a bitter, disappointed, angry journey. I only began to feel better once I'd finally reached home, and the welcome that awaited me there – but my feelings of happiness and relief made me even more conscious that for the Harper family and for Matthew himself, the misery went on.

I would have to put his ordeal in a box in my mind, I realised, knowing that the ending of the crisis might be months or even years away, if it ever came at all. And crime doesn't stop – it has no regard for how you feel, or for whatever else might be going on in your life. I needed to find a way to cope with the limbo and give my full attention to the cases I was working on, cases where I might be able to make a difference. My years of police experience had taught me how to compartmentalise like this, but it was going to be tough.

And then, after all the international travelling, the dramas in the hotel, the grim night in the Australian police station, the hopeful suspense that had ended in crushing disappointment – the final resolution to the crisis was simple and low-key. As I was sitting in my office one morning three weeks later, a member of our support team walked in and said to me with a grin: 'Great news – Matthew Harper's on his way home.' This time the fragile network of uncertain arrangements had held up, a second ransom had been paid, and he was free.

I gasped with relief. A massive weight lifted from my shoulders. That was when I understood how much I had been carrying this case with me. His relatives sent us a photo of him and a thank-you card, which touched us all deeply, and the atmosphere on the fifth floor at New Scotland Yard that day was one of joy and the satisfaction of a job well done. There was much to reflect on and to learn, but for now we were all just grateful that Matthew was back with his family at last.

Chapter 11

THE POWER OF BECAUSE

'Brad – can I have a word?'

'Sure.' My student looked surprised, and followed me into the small room I used as my office when I was on site at Hendon running negotiator training.

'Sit down,' I told him. Brad had arrived at Hendon on Monday to start the course. On Tuesday afternoon I began to have concerns and by Thursday they were becoming more serious. Now it was Friday morning, and before going any further I needed to make him aware of them.

As training director of hostage and crisis negotiation, I was responsible for training negotiators from all UK police services and providing teaching to partners (front-line police officers, mental health teams in prisons, lifeboat crew, aeroplane anti-hijack courses). I was always intensely conscious that the trainees I worked with would face life-and-death decisions. Their judgements and actions could make all the difference, so who passed the course and who failed it was always a very big decision. I knew how much satisfaction my own career had given me, and what a dream-come-true it had been, and felt the weight of knowing that I had the power to deprive someone else of the same opportunity. I also had respect for anyone who put themselves forward for negotiation training: it's a big, unpaid commitment. When a person has been willing to step up like this, to then fail the course is a career-changing, even a life-changing moment.

But at the end of week one, I and the other course directors had to decide who'd proceed to week two, and sometimes not everybody could. We never just waited and then said to them: 'Sorry – you're out.' When we saw problems developing, we made the effort to head them off because if someone's motivated enough to be here, hopefully they're also motivated enough to address any issues they're having. But if they didn't – or couldn't – respond to our concerns, there was no way we could pass them.

'So, Brad, I've been talking with the other instructors about your performance on the course so far. The feedback I have from them, and my own observations, are worrying me.'

He looked very taken aback.

'What we do here isn't easy,' I went on. 'We're teaching communication skills that aren't based on problem-solving or on telling people what to do. But as police officers, we've been trained throughout our careers to do just that – to problem-solve. We're used to a directive way of thinking. And we know it can be a challenge to step away from it.'

Training sessions are all recorded, so I was able to give him specific examples of where he was going wrong. 'Yesterday, when a woman told you that she didn't see any point in life anymore because nobody cared, your response was: "Sure, we can talk about that once you get down off this roof. There are loads of people who can help." That's not factually wrong because there *are* people who can help her, but it didn't address how she was feeling. You jumped straight to offering a solution.'

'Hmm.' Brad nodded uncertainly.

'And in yesterday afternoon's scenario, you told someone in crisis that you could relate to them because the same thing happened to you. You need to move away from your own agenda. This is about mirroring what they're feeling, letting them feel heard. Do you understand?'

Brad nodded again.

'What I want you to do over the weekend is have a think,' I told him. 'Go through your notes carefully and think about what I've said. We need to see improvement, and we need to see you taking on board what I'm saying.'

I hoped he'd be able to respond. Where some students struggled was in finding the dexterity and quickness of mind to think outside the box under pressure: this creativity is where negotiation differs from any other aspect of police work. We didn't want people to fail – after all, it never feels good to break anyone's heart – but if they just didn't get it then we had to be honest, even if it meant a tricky conversation.

Telling people what they don't want to hear can provoke a range of reactions, from tears to fury. My most difficult challenge as a teacher came when another student became angry and defensive after I gave him similar feedback to Brad's. The way he was going, he clearly wasn't going to pass the course: stuck in his own agenda from the start, all he'd done was relate everything to himself. In the team exercises, he didn't pay attention to others at all: his own idea was always the one he would go with. Still, rather than just dropping failure on him at the end of the first week, I drew him aside for a chat – then found he wouldn't accept anything I told him. First he didn't agree with my assessment, then he announced that the problems he was having weren't his fault, and finally he accused me of bullying him. I was absolutely confident that this wasn't true: all our students are under the microscope for two weeks and are assessed by a number of different instructors to avoid any kind of confirmation bias. After he was asked to leave the course, he escalated his complaint anyway and there was a detailed investigation which found – to my great relief – that he hadn't been bullied.

Being a negotiator isn't for everyone. The truth is that we don't all have what it takes. The training is tough: it takes you away from friends and family, it demands long hours and can be exhausting. But the outcome I was working towards was clear: I was building a team whose members I could call upon at 2 a.m. and know that they'd respond and bring their A game. This was what I needed to see if a student was going to make the grade.

Our students also gave feedback to their instructors, and that included me. We were always seeking to improve our teaching performance, and as police officers we were used to getting honest comments right from the start of our careers. Instructors don't mince their words and you're expected to take it on board – but on one memorable occasion, I found my own ability to do this was seriously tested. The training in question took place at a challenging time: my dad had been unwell, I wasn't feeling great, and I'd had solo childcare responsibilities throughout because Jules was away on a course of her own. It's wonderful to be part of a family unit but also a massive learning curve, and looking after a child on your own, as I've discovered, is incredibly full-on. No one can be on top of their game every minute of every day, but I'd done my best and still felt I'd managed to give my full focus to my work and deliver the course well.

This student disagreed. He was from overseas with a military background, and his impressions of me were very negative: he felt I didn't care about the students I'd been with, and had found me cold, unavailable, and dismissive. Rather than using the feedback form which was issued to everyone, and which I would immediately have read, he'd also gone to my boss with his comments and that made it worse: I was distressed that he'd been so indirect. I got his feedback at a particularly happy time: I'd travelled to Barcelona with Jules and Megan for the presentation of an award Jules had received from the International Women's Association of Policing. I was feeling super-proud of her achievement and all ready to celebrate. While we were there I took a minute to quickly check my email, opened this one and felt my stomach drop.

Other feedback on the course wasn't so bad and there were positive comments – but the negative is what always sticks with you. This was *really* negative. This student had also criticised the thing which forms the core of my identity – my performance in my work – and that's extremely hard to take. Jules is always so considerate to me so I made a big effort to act okay and not ruin her enjoyment of the trip, but for me it wrecked the whole day. And the next one. And it spoiled quite a few after that. I bottled up my unhappiness until we were on the plane heading home, then showed the email to her and said shakily, 'Um – I got this. And – wow – it's pretty honest.'

By chance, I'd recently been learning about the Kübler-Ross Grief Cycle. Elisabeth Kübler-Ross was a psychiatrist who identified five stages we all go through after bereavement: denial (we blank our loss out and refuse to believe it), anger (we furiously reject it and might even feel cross with the person who has died), bargaining (we make magical deals in our heads to get it reversed, even though we know that's irrational), depression (misery and despair), and finally acceptance that the world has changed. It's not just the bereaved who go through this: people in crisis experience it too, as do the terminally ill and – much more rapidly – a child who's lost a toy. Negotiators see the process in our work and it's helpful to understand it better.

This student's feedback gave me a chance to observe the Kübler-Ross Cycle in myself. To begin with, I rejected everything he'd said. Then I was furious with him. Then I thought there'd probably just been a misunderstanding and perhaps if I contacted him he'd change it. Then I felt really, really sad. And finally, I was able to get my head around it. *Why did he feel like this? What had his experience on the course been?* After that, I was able to take ownership of what I'd got wrong and work out how to learn from it and do better next time.

I faced another teaching challenge when my colleague Connor was called away to a meeting and his work needed covering. This included a PowerPoint presentation to be given in two days' time in the briefing room at New Scotland Yard – a large, tiered room which seats over a hundred people. Stepping up and filling in for each other was just what the team had to do sometimes, so I agreed that I'd do it without really finding out what it involved. But as I went through his slides, I began to have misgivings: there weren't a lot of lesson plan notes to guide me, and because I hadn't created this presentation it was hard to get a feel of how Connor intended it to go.

I ended up delivering it very uneasily, aware the whole time that it wasn't going well. I didn't have the expertise on the topic, which really came across, and the more conscious of this I became, the more nervous and hesitant I got. By the end I was just glad that it was over. I realised how substandard my performance had been when Harry jumped in afterwards, free-styling away and padding out the time with some spur-of-the-moment content. *Ouch*, I thought. *That really did not go well*. But it did have value in the end, as uncomfortable things often can, because it showed me what I must never do as an instructor. It's difficult to deliver someone else's material and if you're going to speak on a subject, you must know it both practically and from a human behaviour perspective. Unless you're right across the content of a lesson – *just don't teach it*. And I'd also add: *know your own style*. I have a naturally coaching approach as an instructor – I want to make connections with my students. I'm at my best when I play to that and use the strengths I have, rather than trying to do what someone else would.

*

'Hi, Brad. Nice to see you.'

'Nick!' Brad looked startled for a second, then worried. We were standing with the incident coordinator in the tiny porch of a narrow Victorian terraced house in east London, where I'd just arrived to provide support in an ongoing crisis negotiation.

I didn't realise until I got there that Brad – who'd passed the course at Hendon a few weeks before, after making a big effort to take on board what he'd been told and showing real improvement in his second week – was involved in it.

'It's okay. I'm not here to assess you,' I reassured him. 'I'm here to help.'

'Right.'

He cleared his throat nervously. I had vivid memories of feeling like this myself, standing in the corridor at Hendon with my heart thumping as I worked out how to impress my own teachers and pass the course I felt so passionately about. It struck me how much my role had changed. Now I was the person in authority, and Brad felt just the same anxiety and wanted to please me.

'So this guy upstairs – Leon – what's he doing now?'

'Pointing his gun out of the front bedroom window,' Brad told me, 'and shouting. Can't tell what he's saying, though. The last thing I could make out was him saying that the police want to kill him and set the house on fire.'

Two firearms officers who'd been called to the incident, one armed with a Glock and the other with an MP5, were in the little front porch with us. The atmosphere was extremely tense and being crushed together like this only added to the pressure-cooker stress we all felt.

'How long ago did he say that?' I asked Brad.

'Twenty minutes, maybe. He seemed calmer for a while and I stood on the bottom step inside and we talked. But then he became very agitated – there didn't seem to be a trigger – and he started waving the gun again so I had to pull back.'

'You got a look at his weapon. Is it real, do we think?'

'Hard to say. He doesn't have a licence.'

I glanced around at the firearms officer behind me to see what she thought. She grimaced. 'If it's a fake,' she said, 'it's a good one.'

We heard loud banging coming towards us as Leon stamped his way along the narrow upper landing from the rear of the house. I peered into the gloomy hall and could just see his feet at the top of the steep flight of stairs.

'Get out of my house!' he screamed. 'All of you! Just fuckin' get out!' He hurled an object down the stairway into the hall – a heavy tube of something: hair gel, maybe, or shampoo. It skidded along the floor almost to the front door.

'The fuckin' pigs gonna shoot me and burn me!' Leon yelled. 'Where's the fuckin' reporters? Where's the people from the telly? The pigs gonna –' The rest of what he said was lost in more crashing as he stormed back along the landing and out of sight.

'Leon!' Brad shouted. 'You need to listen! No one's going to set fire to the house!'

That wasn't how I wanted to hear a negotiator reacting. 'Brad,' I said to him quietly, 'we need to try to calm this down.'

'It's on fire!' Leon's voice screamed. 'It's all on fire! They're burning down the house!' More crashing, and something falling, as though he might have tipped a table over. Then his footsteps pounded back to the staircase, and this time he ran down the top two steps. Now I could see most of his legs and the black lump of the gun in his hand. The firearms officers' fingers moved to their triggers as his behaviour became more menacing. The restraint they were showing was remarkable – but if they judged that their personal safety was threatened, I knew that they would fire.

'I'll blow your fuckin' heads off if you try to come up here!' Leon screamed.

'Leon!' Brad shouted to him again. 'Put the gun down! Just put it down! Then we can talk!'

Again I was concerned by his reaction. It's not at all helpful if a negotiator starts giving orders. Then the negotiator coordinator spoke from just behind me.

'Nick,' he said, 'Mrs Brian's here. Leon's mum.'

I quickly went out into the street to speak to her. Mrs Brian was a smartly dressed elderly lady who explained in a trembling voice that her son was ill – he suffered from hallucinations and sometimes refused to take the drugs he'd been prescribed to treat them.

'Do you get on with him, Mrs Brian?' I asked her. 'Would he listen if the two of you talked?'

She wiped away a tear that was slowly trickling down her cheek.

'Maybe. He don't always listen. But he don't mean no harm, you know. He's not well – not for a long time.'

'We want to end this peacefully,' I said, 'and take Leon to hospital to make sure he's okay. But he seems to think we're going to attack him. It might help if you could try to explain.'

'Um. Okay,' she said nervously. 'I'll try.'

The porch became even more tightly packed as she shuffled in alongside us and peered into the hall. She was pressed closely against me and I could feel her body trembling. My heart went out to her.

'Leon?' she called shakily. 'Lee? It's Mama.'

There was silence.

'Is he in there?' she whispered.

'Yes,' I said in her ear. 'He's upstairs. If you call to him, he can hear you.'

'Lee,' she called out shakily. 'I just been talkin' to the police lady. She says nobody will hurt you. They want to –'

'They got guns in here, Mama!' Leon yelled. I felt Mrs Brian flinch. 'Fuckin' assault rifles! Don't look like they don't wanna hurt me!'

'Lee, baby, if you just come down the stairs now, the police lady says –'

'The police lady can go fuck herself!'

Mrs Brian swayed on her feet. I thought for a moment she might faint. Brad touched her arm reassuringly. 'Let's try again,' he advised her. 'Tell him that you understand he's scared but he can trust you.' I nodded affirmingly, hoping to boost Brad's confidence in his new negotiator's role, as well as comforting Mrs Brian.

In a wavering voice she called up to her son again: 'Lee? I know you're frightened, baby. I –'

'And you can fuck off too, you dumb old slag!' Leon yelled.

That was too much for her. She burst into floods of tears, and I put my arm around her shoulder and guided her outside into the street.

'He don't mean that!' she sobbed. 'He don't mean what he said. My boy's not well!'

'It's okay, Mrs Brian. It's okay.' We decided she shouldn't stay here; she phoned a friend and the friend came quickly round to take her home. As she was leaving, she clutched at my arm. 'Please look after him, officer,' she pleaded. 'He don't mean to be so angry. He don't mean no harm. Please keep him safe.' I found it deeply moving – this ill, angry, out-of-control man upstairs was her little boy and she loved him very much. It made me determined not to let her down. 'I promise we'll do our very best, Mrs Brian,' I told her.

'Nick,' said the negotiator coordinator, 'I've got one of the psychs on the phone. I rang him for advice and he'd like a word.' The Met has a group of psychologists, vetted and trained so they can work with the police, available to give us advice on crisis situations. Their input can be critically important. Here it was about to change my thinking.

'This man has schizophrenia,' the psychologist told me, 'and I think we can conclude from his behaviour today that he's not taking the medication he was prescribed. This sounds like a full-blown psychotic episode that he's having, and I'm hearing that he's delusional. I don't think you can talk to him.'

'Your opinion is that we're unable to negotiate here?' I asked.

'Yes. This man can't think or process. You won't be able to reason with him.'

It was clear that we needed to act now to protect Leon's well-being, and bring the stand-off to an end. Our firearms officers moved into the house and threw flashbangs up the stairs – devices which make very loud noises and create clouds of smoke to disorientate someone who's barricaded themselves in a building – then rushed up after them. The tactic worked: Leon was temporarily blinded and confused by the bangs and loss of visibility, and they were quickly able to disarm him in the back bedroom. He was taken away to hospital unhurt, and his gun turned out to be a replica. But although the crisis concluded successfully, I was left with real concerns about what I'd seen and heard.

'Brad,' I said to him, 'can we have a chat?'

'Sure, Nick.'

'As you were speaking to Leon in there, I noticed that you were relating to him like a police officer, or like one of the firearms team. Telling him to put the gun down like that might be their job, but as a negotiator you're here to listen to him. To try to tap into what he's going through.'

Brad thought for a moment.

'Right,' he said. 'So you're saying I was going back into problem-solving? Acting as a police officer, not a negotiator?'

'Yes.' I was relieved by how well he remembered the training and understood. He'd not yet fully overcome his natural default setting, I thought – to take charge, to give instructions – but he was working on it and developing the potential that he had to be a negotiator. 'Yes,' I said, 'that's exactly what you were doing.'

'Right,' Brad said carefully. 'Hmm. I see what you mean. It was a stressful situation, I guess, so that's why it happened. I think I need to work on this some more.'

And we all do. Learning is constant for everyone, and that's the way it's always been for me. One of the best things about the negotiation community is its self-reflection: the way people take feedback on board, or consider how something has played out and how things might be done differently next time. It's something that I've found to be true all over the world, in the many countries I've travelled to in order to train others or to gain new knowledge myself. Even when the approaches taken differ – and they do sometimes, from country to country – I've never found a place where there wasn't that willingness to learn and to get better.

Sometimes, these lessons can be painful and shocking. I travelled to Oslo early on in my career at HCNU, not long after a terrorist called Anders Breivik had killed seventy-seven people in a series of attacks on and around the Norwegian capital. To start with, Breivik set off a home-made explosive device in a lorry: eight passers-by died. Oslo sits on the coast at the top of a fjord, and Breivik then travelled to one of its offshore islands where a youth camp was underway. Sixty-nine of his victims died there in a shooting spree which lasted for an hour.

I was invited there to run a five-day training course for the city's military and police in negotiation techniques – my very first teaching trip. It was a big deal for me to represent not just the Met Police, but also the British government. I flew out with Mick, and he gave me lots of support and advice throughout. We spent long days in classrooms at an Oslo military base, then our evenings were taken up with role plays. There were twelve students altogether: those from the police had negotiation experience and were there to consolidate their skills, but for the military personnel it was a totally new experience. The heads of the departments involved had arranged for enthusiastic actors to enact crisis scenarios, instructing them to vary their performances depending on how effectively the trainees responded, and the trainings all went well.

In the short amount of time that we had off, we took a trip to the stunning nearby mountains then explored the centre of the city on foot. It was there we had our greatest surprise: Oslo's security arrangements were amazingly relaxed. As we approached a government building right in the middle of town, we expected every second to find ourselves blocked from going any further, or to encounter security guards. But no – we walked right up to the front entrance and could literally have knocked on the door with no one to prevent us. This was *after* Breivik's atrocity, and Mick and I thought that a sense of disbelief still gripped Norway. Their country had felt so peaceful and safe before the attack that it was difficult for Norwegians to make the adjustment and accept a new, increased level of danger that required preventive action. I would remember that dark, snowy afternoon in Oslo later on in my career, on a very different trip with a very different level of security – to Quantico, Virginia, the headquarters of America's FBI.

On another evening in Norway, I went to a meeting with the country's national negotiation lead. We talked about the official response to the Breivik attacks – what had gone well, what hadn't worked, what the city and the country could learn from it all – and I was chilled to discover that during the shootings on the island, the gunman had actually rung the Norwegian police. I'm pretty sure – although it wasn't absolutely confirmed – that this startling fact was discovered later when his mobile phone number was known and cross-checked against all the calls that the emergency services had received while the attack was underway. Quiet, methodical police work like this doesn't have the drama and excitement of firearms or kidnapping or first response, but what it uncovers can be vital.

'My God – what did Breivik say?' I asked my Norwegian counterpart.

'He said he was the colonel.'

'The colonel?'

'Yes. No one has any idea even now what he meant by this. And he referred to a right-wing organisation of which he claimed to be a member. The operator thought he was crazy. . . ' His voice died away.

It was clear what must have happened. In any kind of emergency situation, operators are flooded with crank calls. Some of these are malicious, made by people trying to disrupt the security services' response, but others are from the vulnerable and delusional, the mentally unwell and confused. In an overwhelming situation, deluged with calls, it had been easy to misidentify this one. *Was there any chance to negotiate at a time like that?* I wondered. It was impossible to say.

'Were negotiators considered at any stage during the shootings?' I enquired.

'I don't think there was time. It was mayhem. Nothing like that had ever occurred here before. And Breivik made no demands.'

Back at New Scotland Yard, our team talked through what Mick and I had learned in Oslo. From what might have been a missed opportunity came a plan to deploy a negotiator to the control room if a British force was faced with a similar event. If suspects rang 999 during a critical incident and could be identified and passed straight to someone who could talk to them, might there be a chance to intervene, perhaps even to save life? It must be worth a try. Our decision was actioned and became part of the national negotiator deployment plan – one positive that could be taken from the terrible experiences of the Norwegian people. I hope it can make a difference at a future time of crisis.

*

There's been another huge change during my time with HCNU
– the rise of social media. Back on Alison Elliott's roof where
I first witnessed negotiators talking to Captain America and Thor,
protestors were entirely dependent on the press. They needed
their photos on the front pages and the journalists writing about
what they were doing. But just a few years later, the balance of
power had shifted completely.

*

April 2016

I spotted Superman and Green Lantern up on the balcony of the
house in north London, waving to the reporters who'd already
gathered down below. I'd been called to another politician's
home – this time, the residence of the Mayor of London. Fathers
4 Justice was campaigning in superhero costumes once again.

They knew the media was useful and they were willing to
engage – but they weren't dependent on that any longer. These
days, their power was in the smartphones in their hands, to
update their own social media, put out any images they wanted
and control the narrative themselves. The police, on the other
hand, didn't seem to be in control of the pavement. As I quickly
assessed the scene, the sense of chaos was concerning: there was
no proper cordon in place and quite a lot of people – passers-
by? journalists? – were strolling around and taking photos up
close. I spoke quickly to the incident commander and the two
negotiators, trying to establish some boundaries.

'There's a third guy down here on the street,' the commander told me. 'He's walking about handing out leaflets and talking to the press or anyone who'll listen. Quite a smart tactic, because what can we charge him with? He's not doing anything wrong. Breach of the peace, maybe?'

'It would help if the guy with the leaflets would stay in one place,' I said. 'Let me have a word with him.'

But as I headed over there, a reporter walked straight up to me and asked, 'Are there negotiators on the scene? Are they talking to the intruders? What's the plan?' I know the press is always interested in the work that we do, but what on earth was he doing so close to the police operation? *This is shambolic.*

The Mayor wasn't in his flat that day and our negotiators started talking to the protestors. Of course I didn't have all the facts in their cases but just as on Alison Elliott's roof, it was hard not to feel sympathy towards them. I'm always aware that there are two sides to a story, but these guys weren't rude or aggressive, just determined. 'It's no good sitting at home getting upset at how much you miss seeing your kids,' said Superman. 'You need to stand up and not accept it. We want equal contact for both parents if they split up.'

Green Lantern told us that he hadn't seen his daughter for six years. *That's such a long time*, I thought. *That's so tough. I can only imagine what it would be like.*

Superman and Green Lantern were talking to the world on their own terms. Their words and photos and videos went straight from their phones to thousands of other phones and were shared on from there. And on, and on. Once they'd made sure of that, they were willing to come down and be arrested. They understood the new social media reality while the authorities were still playing catch-up – everything that went on at the scene underlined it. By the middle of the afternoon, the situation had been peacefully resolved, but the protestors already knew they'd won.

When I thought about it later, it struck me that our difficulty in setting a boundary that day was symbolic of this very different era of communication. Who directs a story now? Who controls what we hear and what we see? The answers to those questions have changed. Negotiators must find a way to do our jobs in a completely different world.

*

I felt strongly that another part of negotiation training was to broaden students' understanding. A considerable number of the people we work with as negotiators are in personal crisis, and this often has a mental health aspect. If you've never felt that way yourself, it's hard to know where others are coming from, and the better negotiators understand what it's like, the more sensitively they'll be able to respond. I thought that the best way to achieve this was to invite people who'd faced mental health challenges to talk to the trainees about their experiences. That's how we ended up working with a group called Hear Us, which is based in south London.

I first became involved with Hear Us through a man called Jonny Benjamin. On 14 January 2008, Jonny was acutely depressed and suicidal, standing on the wrong side of the railings on Westminster Bridge and preparing to end his life, when a passing stranger stopped to talk to him and managed to persuade him not to jump. Some time later, feeling much better, he was grateful to the man who had been prepared to do this but all he knew about him was his first name, so he set out to search for him via social media, calling his campaign 'Finding Mike'. It worked – he and Mike were re-united and they made a documentary together based on their shared experience.

I talked to Jonny about the experience of acute mental health crisis, and he referred me to Hear Us. The group was a tremendous help, sending volunteers to talk openly to our students on the national negotiator training course about what they had been through. These remarkable people included a woman who'd been talked down from an arterial road bridge and an individual suffering from schizophrenia who explained what it's actually like to hear voices. Our visitors were open about the negative attitudes they'd faced, even from professionals who were meant to be there to help them: doctors, they told us, could be unsympathetic to those who were close to killing themselves or had tried to do so.

Meeting these survivors of crisis opened the students' eyes. It allowed them to ask very direct questions and to get practical input about which approaches work and which do not. Our volunteer speakers shared their sense of purpose: they felt that they were making a difference and that what they said might help others in the future. The feedback from everyone was excellent.

I also had another aim in mind – to give our students a human connection. That sometimes feels like a gap in the negotiator's role: we intervene in people's lives and can change them in ways which will stay with them forever, but after that we vanish and the person in crisis never finds out who we are. We have no part in the ongoing story: you never know what someone's going through, or how they got here, or what their next step is going to be.

That's as it should be: a negotiator doesn't seek the limelight. But it does leave you wondering: what happened afterwards? Did I make an impact? Have I saved a life – not just today, but going forward? You're only around for a few hours, or even a few moments, and you'll never really know. The stories from Hear Us gave our students a lasting – and I believe, an inspiring – sense of how much difference they could make.

*

International travel and training were a big part of my role throughout all the time I spent at HCNU. I know how fortunate I've been to see so many places, meet so many interesting people, and hear their stories. But there's a downside to the jet-setting life: on too many occasions, I'd visit a beautiful and fascinating country and find I barely saw it. My time there would be packed with meetings and mostly spent indoors, and conference rooms are pretty much the same all over the world. I'm disappointed sometimes when I look back and find so many amazing destinations blurring together in my mind.

Some trips, however, stand out vividly. My visit to Kenya is one of those. I was sent there to give an intensive five-day training to UN workers stationed in the country who faced the risk of kidnap – far higher for workers for an organisation like this which sends staff into areas of the world with high levels of conflict. It was vital that they all knew the safest way to respond if the worst actually happened.

A few weeks before my visit, Kenya hit the headlines round the world when the Westgate Shopping Mall in Nairobi was attacked by a terrorist group claiming that this was revenge for the involvement of Kenyan troops in Somalia. At least four men armed with assault rifles – the final number was never quite clear – started shooting in the cafe outside the centre and there were also reports of grenade explosions. The men then rushed inside and occupied the place while shoppers and staff fled through any exit they could find, or ran upstairs to hide in offices. The stand-off which followed lasted for four days and was marked by acts of extraordinary bravery, including by an undercover anti-terrorism agent who travelled to the besieged mall armed only with a handgun and successfully rescued a mother and her three daughters, and the retrieval of injured children by security staff who wheeled them out in shopping trolleys. Two hundred people are believed to have been injured and at least seventy-one were killed, but the final death toll was unclear because the storming of the centre by the Kenyan authorities which ended the crisis also caused a fire to break out.

As the day I was due to travel approached, I found I was more and more uneasy – an unusual feeling for me as I'm normally fairly phlegmatic. (I chose, after all, a career in the police and that comes with a certain level of personal risk.) The person responsible for organising UN trainings in Nairobi was an ex-police negotiator who regularly asked Harry for volunteers to help run the course, and he seemed pretty confident that everything was fine, but I was worried enough to speak to Mick, who'd visited a few months before, and find out if he honestly thought the place was safe. Instead of reassuring me, he gave me a beady look.

'Do you want a really honest answer?' he asked.

'Er – yes.'

'Okay, then. No. It's probably not safe. There's a lot of stuff going down out there. And you'll be visiting the UN, which is a target.'

Crikey, I thought. I'd already said I'd go and the arrangements had been made so I kind of felt committed, but this didn't sound too great.

I flew out to Kenya on my own – again not something that would usually bother me at all – but as my plane landed at 4 a.m. local time on a Sunday, the place was almost deserted, with just a few lonely bags going around on the empty carousel. Signs all over the airport warning about the risk of Ebola infection added to my lack of reassurance as I searched for the driver who was supposed to be meeting me. A young man standing in Arrivals held up a sign with my name on it and as I identified myself, a little voice of doubt in my head did wonder if he was who he said. Wasn't it possible that I was about to climb into a random stranger's car in the small hours of the morning in a not particularly safe country, then vanish who knows where?

'Hi, Madam Nicky!' A few minutes' chat reassured me. My driver knew Erik, the local course organiser on the ground, and as he drove me through the streets I was fascinated by everything I saw of the Kenyan capital, a place whose forceful motoring style makes driving in the rush hour in London seem like taking a stroll in the woods. He cheerily pointed out local landmarks and I began to look around and relax a little, but once we reached the gated and guarded UN compound, I was told that I'd be staying inside for my whole visit since it wasn't safe to go out. Not only that, but security was actually at a heightened risk level right now. The compound had its own hotel, which was a charming building, but my ground-floor room didn't feel all that secure, and I'd have preferred to be higher up. I nervously went through my hostile environment checks as I always do when I stay anywhere – pacing the layout of the floor, checking for the exits – but there was definitely a real edge this time.

The rest of Sunday passed uneventfully. Having a meal with some of the compound staff and getting to know them helped me feel a bit more comfortable, and next morning I was driven to the UN building to start the first day of the course. Meeting the class felt very normal but before teaching started, an announcement was suddenly made that an attack on the UN centre was believed to be imminent! The only comfort I could draw from hearing this was that at least I wasn't over-reacting: I was picking up on the real tensions around me, and my anxious response was quite reasonable.

After that, though, things seemed to settle down. The attack didn't materialise, the course went well with great engagement from the students, and I ended up enjoying the classes. The UN's employees weren't police officers or members of the armed forces and I noticed a real difference in their learning style. This was kidnap training for a group of students at far higher risk of actually being kidnapped than most other trainees I've taught (I often open by saying to a class: 'Now, you're probably thinking this could never happen to you . . . ' but I didn't use those words to them: without a doubt, they knew that it could), but they still weren't accustomed to the frank, task-focused teaching and feedback which is the norm with police and military students who've been constantly exposed to critical incidents and people in crisis in their work. These UN staff needed a softer, more reflective approach and more time to consider how to react: reading the room, as always, was the most vital teaching skill. I had to adapt my style to their learning.

I did manage to get out of the compound for two trips, one in the very early morning to the beautiful Nairobi National Park, and another to the orphan elephants' home (where the orphans were too cute and appealing for words to do justice and I realised exactly why people want to adopt them) and the giraffe sanctuary. I found the beauty and grace of these animals deeply moving, and was so pleased to feel that I'd seen at least a little of this remarkable country.

But my most vivid memory of my time in Nairobi is a simple conversation over lunch with one of the trainees. The Westgate Shopping Mall siege was still recent and we'd been discussing it that morning in class, but this man suddenly revealed to me that he'd been in the centre with his family at the time the crisis started. He was an ex-soldier and immediately recognised the sound of shooting, so he, his wife and children rushed to an upper level to hide, taking others with them. As they concealed themselves in an office, the terrified group could hear the gunmen moving through the complex and coming up the stairs. Quickly evaluating the situation with his military training to assist him, my student located a fire exit at the rear. Trying to get out was a risk – but staying put, he decided, was a bigger one and the longer they waited, the more extreme the danger would be. They needed to go now. He persuaded the group to follow him and led them all to safety. They probably owed him their lives.

I was stunned by what he said. He'd not mentioned any of it while we were in the classroom and was understated and matter-of-fact about the whole thing. He didn't seem to realise that what he'd done was amazing. No one had interviewed him for a TV exclusive or offered to write his story – but beyond a doubt this guy was a hero. I felt honoured to meet him.

Another remarkable trip – in a very different way – was one I made to Singapore. My students there were unlike any others I've taught, not in the way they learned in the classroom but in how they acted between their lessons. I'm used to a rush for canteens and break-out areas so that people can top up their caffeine levels and usually take on board some sugar as well, but my Singaporean students all stayed put. I was puzzled.

'Um – don't you guys want a break?' I asked them. The answer was that yes, they did, but for them the best way to take it was by closing their eyes and performing mindfulness meditation. I was fascinated to see the difference this made – and it really was noticeable. These students stayed alert and centred at all times – remarkably calm people who responded to aggression in such natural, relaxed ways. They seemed surprised when their instructors collapsed with exhaustion in our hotel at the end of each day, only able to manage a quick debrief and maybe a drink before we had to fall into bed, and at how we struggled to cope with the time zone changes. For them, perhaps, such adjustments would have been easier. It was a wonderful illustration of the uplifting, energising effects of meditation.

In the Gulf state of Oman, I had my first experience of teaching negotiation skills through a translator. Preparations for working in any foreign country are always made carefully

and we'd thought about how we would dress, eat, and relate to
others, but Oman is a pretty relaxed kind of country with rights
for women, such as driving and working, which you don't always
see in its neighbouring states. I even wore short sleeves during my
visit and everyone was comfortable with this. It's quite common
for British police to work with officials in the area to teach new
methods, and the Sultan of Oman was keen on innovation so
I ended up visiting three times, twice to teach basic negotiation
skills, and a third time to deliver the higher-level coordinators'
course. The terror level wasn't heightened at the time, but ISIS
had been active there in the past and I was quite surprised to
learn that there were also open political disagreements in the
country, with strikes going on, as poorer workers campaigned
for better pay and conditions. My sense was of a place in flux,
with internal pressures that might pull it in different directions
in the future.

Our Arabic–English translators were two young Lebanese
women who did a fantastic job, but their presence in the classroom definitely slowed down communication. However, this
wasn't a negative change as it created more time for reflection.
I also found I didn't have to understand everything people said
to grasp what was going on. As we carried out role plays with
the students, I could readily follow their progress through body
language, tone and facial expressions, picking up not just big
emotions like anger or withdrawal, but also moments of doubt
or hesitation. I was fascinated to discover how not being able
to understand people's words gave me the chance to get attuned
in other, more subtle ways. We may talk differently, but we also
all speak one human language.

*

While I was out in Oman, my phone rang. It was Harry.

'Nick – an opportunity's come up for you to go Quantico. It's a fortnight's course – you'd be teaching some classes and also taking part as a student. What d'you think?'

'*Quantico?*' I said. Just the word gave me a rush of excitement. It's the headquarters of America's Federal Bureau of Investigation. He was offering me the chance to train and work with agents of the FBI.

'The only thing is – it's short notice. I'm going to need an answer pretty fast.'

'How fast?'

'By 4 p.m. today. You'd be leaving on Monday.'

'On Monday. That's six days! And – um – I'm still in Oman.'

'Yep. Not ideal, I know.'

I wanted it – I really, really did. This was a career high for me – probably the greatest there could be. The FBI invented negotiation: they are the creators, innovators, and world leaders in the field, and there's always been an exchange and flow of ideas between them and the British police. But to actually go out there myself . . .

'Harry – this is an amazing opportunity. But I need to check with Jules.'

I'd been away so much. She and I had talked about this when we first became serious: she knew I was passionately committed to my career – as of course she is too – and we'd agreed to give each other support in every way we could. But I'm still not sure she'd realised that I was going to be abroad for almost half the year. Juggling parenting, two dogs, and a demanding full-time job on your own is so tough: I'd had that experience myself now and was in awe of her because she'd been doing it for much longer. I rang home and explained what I'd been offered.

Jules didn't even hesitate. 'Oh my God, Nicky – what an opportunity! Of course you must go!' she said. What can I say? It took me a while to meet the right woman – but it really was worth it when I did.

*

This place is just so familiar. That was my first thought as a group of student FBI agents out for a training run pounded past me along a snowy path towards the woods. The sensation was so strong that I almost did a double-take. *I've seen it before – but that was in the movies. And now I'm here for real, it feels a bit like being on a film set.*

We all know what the FBI's HQ in Quantico, Virginia, looks like because it's appeared in so many films. The most famous of these has to be *The Silence of the Lambs*, released in 1991 and starring Anthony Hopkins and Jodie Foster. It's the one that made the terrifying figure of the murderer Hannibal 'the cannibal' Lecter – who ate his victim's liver with cava beans and a nice Chianti – a household word for horror.

My second thought was – *this place is absolutely huge.* Everything's bigger in the United States anyway, but Quantico is massive. My motel was a half-hour drive away, but it was still specially reserved for police and military staff visiting the site. The complex was accessed by level after level of gated security, it had a shooting range and an onsite helicopter, and while Hendon has a few rooms done out like domestic settings to create immersive role plays for trainee police officers, Quantico has a hangar filled with locations and an entire *street* specially built for the same purpose. They have *everything*, including the best kit for doing the job that I have ever seen, which gave me a flashback to my mum anxiously purchasing a second-hand US stab vest for me early on in my career. Quite a lot of our equipment in the Met was inherited from American police forces. The Quantico staff canteen was five times the size of the one at New Scotland Yard and there was even a gift shop selling sweatshirts, pen-holders, fridge magnets, and other FBI memorabilia. It was easy to feel a bit daunted by it all.

I was there as part of a student group for two weeks of training, but as part of that programme I would also be doing some teaching myself. It was when they introduced me to my first class that I really felt proud. I'd always known that Scotland Yard is a brand – those two iconic words are recognised wherever I've travelled in the world. Now, at the heart of American crime fighting and in the birthplace of negotiation, it was the honour of my life and the pinnacle of my career to represent that brand. Mind you, I scarcely recognised myself from their description as they introduced me: this *Inspector Nicky Perfect from Scotland Yard, London's elite specialist negotiation unit* sounded so important and so grand! I felt a definite twinge of imposter syndrome, and steeled myself to overcome it.

The next thing that's bigger in America is crime itself: there's just so much more of it. The country – which is far larger than Britain, of course – has many, many more incidents of kidnap and hostage-taking, and US law enforcement divides responsibility

for these in a way that British police forces don't. A negotiator for the Met deals with everything: threatened suicides and
domestic stand-offs as well as organised crime and terrorism, but
in the States, there's a division between local forces, which are
responsible for personal crisis negotiation, and the FBI, which
handles kidnaps and events affecting national security.

But what – apart from its sheer scale – is the biggest difference
between British and American law enforcement? The answer is
obvious: it's guns. *Everybody* over there carried a weapon, and
many carried more than one. In an FBI training classroom, although
you can hand them in and place them in a safe, there's no require-
ment for you to do so. This felt very strange to me indeed – and
I've been a member of the firearms squad: I'm trained to fire a gun.
But I've done so in the highly controlled British setting of constant
training and re-training, where any weapon you use must be
checked out and checked back in and you're required to undergo
checks every five weeks to keep your skills and knowledge current
(this is called 'holding a blue ticket'). Quantico was a completely
different – and alien – world where the reasonable assumption was
that just about everyone, at all times, was armed.

I arrived in the middle of winter, with a thick layer of snow
on the ground. It made me vividly recall my experiences in
another wintry city – Oslo, where I'd come across the shock of
Anders Breivik's armed attack and seen how Norwegians were
struggling to compute what this might mean for them and the
relaxed, open society they were accustomed to living in. Breivik's
actions had given them their first taste of mortal danger and they
could scarcely get their heads round it. But here in America, that
danger was part of normal life.

'So how do you police without a gun?'

I was asked the question more than once, in a tone that I can only describe as one of wonder. When a situation is natural to you but absolutely strange to your listeners, it's hard to explain. There's no bridge of understanding to help you out, and absolutely no shared assumptions.

'Well – in the UK we police by consent,' I told them. 'The majority of the British public wants us to be unarmed, so until that changes . . .'

'But if you were called out to attend a burglary – you're saying you'd go without a gun?'

'Well, yes. We have relatively few guns in circulation, don't forget. Even in big cities, only a small minority of criminals will be carrying them. So the chances of us encountering an armed burglar aren't that great.'

'Yeah, but what if they *did* have a gun?'

'We'd call a special firearms team for help.'

'And you'd just have to wait until they got there?'

'Er – yes.'

'So how do you walk around and feel safe at night?'

'Well,' I said, 'that's the point, really. There aren't that many guns in the UK. I'm not likely to walk around the streets at night and get attacked by somebody who's armed.'

But again and again I was met with puzzled faces. The sense of living in two completely different worlds separated by the Atlantic Ocean was acute. I tried to turn the question round. 'So when do you *not* carry one?' I asked one fellow trainee.

'Never.'

'You mean – you're always armed?'

'Always. I take my gun on holiday.'

'Why would you take your gun on holiday?'

'I'm an FBI agent. If something happened – I'd have to deal with it.'

They asked me what the British police *did* use to enforce order. Truncheons, I explained. Oh, and our retractable asps. They were incredulous. 'What d'ya think you're going to do with those?' It was easy to dismiss all this as 'US gun culture' – something which feels foreign to Britons and is regarded by us as a terrible idea. But one day I saw something which shifted my opinion a little. I was taken on a visit to the National Law Enforcement Officers' Memorial in Washington, D.C.

It's absolutely huge. Right now, there are 23,229 names inscribed on it, and that number goes on rising. They lose a *lot* of officers over there. The Met in London has a beautiful memorial for fallen policemen and women, and every year there's a charity cycle ride for the families involved: it's called We Ride for Those Who Died. Each force has a plaque and at the end of the cycle ride there's a ceremony and the Chief Constable lays flowers in their memory. There are too many names. But in Washington, the inscriptions of the dead seemed never-ending. As I looked at all of this, I could see how my American counterparts got to where they are, and the difference in the sense of threat they feel. What they experience, I think, is closer to absolute peril, off the scale in comparison with ours. I can grasp why they're unwilling to face the streets unarmed.

*

All the FBI trainees were super-friendly and naturally good communicators – so good that I began to wonder how they got to be that way. There had to be a reason for the stand-out contrast in behaviour between them and the students I taught in the UK and in many other countries.

I don't think there's one simple answer, but it might be something to do with problem-solving. That's what police officers in the UK learn to do: they work out answers in tricky situations and then direct others to follow their lead. So, as we train negotiators, our goal is to overcome all that conditioning: we're asking them to shut down all the doing and directing and turn on their empathy and listening. Our FBI trainees, on the other hand, weren't police officers to start with – not in the same way that their British counterparts were. They'd not worked in uniform, out on the streets directing traffic or intervening in domestic violence cases or handling crowd control at football matches. They thought like investigators, so it was easier for them to be in the moment, to stop taking charge and to be open and curious.

In Quantico, I was honoured to meet one of the most experienced negotiators in the world, a guy named Vince who talked to Somali pirates after they seized the container ship *Maersk Alabama* off the Horn of Africa in 2009. The 2013 film *Captain Phillips*, starring Tom Hanks, told the story of how the ship was eventually retaken by the US Navy. Vince also negotiated with Dzhokhar Tsarnaev, one of the two brothers who carried out the bombing of the Boston Marathon in 2013. After a major manhunt Tsarnaev was eventually discovered hiding in a boat stored in someone's backyard and persuaded by Vince to give himself up. Vince was an incredibly humble and self-effacing guy who didn't take over the sessions of training he took part in, but simply talked with the group and shared his knowledge. His instruction on active listening has always stayed with me: the only thing that we can ever control as negotiators is how we respond to what others say and do. He also gave up his Sunday to take a group of us out on a fascinating trip to historic Civil War sites in the area, and talked knowledgeably about what had happened there. I felt a real kinship with him, which is something I've experienced in many other places too. Wherever I've gone in the world and whenever I've met other negotiators, I've found this sense of shared values; it's made it easy to form close and trusting relationships.

The US is where negotiation began. It's a modern skill set which arose from traumatic events including the hostage-taking crisis at the Olympic Games in Munich, West Germany, in 1972, the eleven-day stand-off by the Weaver family with the FBI at Ruby Ridge in Idaho following an attempted arrest of one of them, and the siege of the headquarters of a religious cult called the Branch Davidians at Waco, Texas, in 1993, which lasted seven weeks and led to the deaths of seventy-six cult members. These tragedies caused the authorities to closely analyse what had happened, and in particular how well – or otherwise – communication had worked, to ensure that events like these could not occur again. Negotiation is still developing as a tool, and knowledge in the field is increasing as new psychological insights are incorporated into training.

An early example of a failure to understand the motivation of an individual under extreme stress took place during a bank siege several decades ago when officers talking to the hostage-taker missed the grave risk he posed to his hostages. They failed to read the situation correctly – until a deadline that the man inside the bank had set passed without action and he responded to this by shooting a hostage dead in full view. The police then shot him dead in turn. Reflection on that horrible incident also advanced the understanding of 'suicide by cop' – the phenomenon in which a suicidal individual who doesn't know how to go about killing themselves will deliberately trigger their own shooting by officers.

In the early days, the first negotiators tended to work in silos, attempting to progress by talking while a police operation went ahead alongside them. This, however, led to instances of disastrously mixed messages. During the Ruby Ridge stand-off, some trust had been established between the Weavers and the negotiators – but it was immediately undone by officers firing shots. At Waco, the negotiators assured the Branch Davidians that the authorities sought a peaceful resolution to the crisis which protected the lives of everyone inside their compound, including a number of children. But when electrical power to the compound was suddenly switched off, affecting the ability of those inside to keep their food fresh in the heat – at this point the siege had been going on for weeks – the cult's members began to doubt that the children's welfare was really such a priority. Close communication between negotiators and other arms of the police force is therefore vital, and this understanding has grown over time. Nowadays we train alongside firearms teams, operate from the same buildings and work in tandem. Academic study of negotiation techniques by psychologists such as Harvey Schlossberg has also been crucial in advancing the field. Once established in America through the work of pioneers like Schlossberg, the science of negotiation spread around the world, and one of the first countries to which it was exported was Britain. Now there's a continual flow of shared ideas and experience, and every year the International Negotiation Working Group meets to act as a forum for this to take place.

The training session I led at Quantico was entitled 'The power of because'. It was based on the work of psychologist Robert Cialdini, who wrote about a concept that I've used many times in my teaching: our brains need to hear a reason why. (Any reason will do. It's been shown in experiments that if someone jumps ahead of you in a queue by telling you that 'I need to get to the front' – there's a pretty good chance you'll agree to let them in.) When a hostage-taker demands an escape helicopter, a million dollars and a pizza, that person almost certainly understands that the police won't agree to it. But giving them *reasons* why not – because it's too expensive, because there's no helicopter available right now – meets the human need to hear an explanation while a hard 'no' triggers off aggression. 'No, *because . . .*' – whether or not the reason is true – is therefore more likely to win cooperation.

My time at Quantico was without a doubt the highlight of my career: I'd sometimes pinch myself to check that all this was really happening, and that I was actually instructing and assessing candidates for the FBI. I remembered 18-year-old Nicky arriving on the first day of police cadet training at Hendon, nervously looking around my dorm, incredibly relieved when I found someone to talk to, not quite buckling down to my revision as hard as I should have. I'd never have believed back then that I could come so far, and knowing I had done so made me proud and happy beyond words. Quantico was a unique training experience which I felt incredibly privileged to have.

*

The last time I worked overseas in my role with HCNU was on a visit to the Cayman Islands in the Caribbean. There'd recently been a high-profile kidnapping there – the first time the country had to cope with such an event – and the authorities realised that they didn't have the specialist knowledge to address it. They wanted to be ready for next time, and when an ex-Met superintendent who was living out there offered negotiation training to the local police, they accepted. He then hosted our team when we went out to deliver it.

The Caymans were beautiful – an actual island paradise with everything you could ever dream of, from shining white beaches to coconut palms to sparkling turquoise sea. Our working days were long and demanding, as always, but we squeezed in a bit of down time too and our host was really welcoming, taking us to visit amazing locations in the two days we had off and treating us to dinner in a beautiful beach cafe.

At the end of any negotiating course, the students who've succeeded in passing really know that they've earned their certificate. They'd competed for their places, then worked really hard to turn their thinking around.

We didn't just hand out pieces of paper: we also gave our newly qualified trainees a police coin and a negotiator pin badge. The badge has recognition around the world, marking out any officer who wears it as a part of the international negotiation family. As I'd noticed so many times before, the trainees were excited to work with us – it was the power of that 'brand' thing again, and I was incredibly proud to represent New Scotland Yard and the Hostage and Crisis Negotiation Unit. As we handed them their certificates, we could see how special they felt to be part of it.

I understood completely; it's the way that I feel too. And as the time approached for me to move on from my role as a police negotiator, I knew I always would.

Chapter 12

AFTERWARDS
Summer 2018

I thought that I could just walk away. Retire and find a different kind of life. No more being woken by the phone at 3 a.m. No more dread and suspense, hoping for a positive conclusion to the latest crisis but fearing that something would go wrong. There'd be less excitement, sure, but there'd be more peace of mind.

Looking back, that belief of mine seems a bit naive. Did I really think that all the trauma I'd witnessed during my career would leave me unscathed? I know now that many front-line emergency staff and first responders feel the same as I did – they're aware that what they've seen and heard can affect people . . . but they still can't quite believe that they, personally, will be one of the ones who are affected. *I didn't think it would happen to me.*

It was a sunny summer morning in 2018. I'd been retired from the Met for six months and I hadn't wasted any time. I'm oriented to taking action – and I also might just be an adrenaline junkie – so I'd satisfied my need for action and excitement by starting not one but *four* businesses, one online and three smaller ones based close to my home. Life as an entrepreneur meant a steep and sometimes stressful learning curve, and there were days when I certainly got my adrenaline fix! One of my small businesses was a gym, so I'd completed a course to qualify as a personal trainer. It allowed me to run classes and teach others to find the enjoyment and mental and physical release that fitness has always provided for me.

This morning I had twelve students with me in the room. We were concentrating on building core strength and the atmosphere was focused. I could hear my students' breathing getting heavier as their hearts and lungs worked harder. The next exercise was a shoulder press from a kneeling position.

'Everybody down on their knees,' I said to the class. That was when it happened.

All of sudden, all of them were wearing orange jumpsuits like the ones that the prisoners of ISIS were forced to wear in Syria. The images were incredibly clear. They were kneeling, but not by choice to do an exercise that would train them to get stronger – they were helpless and about to die, just like the men and women who'd been murdered in the videos Connor had to watch in the ops rooms as he drilled into them for evidence.

I froze. I couldn't make a sound. My chest felt tight. Whatever this was – hallucination? flashback? – must have lasted six or seven seconds, then it vanished as instantly as it had appeared. I let myself lean back against the wall, taking a moment to recover. There was a break in my instructions, but not long enough for anyone else to realise what had happened. Then I was able to refocus and speak, even though my heart was still racing, and the class carried on.

Where the hell did that come from? It left me feeling very shaky, and with a whole load of questions. *What caused it? What does it mean? And what can I do to stop it happening again?*

*

Many police officers commit to stay in the force for thirty years. That's what I did too, as a new recruit, but when you're nineteen the idea of ever being as ancient as forty-nine seems remote and what I was going to do afterwards wasn't something I thought about much. Except that now, somehow, those years had all gone by and here I was, looking at the end.

I started to make my retirement plans well in advance, thinking about how best to use the skills I'd gained across my whole career with the Met and in particular in HCNU. I've been told that many former police officers struggle to see how to transfer their skills into civilian life, and I understand why that is: on paper, after all, I only have five O levels. That certificate can't remotely sum up the range of the experience and abilities I gained in my thirty year police career. It doesn't even come close. Knowing that 'you on paper' doesn't at all represent 'you in real life' doesn't exactly give you confidence or help you sell yourself to others.

I was fortunate to have achieved a personal profile in my work, and a little while before I retired I was asked if I was interested in doing some private work teaching communication skills to companies and individual clients. I decided that I was, and in 2017 I set up a company to enable me to take on this kind of role. It was the genesis of The Communication Coach, one of the businesses I run now. I felt a real excitement about my new business: I have so many stories and lessons and if I share them, they can make a difference to others.

*

I approached retirement gradually through the winter of 2017–18, knowing that the change in my life would be enormous and that I needed to prepare for it. If I wasn't a serving police officer and a New Scotland Yard hostage and crisis negotiator anymore . . . who exactly would I be?

The hardest part came first: the last national negotiation course I would ever teach took place at Hendon at the start of December. That course had been my life and although I knew that my successor was just as dedicated as I had been, it still felt hard and strange to let it go. I'd come to Hendon aged nineteen, at the beginning of it all, and it didn't feel quite real to drive away from that place and know that I would never come back.

During the rest of December I used up lots of my annual leave. An extended Christmas holiday sounds great . . . except it wasn't: all I really did was collapse. As I looked ahead into the huge uncertainty of retirement, I felt confused and quite depressed, which drained my energy, which then made it even harder to do anything about the way I felt. Up to now, when anybody asked me: *so – what do you do?* I'd always replied with pride, 'I am a police officer.' *Now what will I say? And what on earth will I do? I'm going from being quite important in my domain to – well – pretty much nobody outside it. How am I going to cope with that?*

At the start of the New Year came my final two weeks at work. As I left New Scotland Yard for the very last time in mid-January, I had to hand in my warrant card in its square black wallet. I had carried it with me every day, everywhere, throughout my adult life, and being without it felt like giving up part of my identity – not to mention where on earth was I going to keep my bank cards now? Jules and I stayed in a hotel in Vauxhall that night so that we didn't have to travel far after my farewell drinks . . . but next morning it was time to leave London, the city I had served as a Met officer for three decades. That's when it really hit me. *It's all over.* I felt sad and lost and – weird.

But also – I was tired. I was really, really tired. Front-line policing is a young person's game, and you get to a level where you've seen and heard as much as you can take. No one approaches a police officer because they're happy, and most people you see or speak to is in trouble in some way. There's crisis all around you, all the time. This dark side of life was all I'd known for thirty years. I was very, very proud – and still am – of the service I had given to the people of London. But now – enough.

*

Am I going to have more flashbacks? I wondered. I knew a bit about the subject from talking to former members of the military and the police force, and retired colleagues had also warned me about the impact of the work I had done. We'd dealt with trauma after trauma until we were normalised to trauma – but it was never really normal. Sometimes it's not until you stop – until you switch off 'coping' mode – that your body and your brain have the time to catch up with what's happened to you.

And for some, the point of becoming overwhelmed arrives long before that. The biggest killer of serving police officers is suicide. I thought back to the time I'd spent at the Flint House Police Rehabilitation Centre for intensive physio after my back injury. Emotional support and counselling were available there too, along with the physical treatments, but (even at the start of the twenty-first century!) they were still slightly sidelined, offered in a different part of the building, and 'suffering from stress' wasn't something that people wanted to talk about. I'd been reluctant myself, I remembered, to discuss how I was feeling while I was there. The new openness around mental health is still so very recent.

So I'm vulnerable, I thought. *I've been affected by trauma – this flashback that I've had is proof of that.* The question now was – *what was I going to do about it?* I decided on some mindfulness training because I remembered the calm and resilience of my negotiation students in Singapore who'd used it as a way to decompress while the Brits just toughed it out, tanked up on coffee to keep going and hit the bar to forget their cares at the end of the day. They'd certainly seemed to be coping better than we were. I also talked to a therapist I met in a small business support group and told her exactly what I'd seen that day in the gym. She reassured me that if my flashback re-occurred, there would be places that I could go for help. It never did happen again, so perhaps the calm this conversation gave me was exactly what I needed.

And I started talking more in general about the way I feel, to Jules and to friends and to colleagues who had been or still were in the police. Talking is so much better than toughing it out. Most of all, I've learned not to bury what I've been through. Ever since I became a police cadet I'd been a do-er, wanting to take action, but if something happens now I turn my feelings into words and I know that it's not weak. The high levels of emotional transference which make someone a strong negotiator – the very qualities we look for, and which we encourage and develop in trainees – can come at a cost. Taking on other people's emotions is exhausting and those who give support to others also need to receive it themselves.

I still feel the on-going impacts of my exposure to violence, crisis and death. I suffer from hyper-vigilance sometimes, particularly in the way that I react to loud bangs. I can't watch violence on TV – not at all, in fact I have to close my eyes. A scene in a TV drama a few years ago when a character unexpectedly jumped from a bridge – it was a plot twist and I didn't see the action coming – upset me terribly. I know that I have lasting trauma responses.

*

My first piece of corporate work for my company The Communication Coach was in Luxembourg. I was hired by an ex-negotiator who'd been asked to provide some communication training at a bank where there'd recently been an awful tragedy: a member of its staff had committed suicide by throwing themselves off the building. Everyone in the place was in shock and the bank's directors were looking for two things: how to help their people to recover, and how to prevent anything like this ever happening again. They wanted to learn communication skills: how teams and their leaders could speak and listen to each other so that future crisis points could be avoided.

The training went well, everyone was very appreciative and I received more referrals. My business began to grow. Most of the jobs I take on – and this is true of corporate clients, individuals, and those who want to improve communication in areas like parenting teenagers – are really teaching how to have difficult conversations: preparing for them, starting them, navigating them, concluding them. The skills of crisis negotiation – not shying away from the awkward discussion, finding the courage to ask the scary question then really listen to the answer – can help so many people, and these are the skills that I have been trained in myself and taught others over many years.

Realising the value of my knowledge and experience helped to give me the confidence I needed, because working for yourself can be scary. That's especially true when you've always been a part of something huge in the way that I had. The Met employs tens of thousands of people: there's a big human resources department, a big payroll department – a big everything, really. To set up on your own after that is a massive adjustment and to be honest, quite a shock.

But running one new business obviously wasn't stressful enough for me, so alongside The Communication Coach I added three more. I'm the type of person who feels the need to constantly test myself – I thrive on challenges. I take these very seriously and always see them through: it's the way I'm wired and

I never do anything by halves. But even for me, this was pretty crazy. There was the gym, then a garage and a coffee shop – all ideas I had for a space that was for sale quite near my home and which presented a chance that just seemed too good to miss. With Jules's support and encouragement, I made the decision to go for it pretty fast and threw myself full-on into getting all three of them up and running. The arrival of the coffee shop in particular caused a stir of surprise in the area. Not everyone – although I only found out about this later – saw the need for it in the very quiet village where I live and one local resident was so astonished to see it actually open with paying customers that he took his eyes off the road and drove his car into the ditch right outside. He shouldn't have been so surprised: plenty of walkers and cyclists pass through, enjoying the countryside, and they've been glad to find a place where they can pause for refreshment.

I couldn't be certain of this until I'd tried, however, so I was extremely nervous myself on the cafe's opening day. *What if nobody comes in?* I still have the photos I gratefully took of my first customers. It felt good at the time to be so busy and to have such a strong sense of new purpose, but as I look back I can see that I was filling in a space, replacing the intensity of the life I'd had before with a blur of new activity. *Who am I now?* is the question I was asking. *And who will I become in the future?* Those are very big questions, so of course it was going to take a while to find the answers. There were also days when the only question I had any time to ask was *what the hell am I doing?* Or *have I bitten off more than I can chew?* And then I'd have to stop asking and thinking and wondering and just get on with the next time-critical, super-urgent task on my endless to-do lists.

In the end, I had two years to get my businesses established. That's how long I'd been doing my new jobs before the Covid-19 pandemic came sweeping around the world and brought normal life in the United Kingdom to a halt. I was still inexperienced as a business owner and employer when this happened, and I found it really painful and difficult to close everything down and furlough the staff who worked for me, so that I could claim government support to help pay their salaries. First the gym had to stop its operations because of social distancing (although it didn't end entirely because I started offering sessions over Zoom. They were pretty well attended: Joe Wicks, eat your heart out!). Then the garage shut because nobody was driving anywhere. During a live video link with my teams to explain what was going to happen, I actually broke down in tears. It felt awful to see people who trusted me for their livelihoods faced with such uncertainty about the future.

The cafe, though, was different. I thought I saw a way to keep it going through the pandemic – which was going to last how long? None of us had any way to know – and to make it into something more than it had been when it started. As a police officer, I'm trained to walk towards a crisis: this is what all of us instinctively do. And right here was a huge one, a scary new disease, tearing people's lives apart. So this was a time to walk towards it, to step up and to help, and I could see that the cafe offered a way.

It had already found a place in the area as a community hub where local people could find friendship, conversation, and laughter, and now there was a chance to build on that. We could do takeaways, I thought, and home deliveries, and pretty soon we were offering a 'meals on wheels'-type service to vulnerable people and seniors who had to isolate in their homes. Customers began to get in touch to order meals to be delivered to their elderly parents. Next we started matching up those in need of help with others who had time to offer – perhaps because they themselves were furloughed from their work – and who could do weekly shops for their neighbours and deliver to their homes. A local supermarket heard about what we were doing and offered us donations. We asked our delivery drivers, who included me, to make as much time as they could to chat at a safe distance with those they were visiting, helping to combat the awful loneliness which made the pandemic such an ordeal for so many people.

It took me a while to work out why I was doing all this and what my deeper purpose was. I've done a lot of personal development work on myself down the years, and what I've learned is that my highest value is to be of service. I'm at my most comfortable and happy at those times. To make a difference is the key motivator that I have in anything I do, and during the pandemic I could see that this was happening. I especially remember three older local people, all retired, two ladies and a gentleman, who lived quite near to one another but were each isolating on their own on a small estate. The two ladies were friends and used to chat by phone, and they started to talk to their neighbour until the three of them were all ordering home delivery meals at the same time on a Friday evening. Their families were very far away and terrified of infecting them with Covid, and this weekly visit on Fridays was the only face-to-face – although masked and at a distance – contact with other people that any of them had. I mostly did these three deliveries myself, and always chatted with the three of them for as long as I could – even better, it turned out that one of the ladies was also the widow of a Met Police officer who knew Perivale, the area of west London where I grew up. These seniors – and others like them – were the reason for everything we did. What we were offering meant so much to them. That's being of service and in that terrible, dark time, it felt like a beam of light.

Then, at the end of the pandemic's first grim year, I was nominated by local residents for a British Empire Medal for my services to my community. When I first got the news, it arrived by letter in a heavy yellow envelope which looked rather puzzling and mysterious. I opened it curiously and read: *Congratulations! You have been nominated for a BEM for meritorious service during the pandemic* . . . and I broke down in tears. Then I phoned Jules. I had to keep the whole thing secret until the New Year Honours were announced, but when I did receive the award it was posted on a local Facebook group . . . and suddenly everybody knew.

I was scared to look at the Facebook comments – after all, everyone knows what those can be like and the sort of aggressive attacks that social media sometimes seems to trigger off – but all the comments were wonderful and to feel that love and support from my community was amazing. I'm so deeply touched and grateful, and people still stop and say congratulations to me, which is lovely. But it's also true to say that my real reward was to live into my purpose and fulfil it – and that was mine already.

*

'Do you miss negotiation?' my friend Amy asked me. The question stopped me in my tracks.

I'd trained her when she first started out as a negotiator and it was great to see her again. We'd run into each other on a working trip to Frankfurt, delivering a course in communication to a company there. The teaching had gone well and the feedback we'd received from our students at the end of the day had been great.

As I thought about what she'd asked, something struck me. The best thing about the time that I and the other instructors had just spent together had been the preparation: working closely together, discussing how best to lead each session, taking a deep dive into a subject which gripped us all. It reminded me of the best conversations I'd had down the years with friends and colleagues at HCNU when we'd analyse human behaviour, recommend books to each other, share our expertise, hear more, learn more, increase our understanding, find new ways to do things. Those were times of cutting-edge excitement. It was fulfilling and rewarding to be part of the negotiation family and to feel its shared understanding.

'Yes,' I told her. 'Yes. I think I do miss it. Not the phone ringing at 3 in the morning, obviously. Not standing around in the freezing cold for hours. Not the stress of it. But I do miss sharing our ideas. And knowing that I'm part of a community. I was lucky to experience all that.'

'To carry responsibility for somebody's life,' Amy said. 'The weight of that – it's going to change you, isn't it? You won't be quite the same again.' She was right.

'There's no job like it in the world,' I said to her, and she nodded. I knew she understood.

*

The business that was least affected by the pandemic was The Communication Coach. Thanks to the power of technology, events and talks and trainings could still take place online, and while anything that happens remotely lacks the energy of something happening in real life, it's much better than nothing. In October 2021, I was asked to be a keynote speaker at an event called *Standing on the Shoulders of Giants*, which gives advice and support to former military personnel who are leaving the army and facing the challenges of civilian life. My talk would be on the power of communication.

Instead of a conference hall, due to Covid the event was broadcast from a radio studio in west London. When I got there, however, I was struck by how much buzz there still was about the place. I was mic'd up and had to wait in the shadows to be introduced then walk out onto a spotlit stage to speak, facing my 'audience', which was a huge bank of screens showing all the Zoom attendees who were present. It was the nearest the organisers could manage to the excitement of a crowded auditorium – and it came pretty close.

As I launched into my keynote speech, I realised I was happy. I'm not an extrovert – I quite like to be at home and I'm certainly not always super-sociable. But there's something about teaching communication that brings me to life. That's when I love standing up in front of people and being the centre of attention.

I'm using the same skills as I always did, and doing what I absolutely love. It's my thing – to teach these skills, to share my knowledge, to listen and learn, to see people develop and change. I've found what I love to do, and when you're in your purpose – you know it. I'm incredibly grateful for this.

As I stood there on stage in that radio studio, looking at the faces on the bank of screens, watching them 'getting it' as I used to watch students doing on the negotiation course, I realised that while my life is different now in so many ways, I've kept what I most love.

My job has changed. The work I do has changed. But my chance to make a difference in the world is the same as it was before. I'm still me.

Acknowledgments

This book would not have been possible without the help of so many people. Thank you to each one of you who has supported me on my journey through life and those of you who gave your time and showed me opportunities I never knew existed.

Thank you to those who have shared your stories with me, from each one I have learnt a lesson that has helped me to then help others.

Thank you to Susan Smith and the team at HQ for believing in my story and Liz for somehow taking my words and making the magic happen.

Thank you to those friends and family who have picked me up when I have been down, who have loved me, supported me and allowed me the space to grow and achieve – you know who you are.

To my sister and mum for your never-ending love.

To Jules and Megan: you complete my life.

To my dad, I am just so sorry you couldn't be here to witness this, but I am forever grateful to you and miss you terribly.

I dedicate this book to the memory of Jayne Stratton 1968 – 1998. Taken from us far too soon, never once forgotten.

Finally, to each negotiator out there, thank you for the time you give to others, never ever underestimate the difference you make.

Each one of us has a story, this is a part of mine, I hope you the reader find it useful in some way and I wish you well on your own journey.

Nicky

ONE PLACE. MANY STORIES

Bold, innovative and
empowering publishing.

FOLLOW US ON:

@HQStories